OF
HUMAN
BONDAGE
II

W. Somerset Maugham

Chapter 63

Philip did not pass the examination in anatomy at the end of March. He and Dunsford had worked at the subject together on Philip's skeleton, asking each other questions till both knew by heart every attachment and the meaning of every nodule and groove on the human bones; but in the examination room Philip was seized with panic, and failed to give right answers to questions from a sudden fear that they might be wrong. He knew he was ploughed and did not even trouble to go up to the building next day to see whether his number was up. The second failure put him definitely among the incompetent and idle men of his year.

He did not care much. He had other things to think of. He told himself that Mildred must have senses like anybody else, it was only a question of awakening them; he had theories about woman, the rip at heart, and thought that there must come a time with everyone when she would yield to persistence. It was a question of watching for the opportunity, keeping his temper, wearing her down with small attentions, taking advantage of the physical exhaustion which opened the heart to tenderness, making himself a refuge from the petty vexations of her work. He talked to her of the relations between his friends in Paris and the fair ladies they admired. The life he described had a charm, an easy gaiety, in which was no grossness. Weaving nto his own recollections the adventures of Mimi and Rodolphe, of Musette and the rest of them, he poured into Mildred's ears a story of poverty made picturesque by song and laughter, of lawless love made romantic by beauty and youth. He never attacked her prejudices directly, but sought to combat them by the suggestion that they were suburban. He never let himself be disturbed by her inattention, nor irritated by her indifference. He thought he had bored her. By an effort he made himself affable and entertaining; he never let himself be angry, he never asked for anything, he never complained, he never scolded. When she made engagements and broke them, he met her next day with a smiling face; when she excused herself, he said it did not matter. He never let her see that she pained him. He understood that his passionate grief had wearied her, and he took care to hide every sentiment which could be in the least degree troublesome. He was heroic.

Though she never mentioned the change, for she did not take any conscious notice of it, it affected her nevertheless; she became more confidential with him; she took her little grievances to him, and she always had some grievance against the manageress of the shop, one of her fellow-waitresses, or her aunt; she was talkative enough now, and though she never said anything that was not trivial Philip was never tired of listening to her.

"I like you when you don't want to make love to me," she told him once.

"That's flattering for me," he laughed.

She did not realize how her words made his heart sink nor what an effort it needed for him to answer so lightly.

"Oh, I don't mind your kissing me now and then. It doesn't hurt me and it gives you pleasure."

Occasionally she went so far as to ask him to take her out to dinner, and the offer, coming from her, filled him with rapture.

"I wouldn't do it to anyone else," she said, by way of apology. "But I know I can with you."

"You couldn't give me greater pleasure," he smiled.

She asked him to give her something to eat one evening towards the end of April.

"All right," he said. "Where would you like to go afterwards?"

"Oh, don't let's go anywhere. Let's just sit and talk. You don't mind, do you?"

"Rather not."

He thought she must be beginning to care for him. Three months before the thought of an evening spent in conversation would have bored her to death. It was a fine day, and the spring added to Philip's high spirits. He was content with very little now.

"I say, won't it be ripping when the summer comes along," he said, as they drove along on the top of a bus to Soho—she had herself suggested that they should not be so extravagant as to go by cab. "We shall be able to spend every Sunday on the River. We'll take our luncheon in a basket."

She smiled slightly, and he was encouraged to take her hand. She did not withdraw it.

"I really think you're beginning to like me a bit," he smiled.

"You *are* silly, you know I like you, or else I shouldn't be here, should I?"

They were old customers at the little restaurant in Soho by now, and the *patronne* gave them a smile as they came in. The waiter was obsequious.

"Let me order the dinner tonight," said Mildred.

Philip, thinking her more enchanting than ever, gave her the menu, and she chose her favourite dishes. The range was small, and they had eaten many times all that the restaurant could provide. Philip was gay. He looked into her eyes, and he dwelt on every perfection of her pale cheeks. When they had finished Mildred by way of exception took a cigarette. She smoked very seldom.

"I don't like to see a lady smoking," she said.

She hesitated a moment and then spoke.

"Were you surprised, my asking you to take me out and give me a bit of dinner tonight?"

"I was delighted."

"I've got something to say to you, Philip."

He looked at her quickly, his heart sank, but he had trained himself well.

"Well, fire away," he said, smiling.

"You're not going to be silly about it, are you? The fact is I'm going to get married."

"Are you?" said Philip.

He could think of nothing else to say. He had considered the possibility often and had imagined to himself what he would do and say. He had suffered agonies when he thought of the despair he would suffer, he had thought of suicide, of the mad passion of anger that would seize him; but perhaps he had too completely anticipated the emotion he would experience, so that now he felt merely exhausted. He felt as one does in a serious illness when the vitality is so low that one is indifferent to the issue and wants only to be left alone.

"You see, I'm getting on," she said. "I'm twenty-four and it's time I settled down."

He was silent. He looked at the *patronne* sitting behind the counter, and his eye dwelt on a red feather one of the diners wore in her hat. Mildred was nettled.

"You might congratulate me," she said.

"I might, mightn't I? I can hardly believe it's true. I've dreamt it so often. It rather tickles me that I should have been so jolly glad that you asked me to take you out to dinner. Whom are you going to marry?"

"Miller," she answered, with a slight blush.

"Miller?" cried Philip, astounded. "But you've not seen him for months."

"He came in to lunch one day last week and asked me then. He's earning very good money. He makes seven pounds a week now and he's got prospects."

Philip was silent again. He remembered that she had always liked Miller; he amused her; there was in his foreign birth an exotic charm which she felt unconsciously.

"I suppose it was inevitable," he said at last. "You were bound to accept the highest bidder. When are you going to marry?"

"On Saturday next. I have given notice."

Philip felt a sudden pang.

"As soon as that?"

"We're going to be married at a registry office. Emil prefers it."

Philip felt dreadfully tired. He wanted to get away from her. He thought he would go straight to bed. He called for the bill.

"I'll put you in a cab and send you down to Victoria. I daresay you won't have to wait long for a train. "

"Won't you come with me? "

"I think I'd rather not, if you don't mind."

"It's just as you please," she answered haughtily. "I suppose I shall see you at tea-time tomorrow?"

"No, I think we'd better make a full stop now. I don't see why I should go on making myself unhappy. I've paid the cab."

He nodded to her and forced a smile on his lips, then jumped on a bus and made his way home. He smoked a pipe before he went to bed, but he could hardly keep his eyes open. He suffered no pain. He fell into a heavy sleep almost as soon as his head touched the pillow.

Chapter 64

But about three in the morning Philip awoke and could not sleep again. He began to think of Mildred. He tried not to, but could not help himself. He repeated to himself the same thing time after time till his brain reeled. It was inevitable that she should marry: life was hard for a girl who had to earn her own living; and if she found someone who could give her a comfortable home she should not be blamed if she accepted. Philip acknowledged that from her point of view it would have been madness to marry him: only love could have made such poverty bearable, and she did not love him. It was no fault of hers; it was a fact that must be accepted like any other. Philip tried to reason with himself. He told himself that deep down in his heart was mortified pride; his passion had begun in wounded vanity, and it was this at bottom which caused now a great part of his wretchedness. He despised himself as much as he despised her. Then he made plans for the future, the same plans over and over again, interrupted by recollections of kisses on her soft pale cheek and by the sound of her voice with its trailing accent; he had a great deal of work to do, since in the summer he was taking Chemistry as well as the two examinations he had failed in. He had separated himself from his friends at the hospital, but now he wanted companionship. There was one happy occurrence: Hayward a fortnight before had written to say that he was passing through London and had asked him to dinner; but Philip, unwilling to be bothered, had refused. He was coming back for the season, and Philip made up his mind to write to him.

He was thankful when eight o'clock struck and he could get up. He was pale and weary. But when he had bathed, dressed, and had breakfast, he felt himself joined up again with the world at large; and his pain was a little easier to bear. He did not feel like going to lectures that morning, but went instead to the Army and Navy Stores to buy Mildred a wedding present. After much wavering he settled on a dressing-bag. It cost twenty pounds, which was much more than he could afford, but it was showy and vulgar: he knew she would be aware exactly how much it cost; he got a melancholy satisfaction in choosing a gift which would give her pleasure and at the same time indicate for himself the contempt he had for her.

Philip had looked forward with apprehension to the day on which Mildred was to be married; he was expecting an intolerable anguish; and it was with relief that he got a letter from Hayward on Saturday morning to say that he was coming up early on that very day and would fetch Philip to help him to find rooms. Philip, anxious to be distracted, looked up a timetable and discovered the only train Hayward was likely to come by; he went to meet him, and the reunion of the friends was enthusiastic. They left the luggage at the station, and set off gaily. Hayward characteristically proposed that first of all they should go for an hour to the National Gallery; he had not seen pictures for some time, and he stated that it needed a glimpse to set him in tune with life. Philip for months had had no one with whom he could talk of art and books. Since the Paris days Hayward had immersed himself in the modern French versifiers, and, such a plethora of poets is there in France, he had several new geniuses to tell Philip about. They walked through the gallery pointing out to one another their favourite pictures; one subject led to another; they talked excitedly. The sun was shining and the air was warm.

"Let's go and sit in the Park," said Hayward. "We'll look for rooms after luncheon."

The spring was pleasant there. It was a day upon which one felt it good merely to live. The young green of the trees was exquisite against the sky; and the sky, pale and blue, was dappled with little white clouds. At the end of the ornamental water was the grey mass of the Horse Guards. The ordered elegance of the scene had the charm of an eighteenth century picture. It reminded you not of Watteau, whose landscapes are so idyllic that they recall only the woodland glens seen in dreams, but of the more prosaic Jean-Baptiste Pater. Philip's heart was filled with lightness. He realized, what he had only read before, that art (for there was art in the manner in which he looked upon nature) might liberate the soul from pain.

They went to an Italian restaurant for luncheon and ordered themselves a *fiaschetto* of Chianti. Lingering over the meal they talked on. They reminded one another of the people they had known at Heidelberg, they spoke of Philip's friends in Paris, they talked of books, pictures, morals, life; and suddenly Philip heard a clock strike three. He remembered that by this time Mildred was married. He felt a sort of stitch in his heart, and for a minute or two he could not hear what Hayward was saying. But he filled his glass with Chianti. He was unaccustomed to alcohol and it had gone to his head. For the time at all events he was free from care. His quick brain had lain idle for so many months that he was intoxicated now with conversation. He was thankful to have someone to talk to who would interest himself in the things that interested him.

"I say, don't let's waste this beautiful day in looking for rooms. I'll put you up tonight. You can look for rooms tomorrow or Monday."

"All right. What shall we do?" answered Hayward.

"Let's get on a penny steamboat and go down to Greenwich."

The idea appealed to Hayward, and they jumped into a cab which took them to Westminster Bridge. They got on the steamboat just as she was starting. Presently Philip, a smile on his lips, spoke.

"I remember when first I went to Paris, Clutton, I think it was, gave a long discourse on the subject that beauty is put into things by painters and poets. They create beauty. In themselves there is nothing to choose between the Campanile of Giotto and a factory chimney. And then beautiful things grow rich with the emotion that they have aroused in succeeding generations. That is why old things are more beautiful than modern. The *Ode to a Grecian Urn* is more lovely now than when it was written, because for a hundred years lovers have read it and the sick at heart taken comfort in its lines."

Philip left Hayward to infer what in the passing scene had suggested these words to him, and it was a delight to know that he could safely leave the inference. It was in sudden reaction from the life he had been leading for so long that he was now deeply affected. The delicate iridescence of the London air gave the softness of a pastel to the grey stone of the buildings; and in the wharves and storehouses there was the severity of grace of a Japanese print. They went further down, and the splendid channel, a symbol of the great empire, broadened, and it was crowded with traffic; Philip thought of the painters and the poets who had made all these things so beautiful, and his heart was filled with gratitude. They came to the Pool of London, and who can describe its majesty? The imagination thrills, and Heaven knows what figures people still its broad stream, Doctor Johnson with Boswell by his side, an old Pepys going on board a man-o'-war: the pageant of English history, and romance, and high adventure. Philip turned to Hayward with shining eyes.

"Dear Charles Dickens," he murmured, smiling a little at his own emotion.

"Aren't you rather sorry you chucked painting?" asked Hayward.

"No."

"I suppose you like doctoring?"

"No, I hate it; but there was nothing else to do. The drudgery of the first two years is awful, and unfortunately I haven't got the scientific temperament."

"Well, you can't go on changing professions."

"Oh, no. I'm going to stick to this. I think I shall like it better when I get into the wards. I have an idea that I'm more interested in people than in anything else in the world. And as far as I can see, it's the only profession in which you have your freedom. You carry your knowledge in your head; with a box of instruments and a few drugs you can make your living anywhere."

"Aren't you going to take a practice then?"

"Not for a good long time at any rate," Philip answered. "As soon as I've got through my hospital appointments I shall get a ship; I want to go to the East—the Malay Archipelago, Siam, China, and all that sort of thing—and then I shall take odd jobs. Something always comes along—cholera duty in India and things like that. I want to go from place to place. I want to see the world. The only way a poor man can do that is by going in for the medical."

They came to Greenwich then. The noble building of Inigo Jones faced the river grandly.

"I say, look, that must be the place where Poor Jack dived into the mud for pennies," said Philip.

They wandered in the park. Ragged children were playing in it, and it was noisy with their cries: here and there old seamen were basking in the sun. There was an air of a hundred years ago.

"It seems a pity you wasted two years in Paris," said Hayward.

"Waste? Look at the movement of that child, look at the pattern which the sun makes on the ground, shining through the trees, look at that sky—why, I should never have seen that sky if I hadn't been to Paris."

Hayward thought that Philip choked a sob, and he looked at him with astonishment.

"What's the matter with you?"

"Nothing. I'm sorry to be so damned emotional, but for six months I've been starved for beauty."

"You used to be so matter-of-fact. It's very interesting to hear you say that."

"Damn it all, I don't want to be interesting," laughed Philip. "Let's go and have a stodgy tea."

Chapter 65

Hayward's visit did Philip a great deal of good. Each day his thoughts dwelt less on Mildred. He looked back upon the past with disgust. He could not understand how he had submitted to the dishonour of such a love; and when he thought of Mildred it was with angry hatred, because she had submitted to him to so much humiliation. His imagination presented her to him now with her defects of person and manner exaggerated, so that he shuddered at the thought of having been connected with her.

"It just shows how damned weak I am," he said to himself. The adventure was like a blunder that one had committed at a party so horrible that one felt nothing could be done to excuse it: the only remedy was to forget. His horror at the degradation he had suffered helped him. He was like a snake casting its skin and he looked upon the old covering with nausea. He exulted in the possession of himself once more; he realized how much of the delight of the world he had lost when he was absorbed in that madness which they called love; he had had enough of it; he did not want to be in love any more if love was that. Philip told

Hayward something of what he had gone through.

"Wasn't it Sophocles," he asked, "who prayed for the time when he would be delivered from the wild beast of passion that devoured his heart-strings?"

Philip seemed really to be born again. He breathed the circumambient air as though he had never breathed it before, and he took a child's pleasure in all the facts of the world. He called his period of insanity six months' hard labour.

Hayward had only been settled in London a few days when Philip received from Blackstable, where it had been sent, a card for a private view at some picture gallery. He took Hayward, and, on looking at the catalogue, saw that Lawson had a picture in it.

"I suppose he sent the card," said Philip. "Let's go and find him, he's sure to be in front of his picture."

This, a profile of Ruth Chalice, was tucked away in a corner, and Lawson was not far from it. He looked a little lost, in his large soft hat and loose, pale clothes, amongst the fashionable throng that had gathered for the private view. He greeted Philip with enthusiasm, and with his usual volubility told him that he had come to live in London, Ruth Chalice was a hussy, he had taken a studio, Paris was played out, he had a commission for a portrait, and they'd better dine together and have a good old talk. Philip reminded him of his acquaintance with Hayward, and was entertained to see that Lawson was slightly awed by Hayward's elegant clothes and grand manner. They sat upon him better than they had done in the shabby little studio which Lawson and Philip had shared.

At dinner Lawson went on with his news. Flanagan had gone

back to America. Clutton had disappeared. He had come to the conclusion that a man had no chance of doing anything so long as he was in contact with art and artists: the only thing was to get right away. To make the step easier he had quarrelled with all his friends in Paris. He developed a talent for telling them home truths, which made them bear with fortitude his declaration that he had done with that city and was settling in Gerona, a little town in the north of Spain which had attracted him when he saw it from the train on his way to Barcelona. He was living there now alone.

"I wonder if he'll ever do any good," said Philip.

He was interested in the human side of that struggle to express something which was so obscure in the man's mind that he was become morbid and querulous. Philip felt vaguely that he was himself in the same case, but with him it was the conduct of his life as a whole that perplexed him. That was his means of self-expression, and what he must do with it was not clear. But he had no time to continue with this train of thought, for Lawson poured out a frank recital of his affair with Ruth Chalice. She had left him for a young student who had just come from England, and was behaving in a scandalous fashion. Lawson really thought someone ought to step in and save the young man. She would ruin him. Philip gathered that Lawson's chief grievance was that the rupture had come in the middle of a portrait he was painting.

"Women have no feeling for art," he said. "They only pretend they have." But he finished philosophically enough: "However, I got four portraits out of her, and I'm not sure if the last I was working on would ever have been a success."

Philip envied the easy way in which the painter managed his love affairs. He had passed eighteen months pleasantly enough, had got an excellent model for nothing, and had parted from her at the end with no great pang.

"And what about Cronshaw?" asked Philip.

"Oh, he's done for," answered Lawson, with the cheerful callousness of his youth. "He'll be dead in six months. He got pneumonia last winter. He was in the English hospital for seven weeks, and when he came out they told him his only chance was to give up liquor."

"Poor devil," smiled the abstemious Philip.

"He kept off for a bit. He used to go to the Lilas all the same, he couldn't keep away from that, but he used to drink hot milk, *avec de la fleur d'oranger*, and he was damned dull."

"I take it you did not conceal the fact from him."

"Oh, he knew it himself. A little while ago he started on whisky again. He said he was too old to turn over any new leaves. He would rather be happy for six months and die at the end of it than linger on for five years. And then I think he's been awfully hard up lately. You see, he didn't earn anything while he was ill, and the slut he lives with has been giving him a rotten time."

"I remember, the first time I saw him I admired him awfully," said Philip. "I thought he was wonderful. It is sickening that vulgar, middle-class virtue should pay."

"Of course he was a rotter. He was bound to end in the gutter sooner or later," said Lawson.

Philip was hurt because Lawson would not see the pity of it. Of course it was cause and effect, but in the necessity with which one follows the other lay all the tragedy of life.

"Oh, I'd forgotten," said Lawson. "Just after you left he sent round a present for you. I thought you'd be coming back and I didn't bother about it, and then I didn't think it worth sending on; but it'll come over to London with the rest of my things, and you can come to my studio one day and fetch it away if you want it."

"You haven't told me what it is yet."

"Oh, it's only a ragged little bit of carpet. I shouldn't think it's worth anything. I asked him one day what the devil he'd sent the filthy thing for. He told me he'd seen it in a shop in the Rue de Rennes and bought it for fifteen francs. It appears to be a Persian rug. He said you'd asked him the meaning of life and that was the answer. But he was very drunk."

Philip laughed.

"Oh yes, I know. I'll take it. It was a favourite wheeze of his. He said I must find out for myself, or else the answer meant nothing."

Chapter 66

Philip worked well and easily; he had a good deal to do, since he was taking in July the three parts of the First Conjoint examination, two of which he had failed in before; but he found life pleasant. He made a new friend. Lawson, on the lookout for models, had discovered a girl who was understudying at one of the theatres, and in order to induce her to sit to him arranged a little luncheon-party one Sunday. She brought a chaperon with her; and to her Philip, asked to make a fourth, was instructed to confine his attentions. He found this easy, since she turned out to be an agreeable chatterbox with an amusing tongue. She asked Philip to go and see her; she had rooms in Vincent Square, and was always in to tea at five o'clock; he went, was delighted with his welcome, and went again. Mrs. Nesbit was not more than twenty-five, very small, with a pleasant, ugly face; she had very bright eyes, high cheekbones, and a large mouth: the excessive contrasts of her colouring reminded one of a portrait by one of the modern French painters; her skin was very white, her cheeks were very red, her thick eyebrows, her hair, were very black. The effect was odd, a little unnatural, but far from unpleasing. She was separated from her husband and earned her living and her child's by writing penny novelettes. There were one or two publishers who made a specialty of that sort of thing, and she had as much work as she could do. It was ill-paid, she received fifteen pounds for a story of thirty thousand words; but she was satisfied.

"After all, it only costs the reader twopence," she said, "and they like the same thing over and over again. I just change the names and that's all. When I'm bored I think of the washing and the rent and clothes for baby, and I go on again."

Besides, she walked on at various theatres where they wanted supers and earned by this when in work from sixteen shillings to a guinea a week. At the end of her day she was so tired that she slept like a top. She made the best of her difficult lot. Her keen sense of humour enabled her to get amusement out of every vexatious circumstance. Sometimes things went wrong, and she found herself with no money at all; then her trifling possessions found their way to a pawnshop in the Vauxhall Bridge Road, and she ate bread and butter till things grew brighter. She never lost her cheerfulness.

Philip was interested in her shiftless life, and she made him laugh with the fantastic narration of her struggles. He asked her why she did not try her hand at literary work of a better sort, but she knew that she had no talent, and the abominable stuff she turned out by the thousand words was not only tolerably paid, but was the best she could do. She had nothing to look forward to but a continuation of the life she led. She seemed to have no relations, and her friends were as poor as herself.

"I don't think of the future," she said. "As long as I have enough money for three weeks' rent and a pound or two over for food I never bother. Life wouldn't be worth living if I worried over the future as well as the present. When things are at their worst I find something always happens."

Soon Philip grew in the habit of going in to tea with her every day, and so that his visits might not embarrass her he took in a cake or a pound of butter or some tea. They started to call one another by their Christian names. Feminine sympathy was new to him, and he delighted in someone who gave a willing ear to all his troubles. The hours went quickly. He did not hide his admiration for her. She was a delightful companion. He could not help comparing her with Mildred; and he contrasted with the one's obstinate stupidity, which refused interest to everything she did not know, the other's quick appreciation and ready intelligence. His heart sank when he thought that he might have been tied for life to such a woman as Mildred. One evening he told Norah the whole story of his love. It was not one to give him much reason for self-esteem, and it was very pleasant to receive such charming sympathy.

"I think you're well out of it," she said, when he had finished.

She had a funny way at times of holding her head on one side like an Aberdeen puppy. She was sitting in an upright chair, sewing, for she had no time to do nothing, and Philip had made himself comfortable at her feet.

"I can't tell you how heartily thankful I am it's all over," he sighed.

"Poor thing, you must have had a rotten time," she murmured, and by way of showing her sympathy put her hand on his shoulder.

He took it and kissed it, but she withdrew it quickly.

"Why did you do that?" she asked, with a blush.

"Have you any objection?"

She looked at him for a moment with twinkling eyes, and she smiled.

"No," she said.

He got up on his knees and faced her. She looked into his eyes steadily, and her large mouth trembled with a smile.

"Well?" she said.

"You know, you are a ripper. I'm so grateful to you for being nice to me. I like you so much."

"Don't be idiotic," she said.

Philip took hold of her elbows and drew her towards him. She made no resistance, but bent forward a little, and he kissed her red lips.

"Why did you do that?" she asked again.

"Because it's comfortable."

She did not answer, but a tender look came into her eyes, and she passed her hand softly over his hair.

"You know, it's awfully silly of you to behave like this. We were such good friends. It would be so jolly to leave it at that."

"If you really want to appeal to my better nature," replied Philip, "you'll do well not to stroke my cheek while you're doing it."

She gave a little chuckle, but she did not stop.

"It's very wrong of me, isn't it?" she said.

Philip, surprised and a little amused, looked into her eyes, and as he looked he saw them soften and grow liquid, and there was an expression in them that enchanted him. His heart was suddenly stirred, and tears came to his eyes.

"Norah, you're not fond of me, are you?" he asked, incredulously.

"You clever boy, you ask such stupid questions."

"Oh, my dear, it never struck me that you could be."

He flung his arms round her and kissed her, while she, laughing, blushing, and crying, surrendered herself willingly to his embrace.

Presently he released her and sitting back on his heels looked at her curiously.

"Well, I'm blowed!" he said.

"Why?"

"I'm so surprised."

"And pleased?"

"Delighted," he cried with all his heart, "and so proud and so happy and so grateful."

He took her hands and covered them with kisses. This was the beginning for Philip of a happiness which seemed both solid and durable. They became lovers but remained friends. There was in Norah a maternal instinct which received satisfaction in her love for Philip; she wanted someone to pet, and scold, and make a fuss of; she had a domestic temperament and found pleasure in looking after his health and his linen. She pitied his deformity, over which he was so sensitive, and her pity expressed itself instinctively in tenderness. She was young, strong, and healthy, and it seemed quite natural to her to give her love. She had high spirits and a merry soul. She liked Philip because he laughed with her at all the amusing things in life that caught her fancy, and above all she liked him because he was he.

When she told him this he answered gaily:

"Nonsense. You like me because I'm a silent person and never want to get a word in."

Philip did not love her at all. He was extremely fond of her, glad to be with her, amused and interested by her conversation. She restored his belief in himself and put healing ointments, as it were, on all the bruises of his soul. He was immensely flattered that she cared for him. He admired her courage, her optimism, her impudent defiance of fate; she had a little philosophy of her own, ingenuous and practical.

"You know, I don't believe in churches and parsons and all that," she said, "but I believe in God, and I don't believe He minds much about what you do as long as you keep your end up and help a lame dog over a stile when you can. And I think people on the whole are very nice, and I'm sorry for those who aren't."

"And what about afterwards?" asked Philip.

"Oh, well, I don't know for certain, you know," she smiled, "but I hope for the best. And anyhow there'll be no rent to pay and no novelettes to write."

She had a feminine gift for delicate flattery. She thought that Philip did a brave thing when he left Paris because he was conscious he could not be a great artist; and he was enchanted when she expressed enthusiastic admiration for him. He had never been quite certain whether this action indicated courage or infirmity of purpose. It was delightful to realize that she considered it heroic. She ventured to tackle him on a subject which his friends instinctively avoided.

"It's very silly of you to be so sensitive about your club-foot," she said. She saw him flush darkly, but went on. "You know, people don't think about it nearly as much as you do. They notice it the first time they see you, and then they forget about it."

He would not answer.

"You're not angry with me, are you?"

"No."

She put her arm round his neck.

"You know, I only speak about it because I love you. I don't want it to make you unhappy."

"I think you can say anything you choose to me," he answered, smiling. "I wish I could do something to show you how grateful I am to you."

She took him in hand in other ways. She would not let him be bearish and laughed at him when he was out of temper. She made him more urbane.

"You can make me do anything you like," he said to her once.

"D'you mind?"

"No, I want to do what you like."

He had the sense to realize his happiness. It seemed to him that she gave him all that a wife could, and he preserved his freedom; she was the most charming friend he had ever had, with a sympathy that he had never found in a man. The sexual relationship was no more than the strongest link in their friendship. It completed it, but was not essential. And because Philip's appetites were satisfied, he became more equable and easier to live with. He felt in complete possession of himself. He thought sometimes of the winter, during which he had been obsessed by a hideous passion, and he was filled with loathing for Mildred and with horror of himself.

His examinations were approaching, and Norah was as interested in them as he. He was flattered and touched by her eagerness. She made him promise to come at once and tell her the result. He passed the three parts this time without mishap, and when he went to tell her she burst into tears.

"Oh, I'm so glad, I was so anxious."

"You silly little thing," he laughed, but he was choking.

No one could help being pleased with the way she took it.

"And what are you going to do now?" she asked.

"I can take a holiday with a clear conscience. I have no work to do till the winter session begins in October."

"I suppose you'll go down to your uncle's at Blackstable?"

"You suppose quite wrong. I'm going to stay in London and play with you."

"I'd rather you went away."

"Why? Are you tired of me?"

She laughed and put her hands on his shoulders.

"Because you've been working hard, and you look utterly washed out. You want some fresh air and a rest. Please go."

He did not answer for a moment. He looked at her with loving eyes.

"You know, I'd never believe it of anyone but you. You're only thinking of my good. I wonder what you see in me."

"Will you give me a good character with my month's notice?" she laughed gaily.

"I'll say that you're thoughtful and kind, and you're not exacting; you never worry, you're not troublesome, and you're easy to please."

"All that's nonsense," she said, "but I'll tell you one thing: I'm one of the few persons I ever met who are able to learn from experience."

Chapter 67

Philip looked forward to his return to London with impatience. During the two months he spent at Blackstable Norah wrote to him frequently, long letters in a bold, large hand, in which with cheerful humour she described the little events of the daily round, the domestic troubles of her landlady, rich food for laughter, the comic vexations of her rehearsals—she was walking on in an important spectacle at one of the London theatres—and her odd adventures with the publishers of novelettes. Philip read a great deal, bathed, played tennis, and sailed. At the beginning of October he settled down in London to work for the Second Conjoint examination. He was eager to pass it, since that ended the drudgery of the curriculum; after it was done with the student became an out-patients' clerk, and was brought in contact with men and women as well as with textbooks. Philip saw Norah every day.

Lawson had been spending the summer at Poole, and had a number of sketches to show of the harbour and of the beach. He had a couple of commissions for portraits and proposed to stay in London till the bad light drove him away. Hayward, in London too, intended to spend the winter abroad, but remained week after week from sheer inability to make up his mind to go. Hayward had run to fat during the last two or three years—it was five years since Philip first met him in Heidelberg—and he was prematurely bald. He was very sensitive about it and wore his hair long to conceal the unsightly patch on the crown of his head. His only consolation was that his brow was now very noble. His blue eyes had lost their colour; they had a listless droop; and his mouth, losing the fulness of youth, was weak and pale. He still talked vaguely of the things he was going to do in the future, but with less conviction; and he was conscious that his friends no longer believed in him: when he had drunk two or three glasses of whisky he was inclined to be elegiac.

"I'm a failure," he murmured, "I'm unfit for the brutality of the struggle of life. All I can do is to stand aside and let the vulgar throng hustle by in their pursuit of the good things."

He gave you the impression that to fail was a more delicate, a more exquisite thing than to succeed. He insinuated that his aloofness was due to distaste for all that was common and low. He talked beautifully of Plato.

"I should have thought you'd got through with Plato by now," said Philip impatiently.

"Would you?" he asked, raising his eyebrows.

He was not inclined to pursue the subject. He had discovered of late the effective dignity of silence.

"I don't see the use of reading the same thing over and over again," said Philip. "That's only a laborious form of idleness."

"But are you under the impression that you have so great a mind that you can understand the most profound writer at a first reading?"

"I don't want to understand him, I'm not a critic. I'm not interested in him for his sake but for mine."

"Why d'you read then?"

"Partly for pleasure, because it's a habit and I'm just as uncomfortable if I don't read as if I don't smoke, and partly to know myself. When I read a book I seem to read it with my eyes only, but now and then I come across a passage, perhaps only a phrase, which has a meaning for *me*, and it becomes part of me; I've got out of the book all that's any use to me, and I can't get anything more if I read it a dozen times. You see, it seems to me, one's like a closed bud, and most of what one reads and does has no effect at all; but there are certain things that have a peculiar significance for one, and they open a petal; and the petals open one by one; and at last the flower is there."

Philip was not satisfied with his metaphor, but he did not know how else to explain a thing which he felt and yet was not clear about.

"You want to do things, you want to become things," said Hayward, with a shrug of the shoulders. "It's so vulgar."

Philip knew Hayward very well by now. He was weak and vain, so vain that you had to be on the watch constantly not to hurt his feelings; he mingled idleness and idealism so that he could not separate them. At Lawson's studio one day he met a journalist, who was charmed by his conversation, and a week later the editor of a paper wrote to suggest that he should do some criticism for him. For forty-eight hours Hayward lived in an agony of indecision. He had talked of getting occupation of this sort so long that he had not the face to refuse outright, but the thought of doing anything filled him with panic. At last he declined the offer and breathed freely.

"It would have interfered with my work," he told Philip.

"What work?" asked Philip brutally.

"My inner life," he answered.

Then he went on to say beautiful things about Amiel, the professor of Geneva, whose brilliancy promised achievement which was never fulfilled; till at his death the reason of his failure and the excuse were at once manifest in the minute, wonderful journal which was found among his papers. Hayward smiled enigmatically.

But Hayward could still talk delightfully about books; his taste was exquisite and his discrimination elegant; and he had a constant interest in ideas, which made him an entertaining companion. They meant nothing to him really, since they never had any effect on him; but he treated them as he might have pieces of china in an auction-room, handling them with pleasure in their shape and their glaze, pricing them in his mind; and then, putting them back into their case, thought of them no more.

And it was Hayward who made a momentous discovery. One evening, after due preparation, he took Philip and Lawson to a tavern situated in Beak Street, remarkable not only in itself and for its history—it had memories of eighteenth century glories which excited the romantic imagination—but for its snuff, which was the best in London, and above all for its punch. Hayward

513

led them into a large, long room, dingily magnificent, with huge pictures on the walls of nude women: they were vast allegories of the school of Haydon; but smoke, gas, and the London atmosphere had given them a richness which made them look like old masters. The dark panelling, the massive, tarnished gold of the cornice, the mahogany tables, gave the room an air of sumptuous comfort, and the leather-covered seats along the wall were soft and easy. There was a ram's head on a table opposite the door, and this contained the celebrated snuff. They ordered punch. They drank it. It was hot rum punch. The pen falters when it attempts to treat of the excellence thereof; the sober vocabulary, the sparse epithet of this narrative, are inadequate to the task; and pompous terms, jewelled, exotic phrases rise to the excited fancy. It warmed the blood and cleared the head; it filled the soul with well-being; it disposed the mind at once to utter wit, and to appreciate the wit of others; it had the vagueness of music and the precision of mathematics. Only one of its qualities was comparable to anything else; it had the warmth of a good heart; but its taste, its smell, its feel, were not to be described in words. Charles Lamb, with his infinite tact, attempting to, might have drawn charming pictures of the life of his day; Lord Byron in a stanza of *Don Juan*, aiming at the impossible, might have achieved the sublime; Oscar Wilde, heaping jewels of Ispahan upon brocades of Byzantium, might have created a troubling beauty. Considering it, the mind reeled under visions of the feasts of Elagabalus; and the subtle harmonies of Debussy mingled with the musty, fragrant romance of chests in which have been kept old clothes, ruffs, hose, doublets, of a forgotten generation, and the wan odour of lilies of the valley and the savour of Cheddar cheese.

Hayward discovered the tavern at which this priceless beverage was to be obtained, by meeting in the street a man called Macalister who had been at Cambridge with him. He was a stockbroker and a philosopher. He was accustomed to go to the tavern once a week; and soon Philip, Lawson, and Hayward got into the habit of meeting there every Tuesday evening: change of manners made it now little frequented, which was an advantage to persons who took pleasure in conversation. Macalister was a big-boned fellow, much too short for his width, with a large, fleshy face and a soft voice. He was a student of Kant and judged everything from the standpoint of pure reason. He was fond of expounding his doctrines. Philip listened with excited interest. He had long come to the conclusion that nothing amused him more than metaphysics, but he was not so sure of their efficacy in the affairs of life. The neat little system which he had formed as the result of his meditations at Blackstable had not been of conspicuous use during his infatuation for Mildred. He could not be positive that reason was much help in the conduct of life. It seemed to him that life lived itself. He remembered very vividly the violence of the emotion which had possessed him and his inability, as if he were tied down to the ground with ropes, to react against it. He read many wise things in books, but he could only judge from his own experience (he did not know whether he was different from other people); he did not calculate the pros and cons of an action, the benefits which must befall him if he did it, the harm which might result from the omission; but his whole being was urged on irresistibly. He did not act with a part of himself but altogether. The power that possessed him seemed to have nothing to do with reason: all that reason did was to point out the methods of obtaining what his whole soul was striving for.

Macalister reminded him of the Categorical Imperative:

"Act so that every action of yours should be capable of becoming a universal rule of action for all men."

"That seems to me perfect nonsense," said Philip.

"You're a bold man to say that of anything stated by Immanuel Kant," retorted Macalister.

"Why? Reverence for what somebody said is a stultifying quality: there's a damned sight too much reverence in the world. Kant thought things, not because they were true, but because he was Kant."

"Well, what is your objection to the Categorical Imperative?"

(They talked as though the fate of empires were in the balance.)

"It suggests that one can choose one's course by an effort of will. And it suggests that reason is the surest guide. Why should its dictates be any better than those of passion? They're different. That's all."

"You seem to be a contented slave of your passions."

"A slave because I can't help myself, but not a contented one," laughed Philip.

While he spoke he thought of that hot madness which had driven him in pursuit of Mildred. He remembered how he had chafed against it and how he had felt the degradation of it.

"Thank God, I'm free from all that now," he thought.

And yet even as he said it he was not quite sure whether he spoke sincerely. When he was under the influence of passion he had felt a singular vigour, and his mind had worked with unwonted force. He was more alive, there was an excitement in sheer being, an eager vehemence of soul, which made life now a trifle dull. For all the misery he had endured there was a compensation in that sense of rushing, overwhelming existence.

But Philip's unlucky words engaged him in a discussion on the freedom of the will, and Macalister, with his well-stored memory, brought out argument after argument. He had a mind that delighted in dialectics, and he forced Philip to contradict himself; he pushed him into corners from which he could only escape by damaging concessions; he tripped him up with logic and battered him with authorities.

At last Philip said:

"Well, I can't say anything about other people. I can only speak for myself. The illusion of free will is so strong in my mind that I can't get away from it, but I believe it is only an illusion. But it is an illusion which is one of the strongest motives of my actions. Before I do anything I feel that I have choice, and that influences what I do; but afterwards, when the thing is done, I believe that it was inevitable from all eternity."

"What do you deduce from that?" asked Hayward.

"Why, merely the futility of regret. It's no good crying over spilt milk, because all the forces of the universe were bent on spilling it."

Chapter 68

One morning Philip on getting up felt his head swim, and going back to bed suddenly discovered he was ill. All his limbs ached and he shivered with cold. When the landlady brought in his breakfast he called to her through the open door that he was not well, and asked for a cup of tea and a piece of toast. A few minutes later there was a knock at his door, and Griffiths came in. They had lived in the same house for over a year, but had never done more than nod to one another in the passage.

"I say, I hear you're seedy," said Griffiths. "I thought I'd come in and see what was the matter with you."

Philip, blushing he knew not why, made light of the whole thing. He would be all right in an hour or two.

"Well, you'd better let me take your temperature," said Griffiths.

"It's quite unnecessary," answered Philip irritably.

"Come on."

Philip put the thermometer in his mouth. Griffiths sat on the bed and chatted brightly for a moment, then he took it out and looked at it.

"Now, look here, old man, you must stay in bed, and I'll bring old Deacon in to have a look at you."

"Nonsense," said Philip. "There's nothing the matter. I wish you wouldn't bother about me."

"But it isn't any bother. You've got a temperature and you must stay in bed. You will, won't you?"

There was a peculiar charm in his manner, a mingling of gravity and kindliness, which was infinitely attractive.

"You've got a wonderful bedside manner," Philip murmured, closing his eyes with a smile.

Griffiths shook out his pillow for him, deftly smoothed down the bedclothes, and tucked him up. He went into Philip's sitting-room to look for a siphon, could not find one, and fetched it from his own room. He drew down the blind.

"Now, go to sleep and I'll bring the old man round as soon as he's done the wards."

It seemed hours before anyone came to Philip. His head felt as if it would split, anguish rent his limbs, and he was afraid he was going to cry. Then there was a knock at the door and Griffiths, healthy, strong, and cheerful, came in.

"Here's Doctor Deacon," he said.

The physician stepped forward, an elderly man with a bland manner, whom Philip knew only by sight. A few questions, a brief examination, and the diagnosis.

"What d'you make it?" he asked Griffiths, smiling.

"Influenza."

"Quite right."

Doctor Deacon looked round the dingy lodging-house room.

"Wouldn't you like to go to the hospital? They'll put you in a private ward, and you can be better looked after than you can here."

"I'd rather stay where I am," said Philip.

He did not want to be disturbed, and he was always shy of new surroundings. He did not fancy nurses fussing about him, and the dreary cleanliness of the hospital.

"I can look after him, sir," said Griffiths at once.

"Oh, very well."

He wrote a prescription, gave instructions, and left.

"Now you've got to do exactly as I tell you," said Griffiths. "I'm day-nurse and night-nurse all in one."

"It's very kind of you, but I shan't want anything," said Philip.

Griffiths put his hand on Philip's forehead, a large cool, dry hand, and the touch seemed to him good.

"I'm just going to take this round to the dispensary to have it made up, and then I'll come back."

In a little while he brought the medicine and gave Philip a dose. Then he went upstairs to fetch his books.

"You won't mind my working in your room this afternoon, will you?" he said, when he came down. "I'll leave the door open so that you can give me a shout if you want anything."

Later in the day Philip, awaking from an uneasy doze, heard voices in his sitting-room. A friend had come in to see Griffiths.

"I say, you'd better not come in tonight," he heard Griffiths saying.

And then a minute or two afterwards someone else entered the room and expressed his surprise at finding Griffiths there. Philip heard him explain.

"I'm looking after a second year's man who's got these rooms. The wretched blighter's down with influenza. No whist tonight, old man."

Presently Griffiths was left alone and Philip called him.

"I say, you're not putting off a party tonight, are you?" he asked.

"Not on your account. I must work at my surgery."

"Don't put it off. I shall be all right. You needn't bother about me."

"That's all right."

Philip grew worse. As the night came on he became slightly delirious, but towards morning he awoke from a restless sleep. He saw Griffiths get out of an armchair, go down on his knees, and with his fingers put piece after piece of coal on the fire. He was in pyjamas and a dressing-gown.

"What are you doing here?" he asked.

"Did I wake you up? I tried to make up the fire without making a row."

"Why aren't you in bed? What's the time?"

"About five. I thought I'd better sit up with you tonight. I brought an armchair in as I thought if I put a mattress down I should sleep so soundly that I shouldn't hear you if you wanted anything."

"I wish you wouldn't be so good to me," groaned Philip. "Suppose you catch it?"

"Then you shall nurse me, old man," said Griffiths, with a laugh.

In the morning Griffiths drew up the blind. He looked pale and tired after his night's watch, but was full of spirits.

"Now, I'm going to wash you," he said to Philip cheerfully.

"I can wash myself," said Philip, ashamed.

"Nonsense. If you were in the small ward a nurse would wash you, and I can do it just as well as a nurse."

Philip, too weak and wretched to resist, allowed Griffiths to wash his hands and face, his feet, his chest and back. He did it with charming tenderness, carrying on meanwhile a stream of friendly chatter; then he changed the sheet just as they did at the hospital, shook out the pillow, and arranged the bedclothes.

"I should like Sister Arthur to see me. It would make her sit up. Deacon's coming in to see you early."

"I can't imagine why you should be so good to me," said Philip.

"It's good practice for me. It's rather a lark having a patient."

Griffiths gave him his breakfast and went off to get dressed and have something to eat. A few minutes before ten he came back with a bunch of grapes and a few flowers.

"You are awfully kind," said Philip.

He was in bed for five days.

Norah and Griffiths nursed him between them. Though Griffiths was the same age as Philip he adopted towards him a humorous, motherly attitude. He was a thoughtful fellow, gentle and encouraging; but his greatest quality was a vitality which seemed to give health to everyone with whom he came in contact.

Philip was unused to the petting which most people enjoy from mothers or sisters and he was deeply touched by the feminine tenderness of this strong young man. Philip grew better. Then Griffiths, sitting idly in Philip's room, amused him with gay stories of amorous adventure. He was a flirtatious creature, capable of carrying on three or four affairs at a time; and his account of the devices he was forced to in order to keep out of difficulties made excellent hearing. He had a gift for throwing a romantic glamour over everything that happened to him. He was crippled with debts, everything he had of any value was pawned, but he managed always to be cheerful, extravagant, and generous. He was the adventurer by nature. He loved people of doubtful occupations and shifty purposes; and his acquaintance among the riff-raff that frequents the bars of London was enormous. Loose women, treating him as a friend, told him the troubles, difficulties, and successes of their lives; and card-sharpers, respecting his impecuniosity, stood him dinners and lent him five-pound notes. He was ploughed in his examinations time after time; but he bore this cheerfully, and submitted with such a charming grace to the parental expostulations that his father, a doctor in practice at Leeds, had not the heart to be seriously angry with him.

"I'm an awful fool at books," he said cheerfully, "but I *can't* work."

Life was much too jolly. But it was clear that when he had got through the exuberance of his youth, and was at last qualified, he would be a tremendous success in practice. He would cure people by the sheer charm of his manner.

Philip worshipped him as at school he had worshipped

boys who were tall and straight and high of spirits. By the time he was well they were fast friends, and it was a peculiar satisfaction to Philip that Griffiths seemed to enjoy sitting in his little parlour, wasting Philip's time with his amusing chatter and smoking innumerable cigarettes. Philip took him sometimes to the tavern off Regent Street. Hayward found him stupid, but Lawson recognized his charm and was eager to paint him; he was a picturesque figure with his blue eyes, white skin, and curly hair. Often they discussed things he knew nothing about, and then he sat quietly, with a good-natured smile on his handsome face, feeling quite rightly that his presence was sufficient contribution to the entertainment of the company. When he discovered that Macalister was a stockbroker he was eager for tips; and Macalister, with his grave smile, told him what fortunes he could have made if he had bought certain stock at certain times. It made Philip's mouth water, for in one way and another he was spending more than he had expected, and it would have suited him very well to make a little money by the easy method Macalister suggested.

"Next time I hear of a really good thing I'll let you know," said the stockbroker. "They do come along sometimes. It's only a matter of biding one's time."

Philip could not help thinking how delightful it would be to make fifty pounds, so that he could give Norah the furs she so badly needed for the winter. He looked at the shops in Regent Street and picked out the articles he could buy for the money. She deserved everything. She made his life very happy.

Chapter 69

One afternoon, when he went back to his rooms from the hospital to wash and tidy himself before going to tea as usual with Norah, as he let himself in with his latchkey, his landlady opened the door for him.

"There's a lady waiting to see you," she said.

"Me?" exclaimed Philip.

He was surprised. It would only be Norah, and he had no idea what had brought her.

"I shouldn't 'ave let her in, only she's been three times, and she seemed that upset at not finding you, so I told her she could wait."

He pushed past the explaining landlady and burst into the room. His heart turned sick. It was Mildred. She was sitting down, but got up hurriedly as he came in. She did not move towards him nor speak. He was so surprised that he did not know what he was saying.

"What the hell d'you want?" he asked.

She did not answer, but began to cry. She did not put her

hands to her eyes, but kept them hanging by the side of her body. She looked like a housemaid applying for a situation. There was a dreadful humility in her bearing. Philip did not know what feelings came over him. He had a sudden impulse to turn round and escape from the room.

"I didn't think I'd ever see you again," he said at last.

"I wish I was dead," she moaned.

Philip left her standing where she was. He could only think at the moment of steadying himself. His knees were shaking. He looked at her, and he groaned in despair.

"What's the matter?" he said.

"He's left me—Emil."

Philip's heart bounded. He knew then that he loved her as passionately as ever. He had never ceased to love her. She was standing before him humble and unresisting. He wished to take her in his arms and cover her tear-stained face with kisses. Oh, how long the separation had been! He did not know how he could have endured it.

"You'd better sit down. Let me give you a drink."

He drew the chair near the fire and she sat in it. He mixed her whisky and soda, and, sobbing still, she drank it. She looked at him with great, mournful eyes. There were large black lines under them. She was thinner and whiter than when last he had seen her.

"I wish I'd married you when you asked me," she said.

Philip did not know why the remark seemed to swell his heart. He could not keep the distance from her which he had forced upon himself. He put his hand on her shoulder.

"I'm awfully sorry you're in trouble."

She leaned her head against his bosom and burst into hysterical crying. Her hat was in the way and she took it off. He had never dreamt that she was capable of crying like that. He kissed her again and again. It seemed to ease her a little.

"You were always good to me, Philip," she said. "That's why I knew I could come to you."

"Tell me what's happened."

"Oh, I can't, I can't," she cried out, breaking away from him.

He sank down on his knees beside her and put his cheek against hers.

"Don't you know that there's nothing you can't tell me. I can never blame you for anything."

She told him the story little by little, and sometimes she sobbed so much that he could hardly understand.

"Last Monday week he went up to Birmingham, and he promised to be back on Thursday, and he never came, and he didn't come on the Friday, so I wrote to ask what was the matter, and he never answered the letter. And I wrote and said that if I didn't hear from him by return I'd go up to Birmingham, and this morning I got a solicitor's letter to say I had no claim on him, and if I molested him he'd seek the protection of the law."

"But it's absurd," cried Philip. "A man can't treat his wife like that. Had you had a row?"

"Oh, yes, we'd had a quarrel on the Sunday, and he said he was sick of me, but he'd said it before, and he'd come back all right. I didn't think he meant it. He was frightened because I told him a baby was coming. I kept it from him as long as I could. Then I had to tell him. He said it was my fault, and I ought to have known better. If you'd only heard the things he said to me! But I found out precious quick that he wasn't a gentleman. He left me without a penny. He hadn't paid the rent, and I hadn't got the money to pay it, and the woman who kept the house said such things to me—well, I might have been a thief the way she talked."

"I thought you were going to take a flat."

"That's what he said, but we just took furnished apartments in Highbury. He was that mean. He said I was extravagant; he didn't give me anything to be extravagant with."

She had an extraordinary way of mixing the trivial with the important. Philip was puzzled. The whole thing was incomprehensible.

"No man could be such a blackguard."

"You don't know him. I wouldn't go back to him now not if he was to come and ask me on his bended knees. I was a fool ever to think of him. And he wasn't earning the money he said he was. The lies he told me!"

Philip thought for a minute or two. He was so deeply moved by her distress that he could not think of himself.

"Would you like me to go to Birmingham? I could see him and try to make things up."

"Oh, there's no chance of that. He'll never come back now, I know him."

"But he must provide for you. He can't get out of that. I don't know anything about these things, you'd better go and see a solicitor."

"How can I? I haven't got the money."

"I'll pay all that. I'll write a note to my own solicitor, the sportsman who was my father's executor. Would you like me to come with you now? I expect he'll still be at his office."

"No, give me a letter to him. I'll go alone."

She was a little calmer now. He sat down and wrote a note. Then he remembered that she had no money. He had fortunately changed a cheque the day before and was able to give her five pounds.

"You are good to me, Philip," she said.

"I'm so happy to be able to do something for you."

"Are you fond of me still?"

"Just as fond as ever."

She put up her lips and he kissed her. There was a surrender in the action which he had never seen in her before. It was worth all the agony he had suffered.

She went away and he found that she had been there for two hours. He was extraordinarily happy.

"Poor thing, poor thing," he murmured to himself, his heart glowing with a greater love than he had ever felt before.

He never thought of Norah at all till about eight o'clock a telegram came. He knew before opening it that it was from her.

Is anything the matter? Norah.

He did not know what to do nor what to answer. He could fetch her after the play, in which she was walking on, was over and stroll home with her as he sometimes did; but his whole soul revolted against the idea of seeing her that evening. He thought of writing to her, but he could not bring himself to address her as usual, *dearest Norah*. He made up his mind to telegraph.

Sorry. Could not get away. Philip.

He visualized her. He was slightly repelled by the ugly little face, with its high cheekbones and the crude colour. There was a coarseness in her skin which gave him goose-flesh. He knew that his telegram must be followed by some action on his part, but at all events it postponed it.

Next day he wired again.

Regret, unable to come. Will write.

Mildred had suggested coming at four in the afternoon, and he would not tell her that the hour was inconvenient. After all she came first. He waited for her impatiently. He watched for her at the window and opened the front door himself.

"Well? Did you see Nixon?"

"Yes," she answered. "He said it wasn't any good. Nothing's to be done. I must just grin and bear it."

"But that's impossible," cried Philip.

She sat down wearily.

"Did he give any reasons?" he asked.

She gave him a crumpled letter.

"There's your letter, Philip. I never took it. I couldn't tell you yesterday, I really couldn't. Emil didn't marry me. He couldn't. He had a wife already and three children."

Philip felt a sudden pang of jealousy and anguish. It was

almost more than he could bear.

"That's why I couldn't go back to my aunt. There's no one I can go to but you."

"What made you go away with him?" Philip asked, in a low voice which he struggled to make firm.

"I don't know. I didn't know he was a married man at first, and when he told me I gave him a piece of my mind. And then I didn't see him for months, and when he came to the shop again and asked me I don't know what came over me. I felt as if I couldn't help it. I had to go with him."

"Were you in love with him?"

"I don't know. I couldn't hardly help laughing at the things he said. And there was something about him—he said I'd never regret it, he promised to give me seven pounds a week—he said he was earning fifteen, and it was all a lie, he wasn't. And then I was sick of going to the shop every morning, and I wasn't getting on very well with my aunt; she wanted to treat me as a servant instead of a relation, said I ought to do my own room, and if I didn't do it nobody was going to do it for me. Oh, I wish I hadn't. But when he came to the shop and asked me I felt I couldn't help it."

Philip moved away from her. He sat down at the table and buried his face in his hands. He felt dreadfully humiliated.

"You're not angry with me, Philip?" she asked piteously.

"No," he answered, looking up but away from her, "only I'm awfully hurt."

"Why?"

"You see, I was so dreadfully in love with you. I did everything I could to make you care for me. I thought you were incapable of loving anyone. It's so horrible to know that you were willing to sacrifice everything for that bounder. I wonder what you saw in him."

"I'm awfully sorry, Philip. I regretted it bitterly afterwards, I promise you that."

He thought of Emil Miller, with his pasty, unhealthy look, his shifty blue eyes, and the vulgar smartness of his appearance; he always wore bright red knitted waistcoats. Philip sighed. She got up and went to him. She put her arm round his neck.

"I shall never forget that you offered to marry me, Philip."

He took her hand and looked up at her. She bent down and kissed him.

"Philip, if you want me still I'll do anything you like now. I know you're a gentleman in every sense of the word."

His heart stood still. Her words made him feel slightly sick.

"It's awfully good of you, but I couldn't."

"Don't you care for me any more?"

"Yes, I love you with all my heart."

"Then why shouldn't we have a good time while we've got the chance? You see, it can't matter now."

He released himself from her.

"You don't understand. I've been sick with love for you ever since I saw you, but now—that man. I've unfortunately got a vivid imagination. The thought of it simply disgusts me."

"You are funny," she said.

He took her hand again and smiled at her.

"You mustn't think I'm not grateful. I can never thank you enough, but, you see, it's just stronger than I am."

"You are a good friend, Philip."

They went on talking, and soon they had returned to the familiar companionship of old days. It grew late. Philip suggested that they should dine together and go to a music hall. She wanted some persuasion, for she had an idea of acting up to her situation, and felt instinctively that it did not accord with her distressed condition to go to a place of entertainment. At last Philip asked her to go simply to please him, and when she could look upon it as an act of self-sacrifice she accepted. She had a new thoughtfulness which delighted Philip. She asked him to take her to the little restaurant in Soho to which they had so often been; he was infinitely grateful to her, because her suggestion showed that happy memories were attached to it. She grew much more cheerful as dinner proceeded. The Burgundy from the public house at the corner warmed her heart, and she forgot that she ought to preserve a dolorous countenance. Philip thought it safe to speak to her of the future.

"I suppose you haven't got a brass farthing, have you?" he asked, when an opportunity presented itself.

"Only what you gave me yesterday, and I had to give the landlady three pounds of that."

"Well, I'd better give you a tenner to go on with. I'll go and see my solicitor and get him to write to Miller. We can make him pay up something, I'm sure. If we can get a hundred pounds out of him it'll carry you on till after the baby comes."

"I wouldn't take a penny from him. I'd rather starve."

"But it's monstrous that he should leave you in the lurch like this."

"I've got my pride to consider."

It was a little awkward for Philip. He needed rigid economy to make his own money last till he was qualified, and he must have something over to keep him during the year he intended to spend as house physician and house surgeon either at his own or at some other hospital. But Mildred had told him various stories of Emil's meanness, and he was afraid to remonstrate with her in case she accused him too of want of generosity.

"I wouldn't take a penny piece from him. I'd sooner beg my bread. I'd have seen about getting some work to do long before now, only it wouldn't be good for me in the state I'm in. You have to think of your health, don't you?"

"You needn't bother about the present," said Philip. "I can let you have all you want till you're fit to work again."

"I knew I could depend on you. I told Emil he needn't think I hadn't got somebody to go to. I told him you was a gentleman in every sense of the word."

By degrees Philip learned how the separation had come about. It appeared that the fellow's wife had discovered the adventure he was engaged in during his periodical visits to London, and had gone to the head of the firm that employed him. She threatened to divorce him, and they announced that they would dismiss him if she did. He was passionately devoted to his children and could not bear the thought of being separated from them. When he had to choose between his wife and his mistress he chose his wife. He had always been anxious that there should be no child to make the entanglement more complicated; and when Mildred, unable longer to conceal its approach, informed him of the fact, he was seized with panic. He picked a quarrel and left her without more ado.

"When d'you expect to be confined?" asked Philip.

"At the beginning of March."

"Three months."

It was necessary to discuss plans. Mildred declared she would not remain in the rooms at Highbury, and Philip thought it more convenient too that she should be nearer to him. He promised to look for something next day. She suggested the Vauxhall Bridge Road as a likely neighbourhood.

"And it would be near for afterwards," she said.

"What do you mean?"

"Well, I should only be able to stay there about two months or a little more, and then I should have to go into a house. I know a very respectable place, where they have a most superior class of people, and they take you for four guineas a week and no extras. Of course the doctor's extra, but that's all. A friend of mine went there, and the lady who keeps it is a thorough lady. I mean to tell her that my husband's an officer in India and I've come to London for my baby, because it's better for my health."

It seemed extraordinary to Philip to hear her talking in this way. With her delicate little features and her pale face she looked cold and maidenly. When he thought of the passions that burnt within her, so unexpectedly, his heart was strangely troubled. His pulse beat quickly.

Chapter 70

Philip expected to find a letter from Norah when he got back to his rooms, but there was nothing; nor did he receive one the following morning. The silence irritated and at the same time alarmed him. They had seen one another every day he had been in London since the previous June, and it must seem odd to her that he should let two days go by without visiting her or offering a reason for his absence; he wondered whether by an unlucky chance she had seen him with Mildred. He could not bear to think that she was hurt or unhappy, and he made up his mind to call on her that afternoon. He was almost inclined to reproach her because he had allowed himself to get on such intimate terms with her. The thought of continuing them filled him with disgust.

He found two rooms for Mildred on the second floor of a house in the Vauxhall Bridge Road. They were noisy, but he knew that she liked the rattle of traffic under her windows.

"I don't like a dead-and-alive street where you don't see a soul pass all day," she said. "Give me a bit of life."

Then he forced himself to go to Vincent Square. He was

sick with apprehension when he rang the bell. He had an uneasy sense that he was treating Norah badly; he dreaded reproaches; he knew she had a quick temper, and he hated scenes: perhaps the best way would be to tell her frankly that Mildred had come back to him and his love for her was as violent as it had ever been; he was very sorry, but he had nothing to offer Norah any more. Then he thought of her anguish, for he knew she loved him; it had flattered him before, and he was immensely grateful; but now it was horrible. She had not deserved that he should inflict pain upon her. He asked himself how she would greet him now, and as he walked up the stairs all possible forms of her behaviour flashed across his mind. He knocked at the door. He felt that he was pale, and wondered how to conceal his nervousness.

She was writing away industriously, but she sprang to her feet as he entered.

"I recognized your step," she cried. "Where have you been hiding yourself, you naughty boy?"

She came towards him joyfully and put her arms round his neck. She was delighted to see him. He kissed her, and then, to give himself countenance, said he was dying for tea. She bustled the fire to make the kettle boil.

"I've been awfully busy," he said lamely.

She began to chatter in her bright way, telling him of a new commission she had to provide a novelette for a firm which had not hitherto employed her. She was to get fifteen guineas for it.

"It's money from the clouds. I'll tell you what we'll do, we'll stand ourselves a little jaunt. Let's go and spend a day at Oxford, shall we? I'd love to see the colleges."

He looked at her to see whether there was any shadow of reproach in her eyes; but they were as frank and merry as ever; she was overjoyed to see him. His heart sank. He could not tell her the brutal truth. She made some toast for him, and cut it into little pieces, and gave it him as though he were a child.

"Is the brute fed?" she asked.

He nodded, smiling; and she lit a cigarette for him. Then, as she loved to do, she came and sat on his knees. She was very light. She leaned back in his arms with a sigh of delicious happiness.

"Say something nice to me," she murmured.

"What shall I say?"

"You might by an effort of imagination say that you rather liked me."

"You know I do that."

He had not the heart to tell her then. He would give her peace at all events for that day, and perhaps he might write to her. That would be easier. He could not bear to think of her crying. She made him kiss her, and as he kissed her he thought of Mildred and Mildred's pale, thin lips. The recollection of Mildred remained with him all the time, like an incorporated form, but more substantial than a shadow; and the sight continually distracted his attention.

"You're very quiet today," Norah said.

Her loquacity was a standing joke between them, and he answered:

"You never let me get a word in, and I've got out of the habit of talking."

"But you're not listening, and that's bad manners."

He reddened a little, wondering whether she had some inkling of his secret; he turned away his eyes uneasily. The weight of her irked him this afternoon, and he did not want her to touch him.

"My foot's gone to sleep," he said.

"I'm so sorry," she cried, jumping up. "I shall have to bant if I can't break myself of this habit of sitting on gentlemen's knees."

He went through an elaborate form of stamping his foot and walking about. Then he stood in front of the fire so that she should not resume her position. While she talked he thought that she was worth ten of Mildred; she amused him much more and was jollier to talk to; she was cleverer, and she had a much nicer nature. She was a good, brave, honest little woman; and Mildred, he thought bitterly, deserved none of these epithets. If he had any sense he would stick to Norah, she would make him much happier than he would ever be with Mildred: after all she loved him, and Mildred was only grateful for his help. But when all was said the important thing was to love rather than to be loved; and he yearned for Mildred with his whole soul. He would sooner have ten minutes with her than a whole afternoon with Norah, he prized one kiss of her cold lips more than all Norah could give him.

"I can't help myself," he thought. "I've just got her in my bones."

He did not care if she was heartless, vicious and vulgar, stupid and grasping, he loved her. He would rather have misery with the one than happiness with the other.

When he got up to go Norah said casually:

"Well, I shall see you tomorrow, shan't I?"

"Yes," he answered.

He knew that he would not be able to come, since he was going to help Mildred with her moving, but he had not the courage to say so. He made up his mind that he would send a wire. Mildred saw the rooms in the morning, was satisfied with them, and after luncheon Philip went up with her to Highbury. She had a trunk for her clothes and another for the various odds and ends, cushions, lampshades, photograph frames, with which she had tried to give the apartments a home-like air; she had two or three large cardboard boxes besides, but in all there was no more than could be put on the roof of a four-wheeler. As they drove through Victoria Street Philip sat well back in the cab in case Norah should happen to be passing. He had not had an opportunity to telegraph and could not do so from the post office in the Vauxhall Bridge Road, since she would wonder what he was doing in that neighbourhood; and if he was there he could have no excuse for not going into the neighbouring square where she lived. He made up his mind that he had better go in and see her for half an hour; but the necessity irritated him: he was angry with Norah, because she forced him to vulgar and degrading shifts. But he was happy to be with Mildred. It amused him to help her with the unpacking; and he experienced a charming sense of possession in installing her in these lodgings which he had found and was paying for. He would not let her exert herself. It was a pleasure to do things for her, and she had no desire to do what somebody else seemed desirous to do for her. He unpacked her clothes and put them away. She was not proposing to go out again, so he got her slippers and took off her boots. It delighted him to perform menial offices.

"You do spoil me," she said, running her fingers affectionately through his hair, while he was on his knees unbuttoning her boots.

He took her hands and kissed them.

"It is ripping to have you here."

He arranged the cushions and the photograph frames. She had several jars of green earthenware.

"I'll get you some flowers for them," he said.

He looked round at his work proudly.

"As I'm not going out any more I think I'll get into a tea gown," she said. "Undo me behind, will you?"

She turned round as unconcernedly as though he were a woman. His sex meant nothing to her. But his heart was filled with gratitude for the intimacy her request showed. He undid the hooks and eyes with clumsy fingers.

"That first day I came into the shop I never thought I'd be doing this for you now," he said, with a laugh which he forced.

"Somebody must do it," she answered.

She went into the bedroom and slipped into a pale blue tea gown decorated with a great deal of cheap lace. Then Philip settled her on a sofa and made tea for her.

"I'm afraid I can't stay and have it with you," he said regretfully. "I've got a beastly appointment. But I shall be back in half an hour."

He wondered what he should say if she asked him what the appointment was, but she showed no curiosity. He had ordered dinner for the two of them when he took the rooms, and proposed to spend the evening with her quietly. He was in such a hurry to get back that he took a tram along the Vauxhall Bridge

Road. He thought he had better break the fact to Norah at once that he could not stay more than a few minutes.

"I say, I've only just got time to say how d'you do," he said, as soon as he got into her rooms. "I'm frightfully busy."

Her face fell.

"Why, what's the matter?"

It exasperated him that she should force him to tell lies, and he knew that he reddened when he answered that there was a demonstration at the hospital which he was bound to go to. He fancied that she looked as though she did not believe him, and this irritated him all the more.

"Oh, well, it doesn't matter," she said. "I shall have you all tomorrow."

He looked at her blankly. It was Sunday, and he had been looking forward to spending the day with Mildred. He told himself that he must do that in common decency; he could not leave her by herself in a strange house.

"I'm awfully sorry, I'm engaged tomorrow."

He knew this was the beginning of a scene which he would have given anything to avoid. The colour on Norah's cheeks grew brighter.

"But I've asked the Gordons to lunch" —they were an actor and his wife who were touring the provinces and in London for Sunday— "I told you about it a week ago."

"I'm awfully sorry, I forgot." He hesitated. "I'm afraid I can't possibly come. Isn't there somebody else you can get?"

"What are you doing tomorrow then?"

"I wish you wouldn't cross-examine me."

"Don't you want to tell me?"

"I don't in the least mind telling you, but it's rather annoying to be forced to account for all one's movements."

Norah suddenly changed. With an effort of self-control she got the better of her temper, and going up to him took his hands.

"Don't disappoint me tomorrow, Philip, I've been looking forward so much to spending the day with you. The Gordons want to see you, and we'll have such a jolly time."

"I'd love to if I could."

"I'm not very exacting, am I? I don't often ask you to do anything that's a bother. Won't you get out of your horrid engagement—just this once?"

"I'm awfully sorry, I don't see how I can," he replied sullenly.

"Tell me what it is," she said coaxingly.

He had had time to invent something.

"Griffiths' two sisters are up for the weekend and we're taking them out."

"Is that all?" she said joyfully. "Griffiths can so easily get another man."

He wished he had thought of something more urgent than that. It was a clumsy lie.

"No, I'm awfully sorry, I can't—I promised and I mean to keep my promise."

"But you promised me too. Surely I come first."

"I wish you wouldn't persist," he said.

She flared up.

"You won't come because you don't want to. I don't know what you've been doing the last few days, you've been quite different."

He looked at his watch.

"I'm afraid I'll have to be going," he said.

"You won't come tomorrow?"

"No."

"In that case you needn't trouble to come again," she cried, losing her temper for good.

"That's just as you like," he answered.

"Don't let me detain you any longer," she added ironically.

He shrugged his shoulders and walked out. He was relieved that it had gone no worse. There had been no tears. As he walked along he congratulated himself on getting out of the affair so easily. He went into Victoria Street and bought a few flowers to take in to Mildred.

The little dinner was a great success. Philip had sent in a small pot of caviare, which he knew she was very fond of, and the landlady brought them up some cutlets with vegetables and a sweet. Philip had ordered Burgundy, which was her favourite wine. With the curtains drawn, a bright fire, and one of Mildred's shades on the lamp, the room was cosy.

"It's really just like home," smiled Philip.

"I might be worse off, mightn't I?" she answered.

When they finished, Philip drew two armchairs in front of the fire, and they sat down. He smoked his pipe comfortably. He felt happy and generous.

"What would you like to do tomorrow?" he asked.

"Oh, I'm going to Tulse Hill. You remember the manageress at the shop, well, she's married now, and she's asked me to go and spend the day with her. Of course she thinks I'm married too."

Philip's heart sank.

"But I refused an invitation so that I might spend Sunday with you."

He thought that if she loved him she would say that in that case she would stay with him. He knew very well that Norah would not have hesitated.

"Well, you were a silly to do that. I've promised to go for three weeks and more."

"But how can you go alone?"

"Oh, I shall say that Emil's away on business. Her husband's in the glove trade, and he's a very superior fellow."

Philip was silent, and bitter feelings passed through his heart. She gave him a sidelong glance.

"You don't grudge me a little pleasure, Philip? You see, it's the last time I shall be able to go anywhere for I don't know how long, and I had promised."

He took her hand and smiled.

"No, darling, I want you to have the best time you can. I only want you to be happy."

There was a little book bound in blue paper lying open, face downwards, on the sofa, and Philip idly took it up. It was a twopenny novelette, and the author was Courtenay Paget. That was the name under which Norah wrote.

"I do like his books," said Mildred. "I read them all. They're so refined."

He remembered what Norah had said of herself.

"I have an immense popularity among kitchen-maids. They think me so genteel."

Chapter 71

Philip, in return for Griffiths' confidences, had told him the details of his own complicated amours, and on Sunday morning, after breakfast, when they sat by the fire in their dressing-gowns and smoked, he recounted the scene of the previous day. Griffiths congratulated him because he had got out of his difficulties so easily.

"It's the simplest thing in the world to have an affair with a woman," he remarked sententiously, "but it's a devil of a nuisance to get out of it."

Philip felt inclined to pat himself on the back for his skill in managing the business. At all events he was immensely relieved. He thought of Mildred enjoying herself in Tulse Hill, and he found in himself a real satisfaction because she was happy. It was an act of self-sacrifice on his part that he did not grudge her pleasure even though paid for by his own disappointment, and it filled his heart with a comfortable glow.

But on Monday morning he found on his table a letter from Norah. She wrote:

Dearest,

I'm sorry I was cross on Saturday. Forgive me and come to tea in the afternoon as usual. I love you.

Your Norah.

His heart sank, and he did not know what to do. He took the note to Griffiths and showed it to him.

"You'd better leave it unanswered," said he.

"Oh, I can't," cried Philip. "I should be miserable if I thought of her waiting and waiting. You don't know what it is to be sick for the postman's knock. I do, and I can't expose anybody else to that torture."

"My dear fellow, one can't break that sort of affair off without somebody suffering. You must just set your teeth to that. One thing is, it doesn't last very long."

Philip felt that Norah had not deserved that he should make her suffer; and what did Griffiths know about the degrees of anguish she was capable of? He remembered his own pain when Mildred had told him she was going to be married. He did not want anyone to experience what he had experienced then.

"If you're so anxious not to give her pain, go back to her," said Griffiths.

"I can't do that."

He got up and walked up and down the room nervously. He was angry with Norah because she had not let the matter rest. She must have seen that he had no more love to give her. They said women were so quick at seeing those things.

"You might help me," he said to Griffiths.

"My dear fellow, don't make such a fuss about it. People do get over these things, you know. She probably isn't so wrapped up in you as you think, either. One's always rather apt to exaggerate the passion one's inspired other people with."

He paused and looked at Philip with amusement.

"Look here, there's only one thing you can do. Write to her, and tell her the thing's over. Put it so that there can be no mistake about it. It'll hurt her, but it'll hurt her less if you do the thing brutally than if you try half-hearted ways."

Philip sat down and wrote the following letter:

My dear Norah,

I am sorry to make you unhappy, but I think we had better let things remain where we left them on Saturday. I don't think there's any use in letting these things drag on when they've ceased to be amusing. You told me to go and I went. I do not propose to come back. Good-bye.

Philip Carey.

He showed the letter to Griffiths and asked him what he thought of it. Griffiths read it and looked at Philip with twinkling eyes. He did not say what he felt.

"I think that'll do the trick," he said.

Philip went out and posted it. He passed an uncomfortable morning, for he imagined with great detail what Norah would feel when she received his letter. He tortured himself with the thought of her tears. But at the same time he was relieved. Imagined grief was more easy to bear than grief seen, and he was free now to love Mildred with all his soul. His heart leaped at the thought of going to see her that afternoon, when his day's work at the hospital was over.

When as usual he went back to his rooms to tidy himself, he had no sooner put the latchkey in his door than he heard a voice behind him.

"May I come in? I've been waiting for you for half an hour."

It was Norah. He felt himself blush to the roots of his hair. She spoke gaily. There was no trace of resentment in her voice and nothing to indicate that there was a rupture between them. He felt himself cornered. He was sick with fear, but he did his best to smile.

"Yes, do," he said.

He opened the door, and she preceded him into his sitting-room. He was nervous and, to give himself countenance, offered her a cigarette and lit one for himself. She looked at him brightly.

"Why did you write me such a horrid letter, you naughty boy? If I'd taken it seriously it would have made me perfectly wretched."

"It was meant seriously," he answered gravely.

"Don't be so silly. I lost my temper the other day, and I wrote and apologized. You weren't satisfied, so I've come here to apologize again. After all, you're your own master and I have no claims upon you. I don't want you to do anything you don't want to."

She got up from the chair in which she was sitting and went towards him impulsively, with outstretched hands.

"Let's make friends again, Philip. I'm so sorry if I offended you."

He could not prevent her from taking his hands, but he could not look at her.

"I'm afraid it's too late," he said.

She let herself down on the floor by his side and clasped his knees.

"Philip, don't be silly. I'm quick-tempered too and I can understand that I hurt you, but it's so stupid to sulk over it. What's the good of making us both unhappy? It's been so jolly, our friendship." She passed her fingers slowly over his hand. "I love you, Philip."

He got up, disengaging himself from her, and went to the other side of the room.

"I'm awfully sorry, I can't do anything. The whole thing's over."

"D'you mean to say you don't love me any more?"

"I'm afraid so."

"You were just looking for an opportunity to throw me over and you took that one?"

He did not answer. She looked at him steadily for a time which seemed intolerable. She was sitting on the floor where he had left her, leaning against the armchair. She began to cry quite silently, without trying to hide her face, and the large tears rolled down her cheeks one after the other. She did not sob. It was horribly painful to see her. Philip turned away.

"I'm awfully sorry to hurt you. It's not my fault if I don't love you."

She did not answer. She merely sat there, as though she were overwhelmed, and the tears flowed down her cheeks. It would have been easier to bear if she had reproached him. He had thought her temper would get the better of her, and he was prepared for that. At the back of his mind was a feeling that a real quarrel, in which each said to the other cruel things, would in some way be a justification of his behaviour. The time passed. At last he grew frightened by her silent crying; he went into his bedroom and got a glass of water; he leaned over her.

"Won't you drink a little? It'll relieve you."

She put her lips listlessly to the glass and drank two or three mouthfuls. Then in an exhausted whisper she asked him for a handkerchief. She dried her eyes.

"Of course I knew you never loved me as much as I loved you," she moaned.

"I'm afraid that's always the case," he said. "There's always one who loves and one who lets himself be loved."

He thought of Mildred, and a bitter pain traversed his heart. Norah did not answer for a long time.

"I'd been so miserably unhappy, and my life was so hateful," she said at last.

She did not speak to him, but to herself. He had never heard her before complain of the life she had led with her husband or of her poverty. He had always admired the bold front she displayed to the world.

"And then you came along and you were so good to me. And I admired you because you were clever and it was so heavenly to have someone I could put my trust in. I loved you. I never thought it could come to an end. And without any fault of mine at all."

Her tears began to flow again, but now she was more mistress of herself, and she hid her face in Philip's handkerchief. She tried hard to control herself.

"Give me some more water," she said.

She wiped her eyes.

"I'm sorry to make such a fool of myself. I was so unprepared."

"I'm awfully sorry, Norah. I want you to know that I'm very grateful for all you've done for me."

He wondered what it was she saw in him.

"Oh, it's always the same," she sighed; "if you want men to behave well to you, you must be beastly to them; if you treat them decently they make you suffer for it."

She got up from the floor and said she must go. She gave Philip a long, steady look. Then she sighed.

"It's so inexplicable. What does it all mean?"

Philip took a sudden determination.

"I think I'd better tell you, I don't want you to think too badly of me; I want you to see that I can't help myself. Mildred's come back."

The colour came to her face.

"Why didn't you tell me at once? I deserved that surely."

"I was afraid to."

She looked at herself in the glass and set her hat straight.

"Will you call me a cab," she said. "I don't feel I *can* walk."

He went to the door and stopped a passing hansom; but

when she followed him into the street he was startled to see how white she was. There was a heaviness in her movements as though she had suddenly grown older. She looked so ill that he had not the heart to let her go alone.

"I'll drive back with you if you don't mind."

She did not answer, and he got into the cab. They drove along in silence over the bridge, through shabby streets in which children, with shrill cries, played in the road. When they arrived at her door she did not immediately get out. It seemed as though she could not summon enough strength to her legs to move.

"I hope you'll forgive me, Norah," he said.

She turned her eyes towards him, and he saw that they were bright again with tears, but she forced a smile to her lips.

"Poor fellow, you're quite worried about me. You mustn't bother. I don't blame you. I shall get over it all right."

Lightly and quickly she stroked his face to show him that she bore no ill-feeling, the gesture was scarcely more than suggested; then she jumped out of the cab and let herself into her house.

Philip paid the hansom and walked to Mildred's lodgings. There was a curious heaviness in his heart. He was inclined to reproach himself. But why? He did not know what else he could have done. Passing a fruiterer's, he remembered that Mildred was fond of grapes. He was so grateful that he could show his love for her by recollecting every whim she had.

Chapter 72

For the next three months Philip went every day to see Mildred. He took his books with him and after tea worked, while Mildred lay on the sofa reading novels. Sometimes he would look up and watch her for a minute. A happy smile crossed his lips. She would feel his eyes upon her.

"Don't waste your time looking at me, silly. Go on with your work," she said.

"Tyrant," he answered gaily.

He put aside his book when the landlady came in to lay the cloth for dinner, and in his high spirits he exchanged chaff with her. She was a little cockney, of middle age, with an amusing humour and a quick tongue. Mildred had become great friends with her and had given her an elaborate but mendacious account of the circumstances which had brought her to the pass she was in. The good-hearted little woman was touched and found no trouble too great to make Mildred comfortable. Mildred's sense of propriety had suggested that Philip should pass himself off as her brother. They dined together, and Philip was delighted when he had ordered something which tempted Mildred's capricious appetite. It enchanted him to see her sitting opposite him, and every now and then from sheer joy he took her hand and pressed it. After dinner she sat in the armchair by the fire, and he settled himself down on the floor beside her, leaning against her knees, and smoked. Often they did not talk at all, and sometimes Philip noticed that she had fallen into a doze. He dared not move then in case he woke her, and he sat very quietly, looking lazily into the fire and enjoying his happiness.

"Had a nice little nap?" he smiled, when she woke.

"I've not been sleeping," she answered. "I only just closed my eyes."

She would never acknowledge that she had been asleep. She had a phlegmatic temperament, and her condition did not seriously inconvenience her. She took a lot of trouble about her health and accepted the advice of anyone who chose to offer it. She went for a "constitutional" every morning that it was fine and remained out a definite time. When it was not too cold she sat in St. James's Park. But the rest of the day she spent quite happily on her sofa, reading one novel after another or chatting with the landlady; she had an inexhaustible interest in gossip, and told Philip with abundant detail the history of the landlady, of the lodgers on the drawing-room floor, and of the people who lived in the next house on either side. Now and then she was seized with panic; she poured out her fears to Philip about the pain of the confinement and was in terror lest she should die; she gave him a full account of the confinements of the landlady and of the lady on the drawing-room floor (Mildred did not know her; "I'm one to keep myself to myself," she said, "I'm not one to go about with anybody"), and she narrated details with a queer mixture of horror and gusto; but for the most part she looked forward to the occurrence with equanimity.

"After all, I'm not the first one to have a baby, am I? And the doctor says I shan't have any trouble. You see, it isn't as if I wasn't well made."

Mrs. Owen, the owner of the house she was going to when her time came, had recommended a doctor, and Mildred saw him once a week. He was to charge fifteen guineas.

"Of course I could have got it done cheaper, but Mrs. Owen strongly recommended him, and I thought it wasn't worth while to spoil the ship for a coat of tar."

"If you feel happy and comfortable I don't mind a bit about the expense," said Philip.

She accepted all that Philip did for her as if it were the most natural thing in the world, and on his side he loved to spend money on her: each five-pound note he gave her caused him a little thrill of happiness and pride; he gave her a good many, for she was not economical.

"I don't know where the money goes," she said herself, "it seems to slip through my fingers like water."

"It doesn't matter," said Philip. "I'm so glad to be able to do anything I can for you."

She could not sew well and so did not make the necessary things for the baby; she told Philip it was much cheaper in the end to buy them. Philip had lately sold one of the mortgages in which his money had been put; and now, with five hundred pounds in the bank waiting to be invested in something that could be more easily realized, he felt himself uncommonly well-to-do. They talked often of the future. Philip was anxious that Mildred should keep the child with her, but she refused; she had her living to earn, and it would be more easy to do this if she had not also to look after a baby. Her plan was to get back into one of the shops of the company for which she had worked before, and the child could be put with some decent woman in the country.

"I can find someone who'll look after it well for seven and sixpence a week. It'll be better for the baby and better for me."

It seemed callous to Philip, but when he tried to reason with her she pretended to think he was concerned with the expense.

"You needn't worry about that," she said. "I shan't ask *you* to pay for it."

"You know I don't care how much I pay."

At the bottom of her heart was the hope that the child would be still-born. She did no more than hint it, but Philip saw that the thought was there. He was shocked at first; and then, reasoning with himself, he was obliged to confess that for all concerned such an event was to be desired.

"It's all very fine to say this and that," Mildred remarked querulously, "but it's jolly difficult for a girl to earn her living by herself; it doesn't make it any easier when she's got a baby."

"Fortunately you've got me to fall back on," smiled Philip, taking her hand.

"You've been good to me, Philip."

"Oh, what rot!"

"You can't say I didn't offer anything in return for what

you've done."

"Good heavens, I don't want a return. If I've done anything for you, I've done it because I love you. You owe me nothing. I don't want you to do anything unless you love me."

He was a little horrified by her feeling that her body was a commodity which she could deliver indifferently as an acknowledgment for services rendered.

"But I do want to, Philip. You've been so good to me."

"Well, it won't hurt for waiting. When you're all right again we'll go for our little honeymoon."

"You are naughty," she said, smiling.

Mildred expected to be confined early in March, and as soon as she was well enough she was to go to the seaside for a fortnight: that would give Philip a chance to work without interruption for his examination; after that came the Easter holidays, and they had arranged to go to Paris together. Philip talked endlessly of the things they would do. Paris was delightful then. They would take a room in a little hotel he knew in the Latin Quarter, and they would eat in all sorts of charming little restaurants; they would go to the play, and he would take her to music halls. It would amuse her to meet his friends. He had talked to her about Cronshaw, she would see him; and there was Lawson, he had gone to Paris for a couple of months; and they would go to the Bal Bullier; there were excursions; they would make trips to Versailles, Chartres, Fontainebleau.

"It'll cost a lot of money," she said.

"Oh, damn the expense. Think how I've been looking forward to it. Don't you know what it means to me? I've never loved anyone but you. I never shall."

She listened to his enthusiasm with smiling eyes. He thought he saw in them a new tenderness, and he was grateful to her. She was much gentler than she used to be. There was in her no longer the superciliousness which had irritated him. She was so accustomed to him now that she took no pains to keep up before him any pretences. She no longer troubled to do her hair with the old elaboration, but just tied it in a knot; and she left off the vast fringe which she generally wore: the more careless style suited her. Her face was so thin that it made her eyes seem very large; there were heavy lines under them, and the pallor of her cheeks made their colour more profound. She had a wistful look which was infinitely pathetic. There seemed to Philip to be in her something of the Madonna. He wished they could continue in that same way always. He was happier than he had ever been in his life.

He used to leave her at ten o'clock every night, for she liked to go to bed early, and he was obliged to put in another couple of hours' work to make up for the lost evening. He generally brushed her hair for her before he went. He had made a ritual of the kisses he gave her when he bade her good night; first he kissed the palms of her hands (how thin the fingers were, the nails were beautiful, for she spent much time in manicuring them), then he kissed her closed eyes, first the right one and then the left, and at last he kissed her lips. He went home with a heart overflowing with love. He longed for an opportunity to gratify the desire for self-sacrifice which consumed him.

Presently the time came for her to move to the nursing-home where she was to be confined. Philip was then able to visit her only in the afternoons. Mildred changed her story and represented herself as the wife of a soldier who had gone to India to join his regiment, and Philip was introduced to the mistress of the establishment as her brother-in-law.

"I have to be rather careful what I say," she told him, "as there's another lady here whose husband's in the Indian Civil."

"I wouldn't let that disturb me if I were you," said Philip. "I'm convinced that her husband and yours went out on the same boat."

"What boat?" she asked innocently.

"The Flying Dutchman."

Mildred was safely delivered of a daughter, and when Philip was allowed to see her the child was lying by her side. Mildred was very weak, but relieved that everything was over. She showed him the baby, and herself looked at it curiously.

"It's a funny-looking little thing, isn't it? I can't believe it's mine."

It was red and wrinkled and odd. Philip smiled when he looked at it. He did not quite know what to say; and it embarrassed him because the nurse who owned the house was standing by his side; and he felt by the way she was looking at him that, disbelieving Mildred's complicated story, she thought he was the father.

"What are you going to call her?" asked Philip.

"I can't make up my mind if I shall call her Madeleine or Cecilia."

The nurse left them alone for a few minutes, and Philip bent down and kissed Mildred on the mouth.

"I'm so glad it's all over happily, darling."

She put her thin arms round his neck.

"You've been a brick to me, Phil dear."

"Now I feel that you're mine at last. I've waited so long for you, my dear."

They heard the nurse at the door, and Philip hurriedly got up. The nurse entered. There was a slight smile on her lips.

Chapter 73

Three weeks later Philip saw Mildred and her baby off to Brighton. She had made a quick recovery and looked better than he had ever seen her. She was going to a boarding-house where she had spent a couple of weekends with Emil Miller, and had written to say that her husband was obliged to go to Germany on business and she was coming down with her baby. She got pleasure out of the stories she invented, and she showed a certain fertility of invention in the working out of the details. Mildred proposed to find in Brighton some woman who would be willing to take charge of the baby. Philip was startled at the callousness with which she insisted on getting rid of it so soon, but she argued with common sense that the poor child had much better be put somewhere before it grew used to her. Philip had expected the maternal instinct to make itself felt when she had had the baby two or three weeks, and had counted on this to help him persuade her to keep it; but nothing of the sort occurred. Mildred was not unkind to her baby, she did all that was necessary; it amused her sometimes, and she talked about it a good deal; but at heart she was indifferent to it. She could not look upon it as part of herself. She fancied it resembled its father already. She was continually wondering how she would manage when it grew older; and she was exasperated with herself for being such a fool as to have it at all.

"If I'd only known then all I do now," she said.

She laughed at Philip because he was anxious about its welfare.

"You couldn't make more fuss if you was the father," she said. "I'd like to see Emil getting into such a stew about it."

Philip's mind was full of the stories he had heard of baby-farming and the ghouls who ill-treat the wretched children that selfish, cruel parents have put in their charge.

"Don't be so silly," said Mildred. "That's when you give a woman a sum down to look after a baby. But when you're going to pay so much a week it's to their interest to look after it well."

Philip insisted that Mildred should place the child with people who had no children of their own and would promise to take no other.

"Don't haggle about the price," he said. "I'd rather pay half a guinea a week than run any risk of the kid being starved or beaten."

"You're a funny old thing, Philip," she laughed.

To him there was something very touching in the child's helplessness. It was small, ugly, and querulous. Its birth had been looked forward to with shame and anguish. Nobody wanted it. It was dependent on him, a stranger, for food, shelter, and clothes to cover its nakedness.

As the train started he kissed Mildred. He would have kissed the baby too, but he was afraid she would laugh at him.

"You will write to me, darling, won't you? And I shall look forward to your coming back with, oh! such impatience."

"Mind you get through your exam."

He had been working for it industriously, and now with only ten days before him he made a final effort. He was very anxious to pass, first to save himself time and expense, for money had been slipping through his fingers during the last four months with incredible speed; and then because this examination marked the end of the drudgery: after that the student had to do with medicine, midwifery, and surgery, the interest of which was more vivid than the anatomy and physiology with which he had been hitherto concerned. Philip looked forward with interest to the rest of the curriculum. Nor did he want to have to confess to Mildred that he had failed: though the examination was difficult and the majority of candidates were ploughed at the first attempt, he knew that she would think less well of him if he did not succeed; she had a peculiarly humiliating way of showing what she thought.

Mildred sent him a postcard to announce her safe arrival, and he snatched half an hour every day to write a long letter to her. He had always a certain shyness in expressing himself by word of mouth, but he found he could tell her, pen in hand, all sorts of things which it would have made him feel ridiculous to say. Profiting by the discovery, he poured out to her his whole heart. He had never been able to tell her before how his adoration filled every part of him so that all his actions, all his thoughts, were touched with it. He wrote to her of the future, the happiness that lay before him, and the gratitude which he owed her. He asked himself (he had often asked himself before but had never put it into words) what it was in her that filled him with such extravagant delight; he did not know; he knew only that when she was with him he was happy, and when she was away from him the world was on a sudden cold and grey; he knew only that when he thought of her his heart seemed to grow big in his body so that it was difficult to breathe (as if it pressed against his lungs) and it throbbed, so that the delight of her presence was almost pain; his knees shook, and he felt strangely weak, as though, not having eaten, he were tremulous from want of food. He looked forward eagerly to her answers. He did not expect her to write often, for he knew that letter-writing came difficultly to her; and he was quite content with the clumsy little note that arrived in reply to four of his. She spoke of the boarding-house in which she had taken a room, of the weather and the baby, told him she had been for a walk on the front with a lady friend whom she had met in the boarding-house and who had taken such a fancy to baby, she was going to the theatre on Saturday night, and Brighton was filling up. It touched Philip because it was so matter-of-fact. The crabbed style, the formality of the matter, gave him a queer desire to laugh and to take her in his arms and kiss her.

He went into the examination with happy confidence. There was nothing in either of the papers that gave him trouble. He knew that he had done well, and though the second part of the examination was *viva voce* and he was more nervous, he managed to answer the questions adequately. He sent a triumphant telegram to Mildred when the result was announced.

When he got back to his rooms Philip found a letter from her, saying that she thought it would be better for her to stay another week in Brighton. She had found a woman who would be glad to take the baby for seven shillings a week, but she wanted to make inquiries about her, and she was herself benefiting so much by the sea air that she was sure a few days more would do her no end of good. She hated asking Philip for money, but would he send some by return, as she had had to buy herself a new hat, she couldn't go about with her lady friend always in the same hat, and her lady friend was so dressy. Philip had a moment of bitter disappointment. It took away all his pleasure at getting through his examination.

"If she loved me one quarter as much as I love her she couldn't bear to stay away a day longer than necessary."

He put the thought away from him quickly; it was pure selfishness; of course her health was more important than anything else. But he had nothing to do now; he might spend the week with her in Brighton, and they could be together all day. His heart leaped at the thought. It would be amusing to appear before Mildred suddenly with the information that he had taken a room in the boarding-house. He looked out trains. But he paused. He was not certain that she would be pleased to see him; she had made friends in Brighton; he was quiet, and she liked boisterous joviality; he realized that she amused herself more with other people than with him. It would torture him if he felt for an instant that he was in the way. He was afraid to risk it. He dared not even write and suggest that, with nothing to keep him in town, he would like to spend the week where he could see her every day.

She knew he had nothing to do; if she wanted him to come she would have asked him to. He dared not risk the anguish he would suffer if he proposed to come and she made excuses to prevent him.

He wrote to her next day, sent her a five-pound note, and at the end of his letter said that if she were very nice and cared to see him for the weekend he would be glad to run down; but she was by no means to alter any plans she had made. He awaited her answer with impatience. In it she said that if she had only known before she could have arranged it, but she had promised to go to a music hall on the Saturday night; besides, it would make the people at the boarding-house talk if he stayed there. Why did he not come on Sunday morning and spend the day? They could lunch at the Metropole, and she would take him afterwards to see the very superior lady-like person who was going to take the baby.

Sunday. He blessed the day because it was fine. As the train approached Brighton the sun poured through the carriage window. Mildred was waiting for him on the platform.

"How jolly of you to come and meet me!" he cried, as he seized her hands.

"You expected me, didn't you?"

"I hoped you would. I say, how well you're looking."

"It's done me a rare lot of good, but I think I'm wise to stay here as long as I can. And there are a very nice class of people at the boarding-house. I wanted cheering up after seeing nobody all these months. It was dull sometimes."

She looked very smart in her new hat, a large black straw with a great many inexpensive flowers on it; and round her neck floated a long boa of imitation swansdown. She was still very thin, and she stooped a little when she walked (she had always done that), but her eyes did not seem so large; and though she never had any colour, her skin had lost the earthy look it had. They walked down to the sea. Philip, remembering he had not walked with her for months, grew suddenly conscious of his limp and walked stiffly in the attempt to conceal it.

"Are you glad to see me?" he asked, love dancing madly in his heart.

"Of course I am. You needn't ask that."

"By the way, Griffiths sends you his love."

"What cheek!"

He had talked to her a great deal of Griffiths. He had told her how flirtatious he was and had amused her often with the narration of some adventure which Griffiths under the seal of secrecy had imparted to him. Mildred had listened, with some pretence of disgust sometimes, but generally with curiosity; and Philip, admiringly, had enlarged upon his friend's good looks and charm.

"I'm sure you'll like him just as much as I do. He's so jolly and amusing, and he's such an awfully good sort."

Philip told her how, when they were perfect strangers, Griffiths had nursed him through an illness; and in the telling Griffiths's self-sacrifice lost nothing.

"You can't help liking him," said Philip.

"I don't like good-looking men," said Mildred. "They're too conceited for me."

"He wants to know you. I've talked to him about you an

awful lot."

"What have you said?" asked Mildred.

Philip had no one but Griffiths to talk to of his love for Mildred, and little by little had told him the whole story of his connection with her. He described her to him fifty times. He dwelt amorously on every detail of her appearance, and Griffiths knew exactly how her thin hands were shaped and how white her face was, and he laughed at Philip when he talked of the charm of her pale, thin lips.

"By Jove, I'm glad I don't take things so badly as that," he said. "Life wouldn't be worth living."

Philip smiled. Griffiths did not know the delight of being so madly in love that it was like meat and wine and the air one breathed and whatever else was essential to existence. Griffiths knew that Philip had looked after the girl while she was having her baby and was now going away with her.

"Well, I must say you've deserved to get something," he remarked. "It must have cost you a pretty penny. It's lucky you can afford it."

"I can't," said Philip. "But what do I care!"

Since it was early for luncheon, Philip and Mildred sat in one of the shelters on the parade, sunning themselves, and watched the people pass. There were the Brighton shop-boys who walked in twos and threes, swinging their canes, and there were the Brighton shop-girls who tripped along in giggling bunches. They could tell the people who had come down from London for the day; the keen air gave a fillip to their weariness. There were many Jews, stout ladies in tight satin dresses and diamonds, little corpulent men with a gesticulative manner. There were middle-aged gentlemen spending a weekend in one of the hotels, carefully dressed; and they walked industriously after too substantial a breakfast to give themselves an appetite for too substantial a luncheon: they exchanged the time of day with friends and talked of Dr. Brighton or London-by-the-Sea. Here and there a well-known actor passed, elaborately unconscious of the attention he excited: sometimes he wore patent leather boots, a coat with an astrakhan collar, and carried a silver-knobbed stick; and sometimes, looking as though he had come from a day's shooting, he strolled in knickerbockers, and ulster of Harris tweed, and a tweed hat on the back of his head. The sun shone on the blue sea, and the blue sea was trim and neat.

After luncheon they went to Hove to see the woman who was to take charge of the baby. She lived in a small house in a back street, but it was clean and tidy. Her name was Mrs. Harding. She was an elderly, stout person, with grey hair and a red, fleshy face. She looked motherly in her cap, and Philip thought she seemed kind.

"Won't you find it an awful nuisance to look after a baby?" he asked her.

She explained that her husband was a curate, a good deal older than herself, who had difficulty in getting permanent work, since vicars wanted young men to assist them; he earned a little now and then by doing locums when someone took a holiday or fell ill, and a charitable institution gave them a small pension; but her life was lonely, it would be something to do to look after a child, and the few shillings a week paid for it would help her to keep things going. She promised that it should be well fed.

"Quite the lady, isn't she?" said Mildred, when they went away.

They went back to have tea at the Metropole. Mildred liked the crowd and the band. Philip was tired of talking, and he watched her face as she looked with keen eyes at the dresses of the women who came in. She had a peculiar sharpness for reckoning up what things cost, and now and then she leaned over to him and whispered the result of her meditations.

"D'you see that aigrette there? That cost every bit of seven guineas."

Or: "Look at that ermine, Philip. That's rabbit, that is—that's not ermine." She laughed triumphantly. "I'd know it a mile off."

Philip smiled happily. He was glad to see her pleasure, and the ingenuousness of her conversation amused and touched him. The band played sentimental music.

After dinner they walked down to the station, and Philip took her arm. He told her what arrangements he had made for their journey to France. She was to come up to London at the end of the week, but she told him that she could not go away till the Saturday of the week after that. He had already engaged a room in a hotel in Paris. He was looking forward eagerly to taking the tickets.

"You won't mind going second-class, will you? We mustn't be extravagant, and it'll be all the better if we can do ourselves pretty well when we get there."

He had talked to her a hundred times of the Quarter. They would wander through its pleasant old streets, and they would sit idly in the charming gardens of the Luxembourg. If the weather was fine perhaps, when they had had enough of Paris, they might go to Fontainebleau. The trees would be just bursting into leaf. The green of the forest in spring was more beautiful than anything he knew; it was like a song, and it was like the happy pain of love. Mildred listened quietly. He turned to her and tried to look deep into her eyes.

"You do want to come, don't you?" he said.

"Of course I do," she smiled.

"You don't know how I'm looking forward to it. I don't know how I shall get through the next days. I'm so afraid something will happen to prevent it. It maddens me sometimes that I can't tell you how much I love you. And at last, at last…"

He broke off. They reached the station, but they had dawdled on the way, and Philip had barely time to say good night. He kissed her quickly and ran towards the wicket as fast as he could. She stood where he left her. He was strangely grotesque when he ran.

Chapter 74

The following Saturday Mildred returned, and that evening Philip kept her to himself. He took seats for the play, and they drank champagne at dinner. It was her first gaiety in London for so long that she enjoyed everything ingenuously. She cuddled up to Philip when they drove from the theatre to the room he had taken for her in Pimlico.

"I really believe you're quite glad to see me," he said.

She did not answer, but gently pressed his hand. Demonstrations of affection were so rare with her that Philip was enchanted.

"I've asked Griffiths to dine with us tomorrow," he told her.

"Oh, I'm glad you've done that. I wanted to meet him."

There was no place of entertainment to take her to on Sunday night, and Philip was afraid she would be bored if she were alone with him all day. Griffiths was amusing; he would help them to get through the evening; and Philip was so fond of them both that he wanted them to know and to like one another. He left Mildred with the words:

"Only six days more."

They had arranged to dine in the gallery at Romano's on Sunday, because the dinner was excellent and looked as though it cost a good deal more than it did. Philip and Mildred arrived first and had to wait some time for Griffiths.

"He's an unpunctual devil," said Philip. "He's probably making love to one of his numerous flames."

But presently he appeared. He was a handsome creature, tall and thin; his head was placed well on the body, it gave him a conquering air which was attractive; and his curly hair, his bold, friendly blue eyes, his red mouth, were charming. Philip saw Mildred look at him with appreciation, and he felt a curious satisfaction. Griffiths greeted them with a smile.

"I've heard a great deal about you," he said to Mildred, as he took her hand.

"Not so much as I've heard about you," she answered.

"Nor so bad," said Philip.

"Has he been blackening my character?"

Griffiths laughed, and Philip saw that Mildred noticed how white and regular his teeth were and how pleasant his smile.

"You ought to feel like old friends," said Philip. "I've talked so much about you to one another."

Griffiths was in the best possible humour, for, having at length passed his final examination, he was qualified, and he had just been appointed house-surgeon at a hospital in the North of London. He was taking up his duties at the beginning of May and meanwhile was going home for a holiday; this was his last week in town, and he was determined to get as much enjoyment into it as he could. He began to talk the gay nonsense which Philip admired because he could not copy it. There was nothing much in what he said, but his vivacity gave it point. There flowed from him a force of life which affected everyone who knew him; it was almost as sensible as bodily warmth. Mildred was more lively than Philip had ever known her, and he was delighted to see that his little party was a success. She was amusing herself enormously. She laughed louder and louder. She quite forgot the genteel reserve which had become second nature to her.

Presently Griffiths said:

"I say, it's dreadfully difficult for me to call you Mrs. Miller. Philip never calls you anything but Mildred."

"I daresay she won't scratch your eyes out if you call her that too," laughed Philip.

"Then she must call me Harry."

Philip sat silent while they chattered away and thought how good it was to see people happy. Now and then Griffiths teased him a little, kindly, because he was always so serious.

"I believe he's quite fond of you, Philip," smiled Mildred.

"He isn't a bad old thing," answered Griffiths, and taking Philip's hand he shook it gaily.

It seemed an added charm in Griffiths that he liked Philip. They were all sober people, and the wine they had drunk went to their heads. Griffiths became more talkative and so boisterous that Philip, amused, had to beg him to be quiet. He had a gift for storytelling, and his adventures lost nothing of their romance and their laughter in his narration. He played in all of them a gallant, humorous part. Mildred, her eyes shining with excitement, urged him on. He poured out anecdote after anecdote. When the lights began to be turned out she was astonished.

"My word, the evening has gone quickly. I thought it wasn't more than half past nine."

They got up to go and when she said good-bye, she added:

"I'm coming to have tea at Philip's room tomorrow. You might look in if you can."

"All right," he smiled back.

On the way back to Pimlico Mildred talked of nothing but Griffiths. She was taken with his good looks, his well-cut clothes, his voice, his gaiety.

"I *am* glad you like him," said Philip. "D'you remember you were rather sniffy about meeting him?"

"I think it's so nice of him to be so fond of you, Philip. He is a nice friend for you to have."

She put up her face to Philip for him to kiss her. It was a thing she did rarely.

"I have enjoyed myself this evening, Philip. Thank you so much."

"Don't be so absurd," he laughed, touched by her appreciation so that he felt the moisture come to his eyes.

She opened her door and, just before she went in, turned again to Philip.

"Tell Harry I'm madly in love with him," she said.

"All right," he laughed. "Good night."

Next day, when they were having tea, Griffiths came in. He sank lazily into an armchair. There was something strangely sensual in the slow movements of his large limbs. Philip remained silent, while the others chattered away, but he was enjoying himself. He admired them both so much that it seemed natural enough for them to admire one another. He did not care if Griffiths absorbed Mildred's attention, he would have her to himself during the evening; he had something the attitude of a loving husband, confident in his wife's affection, who looks on with amusement while she flirts harmlessly with a stranger. But at half past seven he looked at his watch and said:

"It's about time we went out to dinner, Mildred."

There was a moment's pause, and Griffiths seemed to be considering.

"Well, I'll be getting along," he said at last. "I didn't know it was so late."

"Are you doing anything tonight?" asked Mildred.

"No."

There was another silence. Philip felt slightly irritated.

"I'll just go and have a wash," he said, and to Mildred he added: "Would you like to wash your hands?"

She did not answer him.

"Why don't you come and dine with us?" she said to Griffiths.

He looked at Philip and saw him staring at him sombrely.

"I dined with you last night," he laughed. "I should be in the way."

"Oh, that doesn't matter," insisted Mildred. "Make him come, Philip. He won't be in the way, will he?"

"Let him come by all means if he'd like to."

"All right, then," said Griffiths promptly. "I'll just go upstairs and tidy myself."

The moment he left the room Philip turned to Mildred angrily.

"Why on earth did you ask him to dine with us?"

"I couldn't help myself. It would have looked so funny to say nothing when he said he wasn't doing anything."

"Oh, what rot! And why the hell did you ask him if he was doing anything?"

Mildred's pale lips tightened a little.

"I want a little amusement sometimes. I get tired always being alone with you."

They heard Griffiths coming heavily down the stairs, and Philip went into his bedroom to wash. They dined in the neighbourhood in an Italian restaurant. Philip was cross and silent, but he quickly realized that he was showing to disadvantage in comparison with Griffiths, and he forced himself to hide his annoyance. He drank a good deal of wine to destroy the pain that was gnawing at his heart, and he set himself to talk. Mildred, as though remorseful for what she had said, did all she could to make herself pleasant to him. She was kindly and affectionate. Presently Philip began to think he had been a fool to surrender to a feeling of jealousy. After dinner when they got into a hansom to drive to a music hall, Mildred, sitting between the two men, of her own accord gave him her hand. His anger vanished. Suddenly, he knew not how, he grew conscious that Griffiths was holding her other hand. The pain seized him again violently, it was a real physical pain, and he asked himself, panic-stricken, what he might have asked himself before, whether Mildred and Griffiths were in love with one another. He could not see anything of the performance on account of the mist of suspicion, anger, dismay, and wretchedness which seemed to be before his eyes; but he forced himself to conceal the fact that anything was the matter; he went on talking and laughing. Then a strange desire to torture himself seized him, and he got up, saying he wanted to go and drink something. Mildred and Griffiths had never been alone together for a moment. He wanted to leave them by themselves.

"I'll come too," said Griffiths. "I've got rather a thirst on."

"Oh, nonsense, you stay and talk to Mildred."

Philip did not know why he said that. He was throwing them together now to make the pain he suffered more intolerable. He did not go to the bar, but up into the balcony, from where he could watch them and not be seen. They had ceased to look at the stage and were smiling into one another's eyes. Griffiths was talking with his usual happy fluency and Mildred seemed to hang on his lips. Philip's head began to ache frightfully. He stood there motionless. He knew he would be in the way if he went back. They were enjoying themselves without him, and he was suffering, suffering. Time passed, and now he had an extraordinary shyness about rejoining them. He knew they had not thought of him at all, and he reflected bitterly that he had paid for the dinner and their seats in the music hall. What a fool they were making of him! He was hot with shame. He could see how happy they were without him. His instinct was to leave them to themselves and go home, but he had not his hat and coat, and it would necessitate endless explanations. He went back. He felt a shadow of annoyance in Mildred's eyes when she saw him, and his heart sank.

"You've been a devil of a time," said Griffiths, with a smile of welcome.

"I met some men I knew. I've been talking to them, and I couldn't get away. I thought you'd be all right together."

"I've been enjoying myself thoroughly," said Griffiths. "I don't know about Mildred."

She gave a little laugh of happy complacency. There was a vulgar sound in the ring of it that horrified Philip. He suggested that they should go.

"Come on," said Griffiths, "we'll both drive you home."

Philip suspected that she had suggested that arrangement so that she might not be left alone with him. In the cab he did not take her hand nor did she offer it, and he knew all the time that she was holding Griffiths's. His chief thought was that it was all so horribly vulgar. As they drove along he asked himself what plans they had made to meet without his knowledge, he cursed himself for having left them alone, he had actually gone out of his way to enable them to arrange things.

"Let's keep the cab," said Philip, when they reached the house in which Mildred was lodging. "I'm too tired to walk home."

On the way back Griffiths talked gaily and seemed indifferent to the fact that Philip answered in monosyllables. Philip felt he must notice that something was the matter. Philip's silence at last grew too significant to struggle against, and Griffiths, suddenly nervous, ceased talking. Philip wanted to say something, but he was so shy he could hardly bring himself to, and yet the time was passing and the opportunity would be lost. It was best to get at the truth at once. He forced himself to speak.

"Are you in love with Mildred?" he asked suddenly.

"I?" Griffiths laughed. "Is that what you've been so funny about this evening? Of course not. My dear old man."

He tried to slip his hand through Philip's arm, but Philip drew himself away. He knew Griffiths was lying. He could not bring himself to force Griffiths to tell him that he had not been holding the girl's hand. He suddenly felt very weak and broken.

"It doesn't matter to you, Harry," he said. "You've got so many women—don't take her away from me. It means my whole life. I've been so awfully wretched."

His voice broke, and he could not prevent the sob that was torn from him. He was horribly ashamed of himself.

"My dear old boy, you know I wouldn't do anything to hurt you. I'm far too fond of you for that. I was only playing the fool. If I'd known you were going to take it like that I'd have been more careful."

"Is that true?" asked Philip.

"I don't care a twopenny damn for her. I give you my word of honour."

Philip gave a sigh of relief. The cab stopped at their door.

Chapter 75

Next day Philip was in a good temper. He was very anxious not to bore Mildred with too much of his society, and so had arranged that he should not see her till dinner-time. She was ready when he fetched her, and he chaffed her for her unwonted punctuality. She was wearing a new dress he had given her. He remarked on its smartness.

"It'll have to go back and be altered," she said. "The skirt hangs all wrong."

"You'll have to make the dressmaker hurry up if you want to take it to Paris with you."

"It'll be ready in time for that."

"Only three more whole days. We'll go over by the eleven o'clock, shall we?"

"If you like."

He would have her for nearly a month entirely to himself. His eyes rested on her with hungry adoration. He was able to laugh a little at his own passion.

"I wonder what it is I see in you," he smiled.

"That's a nice thing to say," she answered.

Her body was so thin that one could almost see her skeleton. Her chest was as flat as a boy's. Her mouth, with its narrow pale lips, was ugly, and her skin was faintly green.

"I shall give you Blaud's Pills in quantities when we're away," said Philip, laughing. "I'm going to bring you back fat and rosy."

"I don't want to get fat," she said.

She did not speak of Griffiths, and presently while they were dining Philip, half in malice, for he felt sure of himself and his power over her, said:

"It seems to me you were having a great flirtation with Harry last night?"

"I told you I was in love with him," she laughed.

"I'm glad to know that he's not in love with you."

"How d'you know?"

"I asked him."

She hesitated a moment, looking at Philip, and a curious gleam came into her eyes.

"Would you like to read a letter I had from him this morning?"

She handed him an envelope and Philip recognized Griffiths's bold, legible writing. There were eight pages. It was well written, frank and charming; it was the letter of a man who was used to making love to women. He told Mildred that he loved her passionately, he had fallen in love with her the first moment he saw her; he did not want to love her, for he knew how fond Philip was of her, but he could not help himself. Philip was such a dear, and he was very much ashamed of himself, but it was not his fault, he was just carried away. He paid her delightful compliments. Finally he thanked her for consenting to lunch with him next day and said he was dreadfully impatient to see her. Philip noticed that the letter was dated the night before; Griffiths must have written it after leaving Philip, and had taken the trouble to go out and post it when Philip thought he was in bed.

He read it with a sickening palpitation of his heart, but gave no outward sign of surprise. He handed it back to Mildred with a smile, calmly.

"Did you enjoy your lunch?"

"Rather," she said emphatically.

He felt that his hands were trembling, so he put them under the table.

"You mustn't take Griffiths too seriously. He's just a butterfly, you know."

She took the letter and looked at it again.

"I can't help it either," she said, in a voice which she tried to make nonchalant. "I don't know what's come over me."

"It's a little awkward for me, isn't it?" said Philip.

She gave him a quick look.

"You're taking it pretty calmly, I must say."

"What do you expect me to do? Do you want me to tear out my hair in handfuls?"

"I knew you'd be angry with me."

"The funny thing is, I'm not at all. I ought to have known this would happen. I was a fool to bring you together. I know perfectly well that he's got every advantage over me; he's much jollier, and he's very handsome, he's more amusing, he can talk to you about the things that interest you."

"I don't know what you mean by that. If I'm not clever I can't help it, but I'm not the fool you think I am, not by a long way, I can tell you. You're a bit too superior for me, my young friend."

"D'you want to quarrel with me?" he asked mildly.

"No, but I don't see why you should treat me as if I was I don't know what."

"I'm sorry, I didn't mean to offend you. I just wanted to talk things over quietly. We don't want to make a mess of them if we can help it. I saw you were attracted by him and it seemed to me very natural. The only thing that really hurts me is that he should have encouraged you. He knew how awfully keen I was on you. I think it's rather shabby of him to have written that letter to you five minutes after he told me he didn't care twopence about you."

"If you think you're going to make me like him any the less by saying nasty things about him, you're mistaken."

Philip was silent for a moment. He did not know what words he could use to make her see his point of view. He wanted to speak coolly and deliberately, but he was in such a turmoil of emotion that he could not clear his thoughts.

"It's not worth while sacrificing everything for an infatuation that you know can't last. After all, he doesn't care for anyone more than ten days, and you're rather cold; that sort of thing doesn't mean very much to you."

"That's what you think."

She made it more difficult for him by adopting a cantankerous tone.

"If you're in love with him you can't help it. I'll just bear it as best I can. We get on very well together, you and I, and I've not behaved badly to you, have I? I've always known that you're not in love with me, but you like me all right, and when we get over to Paris you'll forget about Griffiths. If you make up your mind to put him out of your thoughts you won't find it so hard as all that, and I've deserved that you should do something for me."

She did not answer, and they went on eating their dinner. When the silence grew oppressive Philip began to talk of different things. He pretended not to notice that Mildred was inattentive. Her answers were perfunctory, and she volunteered no remarks of her own. At last she interrupted abruptly what he was saying.

"Philip, I'm afraid I shan't be able to go away on Saturday. The doctor says I oughtn't to."

He knew this was not true, but he answered:

"When will you be able to come away?"

She glanced at him, saw that his face was white and rigid, and looked nervously away. She was at that moment a little afraid of him.

"I may as well tell you and have done with it, I can't come away with you at all."

"I thought you were driving at that. It's too late to change your mind now. I've got the tickets and everything."

"You said you didn't wish me to go unless I wanted it too, and I don't."

"I've changed my mind. I'm not going to have any more tricks played with me. You must come."

"I like you very much, Philip, as a friend. But I can't bear to think of anything else. I don't like you that way. I couldn't, Philip."

"You were quite willing to a week ago."

"It was different then."

"You hadn't met Griffiths?"

"You said yourself I couldn't help it if I'm in love with him."

Her face was set into a sulky look, and she kept her eyes fixed on her plate. Philip was white with rage. He would have liked to hit her in the face with his clenched fist, and in fancy he saw how she would look with a black eye. There were two lads of eighteen dining at a table near them, and now and then they looked at Mildred; he wondered if they envied him dining with a pretty girl; perhaps they were wishing they stood in his shoes. It was Mildred who broke the silence.

"What's the good of our going away together? I'd be thinking of him all the time. It wouldn't be much fun for you."

"That's my business," he answered.

She thought over all his reply implicated, and she reddened.

"But that's just beastly."

"What of it?"

"I thought you were a gentleman in every sense of the word."

"You were mistaken."

His reply entertained him, and he laughed as he said it.

"For God's sake don't laugh," she cried. "I can't come away with you, Philip. I'm awfully sorry. I know I haven't behaved well to you, but one can't force themselves."

"Have you forgotten that when you were in trouble I did everything for you? I planked out the money to keep you till your baby was born, I paid for your doctor and everything, I paid for you to go to Brighton, and I'm paying for the keep of your baby, I'm paying for your clothes, I'm paying for every stitch you've got on now."

"If you was a gentleman you wouldn't throw what you've done for me in my face."

"Oh, for goodness's sake, shut up. What d'you suppose I care if I'm a gentleman or not? If I were a gentleman I shouldn't waste my time with a vulgar slut like you. I don't care a damn if you like me or not. I'm sick of being made a blasted fool of. You're jolly well coming to Paris with me on Saturday or you can take the consequences."

Her cheeks were red with anger, and when she answered her voice had the hard commonness which she concealed generally by a genteel enunciation.

"I never liked you, not from the beginning, but you forced yourself on me, I always hated it when you kissed me. I wouldn't let you touch me now not if I was starving."

Philip tried to swallow the food on his plate, but the muscles of his throat refused to act. He gulped down something to drink and lit a cigarette. He was trembling in every part. He did not speak. He waited for her to move, but she sat in silence, staring at the white tablecloth. If they had been alone he would have flung his arms round her and kissed her passionately; he fancied the throwing back of her long white throat as he pressed upon her mouth with his lips. They passed an hour without speaking, and at last Philip thought the waiter began to stare at them curiously. He called for the bill.

"Shall we go?" he said then, in an even tone.

She did not reply, but gathered together her bag and her gloves. She put on her coat.

"When are you seeing Griffiths again?"

"Tomorrow," she answered indifferently.

"You'd better talk it over with him."

She opened her bag mechanically and saw a piece of paper in it. She took it out.

"Here's the bill for this dress," she said hesitatingly.

"What of it?"

"I promised I'd give her the money tomorrow."

"Did you?"

"Does that mean you won't pay for it after having told me I could get it?"

"It does."

"I'll ask Harry," she said, flushing quickly.

"He'll be glad to help you. He owes me seven pounds at the moment, and he pawned his microscope last week, because he was so broke."

"You needn't think you can frighten me by that. I'm quite capable of earning my own living."

"It's the best thing you can do. I don't propose to give you a farthing more."

She thought of her rent due on Saturday and the baby's keep, but did not say anything. They left the restaurant, and in the street Philip asked her:

"Shall I call a cab for you? I'm going to take a little stroll."

"I haven't got any money. I had to pay a bill this afternoon."

"It won't hurt you to walk. If you want to see me tomorrow I shall be in about tea-time."

He took off his hat and sauntered away. He looked round in a moment and saw that she was standing helplessly where he had left her, looking at the traffic. He went back and with a laugh pressed a coin into her hand.

"Here's two bob for you to get home with."

Before she could speak he hurried away.

Chapter 76

Next day, in the afternoon, Philip sat in his room and wondered whether Mildred would come. He had slept badly. He had spent the morning in the club of the Medical School, reading one newspaper after another. It was the vacation and few students he knew were in London, but he found one or two people to talk to, he played a game of chess, and so wore out the tedious hours. After luncheon he felt so tired, his head was aching so, that he went back to his lodgings and lay down; he tried to read a novel. He had not seen Griffiths. He was not in when Philip returned the night before; he heard him come back, but he did not as usual look into Philip's room to see if he was asleep; and in the morning Philip heard him go out early. It was clear that he wanted to avoid him. Suddenly there was a light tap at his door. Philip sprang to his feet and opened it. Mildred stood on the threshold. She did not move.

"Come in," said Philip.

He closed the door after her. She sat down. She hesitated to begin.

"Thank you for giving me that two shillings last night," she said.

"Oh, that's all right."

She gave him a faint smile. It reminded Philip of the timid, ingratiating look of a puppy that has been beaten for naughtiness and wants to reconcile himself with his master.

"I've been lunching with Harry," she said.

"Have you?"

"If you still want me to go away with you on Saturday, Philip, I'll come."

A quick thrill of triumph shot through his heart, but it was a sensation that only lasted an instant; it was followed by a suspicion.

"Because of the money?" he asked.

"Partly," she answered simply. "Harry can't do anything. He owes five weeks' here, and he owes you seven pounds, and his tailor's pressing him for money. He'd pawn anything he could, but he's pawned everything already. I had a job to put the woman off about my new dress, and on Saturday there's the book at my lodgings, and I can't get work in five minutes. It always means waiting some little time till there's a vacancy."

She said all this in an even, querulous tone, as though she were recounting the injustices of fate, which had to be borne as part of the natural order of things. Philip did not answer. He knew what she told him well enough.

"You said 'partly'," he observed at last.

"Well, Harry says you've been a brick to both of us. You've been a real good friend to him, he says, and you've done for me what p'raps no other man would have done. We must do the straight thing, he says. And he said what you said about him, that he's fickle by nature, he's not like you, and I should be a fool to throw you away for him. He won't last and you will, he says so himself."

"D'you *want* to come away with me?" asked Philip.

"I don't mind."

He looked at her, and the corners of his mouth turned down in an expression of misery. He had triumphed indeed, and he was going to have his way. He gave a little laugh of derision at his own humiliation. She looked at him quickly, but did not speak.

"I've looked forward with all my soul to going away with you, and I thought at last, after all that wretchedness, I was going to be happy…"

He did not finish what he was going to say. And then on a sudden, without warning, Mildred broke into a storm of tears. She was sitting in the chair in which Norah had sat and wept, and like her she hid her face on the back of it, towards the side where there was a little bump formed by the sagging in the middle, where the head had rested.

"I'm not lucky with women," thought Philip.

Her thin body was shaken with sobs. Philip had never seen a woman cry with such an utter abandonment. It was horribly painful and his heart was torn. Without realizing what he did, he went up to her and put his arms round her; she did not resist, but in her wretchedness surrendered herself to his comforting. He whispered to her little words of solace. He scarcely knew what he was saying, he bent over her and kissed her repeatedly.

"Are you awfully unhappy?" he said at last.

"I wish I was dead," she moaned. "I wish I'd died when the baby come."

Her hat was in her way, and Philip took it off for her. He placed her head more comfortably in the chair, and then he went and sat down at the table and looked at her.

"It is awful, love, isn't it?" he said. "Fancy anyone wanting to be in love."

Presently the violence of her sobbing diminished and she sat in the chair, exhausted, with her head thrown back and her arms hanging by her side. She had the grotesque look of one of those painters' dummies used to hang draperies on.

"I didn't know you loved him so much as all that," said Philip.

He understood Griffiths' love well enough, for he put himself in Griffiths' place and saw with his eyes, touched with his hands; he was able to think himself in Griffiths's body, and he kissed her with his lips, smiled at her with his smiling blue eyes. It was her emotion that surprised him. He had never thought her capable of passion, and this was passion: there was no mistaking it. Something seemed to give way in his heart; it really felt to him as though something were breaking, and he felt strangely weak.

"I don't want to make you unhappy. You needn't come away with me if you don't want to. I'll give you the money all the same."

She shook her head.

"No, I said I'd come, and I'll come."

"What's the good, if you're sick with love for him?"

"Yes, that's the word. I'm sick with love. I know it won't last, just as well as he does, but just now…"

She paused and shut her eyes as though she were going to faint. A strange idea came to Philip, and he spoke it as it came, without stopping to think it out.

"Why don't you go away with him?"

"How can I? You know we haven't got the money."

"I'll give you the money."

"You?"

She sat up and looked at him. Her eyes began to shine, and the colour came into her cheeks.

"Perhaps the best thing would be to get it over, and then you'd come back to me."

Now that he had made the suggestion he was sick with anguish, and yet the torture of it gave him a strange, subtle sensation. She stared at him with open eyes.

"Oh, how could we, on your money? Harry wouldn't think of it."

"Oh yes, he would, if you persuaded him."

Her objections made him insist, and yet he wanted her with all his heart to refuse vehemently.

"I'll give you a fiver, and you can go away from Saturday to Monday. You could easily do that. On Monday he's going home till he takes up his appointment at the North London."

"Oh, Philip, do you mean that?" she cried, clasping her hands. "If you could only let us go—I would love you so much afterwards, I'd do anything for you. I'm sure I shall get over it if you'll only do that. Would you really give us the money?"

"Yes," he said.

She was entirely changed now. She began to laugh. He could see that she was insanely happy. She got up and knelt down by Philip's side, taking his hands.

"You are a brick, Philip. You're the best fellow I've ever known. Won't you be angry with me afterwards?"

He shook his head, smiling, but with what agony in his heart!

"May I go and tell Harry now? And can I say to him that you don't mind? He won't consent unless you promise it doesn't matter. Oh, you don't know how I love him! And afterwards I'll do anything you like. I'll come over to Paris with you or anywhere on Monday."

She got up and put on her hat.

"Where are you going?"

"I'm going to ask him if he'll take me."

"Already?"

"D'you want me to stay? I'll stay if you like."

She sat down, but he gave a little laugh.

"No, it doesn't matter, you'd better go at once. There's only one thing: I can't bear to see Griffiths just now, it would hurt me too awfully. Say I have no ill-feeling towards him or anything like that, but ask him to keep out of my way."

"All right." She sprang up and put on her gloves. "I'll let you know what he says."

"You'd better dine with me tonight."

"Very well."

She put up her face for him to kiss her, and when he pressed his lips to hers she threw her arms round his neck.

"You are a darling, Philip."

She sent him a note a couple of hours later to say that she had a headache and could not dine with him. Philip had almost expected it. He knew that she was dining with Griffiths. He was horribly jealous, but the sudden passion which had seized the pair of them seemed like something that had come from the outside, as though a god had visited them with it, and he felt himself helpless. It seemed so natural that they should love one another. He saw all the advantages that Griffiths had over himself and confessed that in Mildred's place he would have done as Mildred did. What hurt him most was Griffiths's treachery; they had been such good friends, and Griffiths knew how passionately devoted he was to Mildred: he might have spared him.

He did not see Mildred again till Friday; he was sick for a sight of her by then; but when she came and he realized that he had gone out of her thoughts entirely, for they were engrossed in Griffiths, he suddenly hated her. He saw now why she and Griffiths loved one another. Griffiths was stupid, oh, so stupid! he had known that all along, but had shut his eyes to it, stupid and empty-headed: that charm of his concealed an utter selfishness; he was willing to sacrifice anyone to his appetites. And how inane was the life he led, lounging about bars and drinking in music halls, wandering from one light *amour* to another! He never read a book, he was blind to everything that was not frivolous and vulgar; he had never a thought that was fine: the word most common on his lips was "smart"; that was his highest praise for man or woman. Smart! It was no wonder he pleased Mildred. They suited one another.

Philip talked to Mildred of things that mattered to neither

of them. He knew she wanted to speak of Griffiths, but he gave her no opportunity. He did not refer to the fact that two evenings before she had put off dining with him on a trivial excuse. He was casual with her, trying to make her think he was suddenly grown indifferent; and he exercised peculiar skill in saying little things which he knew would wound her; but which were so indefinite, so delicately cruel, that she could not take exception to them. At last she got up.

"I think I must be going off now," she said.

"I daresay you've got a lot to do," he answered.

She held out her hand, he took it, said good-bye, and opened the door for her. He knew what she wanted to speak about, and he knew also that his cold, ironical air intimidated her. Often his shyness made him seem so frigid that unintentionally he frightened people, and, having discovered this, he was able when occasion arose to assume the same manner.

"You haven't forgotten what you promised?" she said at last, as he held open the door.

"What is that?"

"About the money."

"How much d'you want?"

He spoke with an icy deliberation which made his words peculiarly offensive. Mildred flushed. He knew she hated him at that moment, and he wondered at the self-control by which she prevented herself from flying out at him. He wanted to make her suffer.

"There's the dress and the book tomorrow. That's all. Harry won't come, so we shan't want money for that."

Philip's heart gave a great thud against his ribs, and he let the door handle go. The door swung to.

"Why not?"

"He says we couldn't, not on your money."

A devil seized Philip, a devil of self-torture which was always lurking within him, and, though with all his soul he wished that Griffiths and Mildred should not go away together, he could not help himself; he set himself to persuade Griffiths through her.

"I don't see why not, if I'm willing," he said.

"That's what I told him."

"I should have thought if he really wanted to go he wouldn't hesitate."

"Oh, it's not that, he wants to all right. He'd go at once if he had the money."

"If he's squeamish about it I'll give *you* the money."

"I said you'd lend it if he liked, and we'd pay it back as soon as we could."

"It's rather a change for you going on your knees to get a man to take you away for a weekend."

"It is rather, isn't it?" she said, with a shameless little laugh.

It sent a cold shudder down Philip's spine.

"What are you going to do then?" he asked.

"Nothing. He's going home tomorrow. He must."

That would be Philip's salvation. With Griffiths out of the way he could get Mildred back. She knew no one in London, she would be thrown on to his society, and when they were alone together he could soon make her forget this infatuation. If he said nothing more he was safe. But he had a fiendish desire to break down their scruples, he wanted to know how abominably they could behave towards him; if he tempted them a little more they would yield, and he took a fierce joy at the thought of their dishonour. Though every word he spoke tortured him, he found in the torture a horrible delight.

"It looks as if it were now or never."

"That's what I told him," she said.

There was a passionate note in her voice which struck Philip. He was biting his nails in his nervousness.

"Where were you thinking of going?"

"Oh, to Oxford. He was at the 'Varsity there, you know. He said he'd show me the colleges."

Philip remembered that once he had suggested going to Oxford for the day, and she had expressed firmly the boredom she felt at the thought of sights.

"And it looks as if you'd have fine weather. It ought to be very jolly there just now."

"I've done all I could to persuade him."

"Why don't you have another try?"

"Shall I say you want us to go?"

"I don't think you must go as far as that," said Philip.

She paused for a minute or two, looking at him. Philip forced himself to look at her in a friendly way. He hated her, he despised her, he loved her with all his heart.

"I'll tell you what I'll do, I'll go and see if he can't arrange it. And then, if he says yes, I'll come and fetch the money tomorrow. When shall you be in?"

"I'll come back here after luncheon and wait."

"All right."

"I'll give you the money for your dress and your room now."

He went to his desk and took out what money he had. The dress was six guineas; there was besides her rent and her food, and the baby's keep for a week. He gave her eight pounds ten.

"Thanks very much," she said.

She left him.

Chapter 77

After lunching in the basement of the Medical School Philip went back to his rooms. It was Saturday afternoon, and the landlady was cleaning the stairs.

"Is Mr. Griffiths in?" he asked.

"No, sir. He went away this morning, soon after you went out."

"Isn't he coming back?"

"I don't think so, sir. He's taken his luggage."

Philip wondered what this could mean. He took a book and began to read. It was Burton's *Journey to Meccah*, which he had just got out of the Westminster Public Library; and he read the first page, but could make no sense of it, for his mind was elsewhere; he was listening all the time for a ring at the bell. He dared not hope that Griffiths had gone away already, without Mildred, to his home in Cumberland. Mildred would be coming presently for the money. He set his teeth and read on; he tried desperately to concentrate his attention; the sentences etched themselves in his brain by the force of his effort, but they were distorted by the agony he was enduring. He wished with all his heart that he had not made the horrible proposition to give them money; but now that he had made it he lacked the strength to go back on it, not on Mildred's account, but on his own. There was a morbid obstinacy in him which forced him to do the thing he had determined. He discovered that the three pages he had read had made no impression on him at all; and he went back and started from the beginning: he found himself reading one sentence over and over again; and now it weaved itself in with his thoughts, horribly, like some formula in a nightmare. One thing he could do was to go out and keep away till midnight; they could not go then; and he saw them calling at the house every hour to ask if he was in. He enjoyed the thought of their disappointment. He repeated that sentence to himself mechanically. But he could not do that. Let them come and take the money, and he would know then to what depths of infamy it was possible for men to descend. He could not read any more now. He simply could not see the words. He leaned back in his chair, closing his eyes, and, numb with misery, waited for Mildred.

The landlady came in.

"Will you see Mrs. Miller, sir?"

"Show her in."

Philip pulled himself together to receive her without any sign of what he was feeling. He had an impulse to throw himself on his knees and seize her hands and beg her not to go; but he knew there was no way of moving her; she would tell Griffiths what he had said and how he acted. He was ashamed.

"Well, how about the little jaunt?" he said gaily.

"We're going. Harry's outside. I told him you didn't want to see him, so he's kept out of your way. But he wants to know if he can come in just for a minute to say good-bye to you."

"No, I won't see him," said Philip.

He could see she did not care if he saw Griffiths or not. Now that she was there he wanted her to go quickly.

"Look here, here's the fiver. I'd like you to go now."

She took it and thanked him. She turned to leave the room.

"When are you coming back?" he asked.

"Oh, on Monday. Harry must go home then."

He knew what he was going to say was humiliating, but he was broken down with jealousy and desire.

"Then I shall see you, shan't I?"

He could not help the note of appeal in his voice.

"Of course. I'll let you know the moment I'm back."

He shook hands with her. Through the curtains he watched her jump into a four-wheeler that stood at the door. It rolled away. Then he threw himself on his bed and hid his face in his hands. He felt tears coming to his eyes, and he was angry with himself; he clenched his hands and screwed up his body to prevent them; but he could not; and great painful sobs were forced from him.

He got up at last, exhausted and ashamed, and washed his face. He mixed himself a strong whisky and soda. It made him feel a little better. Then he caught sight of the tickets to Paris, which were on the chimney-piece, and, seizing them, with an impulse of rage he flung them in the fire. He knew he could have got the money back on them, but it relieved him to destroy them. Then he went out in search of someone to be with. The club was empty. He felt he would go mad unless he found someone to talk to; but Lawson was abroad; he went on to Hayward's rooms; the maid who opened the door told him that he had gone down to Brighton for the weekend. Then Philip went to a gallery and found it was just closing. He did not know what to do. He was distracted. And he thought of Griffiths and Mildred going to Oxford, sitting opposite one another in the train, happy. He went back to his rooms, but they filled him with horror, he had been so wretched in them; he tried once more to read Burton's book, but, as he read, he told himself again and again what a fool he had been; it was he who had made the suggestion that they should go away, he had offered the money, he had forced it upon them; he might have known what would happen when he introduced Griffiths to Mildred; his own vehement passion was enough to arouse the other's desire. By this time they had reached Oxford. They would put up in one of the lodging-houses in John Street; Philip had never been to Oxford, but Griffiths had talked to him about it so much that he knew exactly where they would go; and they would dine at the Clarendon; Griffiths had been in the habit of dining there when he went on the spree. Philip got himself something to eat in a restaurant near Charing Cross; he had made up his mind to go to a play, and afterwards he fought his way into the pit of a theatre at which one of Oscar Wilde's pieces was being performed. He wondered if Mildred and Griffiths would go to a play that evening: they must kill the evening somehow; they were too stupid, both of them, to content themselves with conversation; he got a fierce delight in reminding himself of the vulgarity of their minds which suited them so exactly to one another. He watched the play with an abstracted mind, trying to give himself gaiety by drinking whisky in each interval; he was unused to alcohol, and it affected him quickly, but his drunkenness was savage and morose. When the play was over he had another drink. He could not go to bed, he knew he would not sleep, and he dreaded the pictures which his vivid imagination would place before him. He tried not to think of them. He knew he had drunk too much. Now he was seized with a desire to do horrible, sordid things; he wanted to roll himself in gutters; his whole being yearned for beastliness; he wanted to grovel.

He walked up Piccadilly, dragging his club-foot, sombrely drunk, with rage and misery clawing at his heart. He was stopped by a painted harlot, who put her hand on his arm; he pushed her violently away with brutal words. He walked on a few steps and then stopped. She would do as well as another. He was sorry he had spoken so roughly to her. He went up to her.

"I say," he began.

"Go to hell," she said.

Philip laughed.

"I merely wanted to ask if you'd do me the honour of supping with me tonight."

She looked at him with amazement, and hesitated for a while. She saw he was drunk.

"I don't mind."

He was amused that she should use a phrase he had heard so often on Mildred's lips. He took her to one of the restaurants he had been in the habit of going to with Mildred. He noticed as they walked along that she looked down at his limb.

"I've got a club-foot," he said. "Have you any objection?"

"You are a cure," she laughed.

When he got home his bones were aching, and in his head there was a hammering that made him nearly scream. He took another whisky and soda to steady himself, and going to bed sank into a dreamless sleep till midday.

Chapter 78

At last Monday came, and Philip thought his long torture was over. Looking out the trains he found that the latest by which Griffiths could reach home that night left Oxford soon after one, and he supposed that Mildred would take one which started a few minutes later to bring her to London. His desire was to go and meet it, but he thought Mildred would like to be left alone for a day; perhaps she would drop him a line in the evening to say she was back, and if not he would call at her lodgings next morning: his spirit was cowed. He felt a bitter hatred for Griffiths, but for Mildred, notwithstanding all that had passed, only a heart-rending desire. He was glad now that Hayward was not in London on Saturday afternoon when, distraught, he went in search of human comfort: he could not have prevented himself from telling him everything, and Hayward would have been astonished at his weakness. He would despise him, and perhaps be shocked or disgusted that he could envisage the possibility of making Mildred his mistress after she had given herself to another man. What did he care if it was shocking or disgusting? He was ready for any compromise, prepared for more degrading humiliations still, if he could only gratify his desire.

Towards the evening his steps took him against his will to the house in which she lived, and he looked up at her window. It was dark. He did not venture to ask if she was back. He was confident in her promise. But there was no letter from her in the morning, and, when about midday he called, the maid told him she had not arrived. He could not understand it. He knew that Griffiths would have been obliged to go home the day before, for he was to be best man at a wedding, and Mildred had no money. He turned over in his mind every possible thing that might have happened. He went again in the afternoon and left a note, asking her to dine with him that evening as calmly as though the events of the last fortnight had not happened. He mentioned the place and time at which they were to meet, and hoping against hope kept the appointment: though he waited for an hour she did not come. On Wednesday morning he was ashamed to ask at the house and sent a messenger-boy with a letter and instructions to bring back a reply; but in an hour the boy came back with Philip's letter unopened and the answer that the lady had not returned from the country. Philip was beside himself. The last deception was more than he could bear. He repeated to himself over and over again that he loathed Mildred, and, ascribing to Griffiths this new disappointment, he hated him so much that he knew what was the delight of murder: he walked about considering what a joy it would be to come upon him on a dark night and stick a knife into his throat, just about the carotid artery, and leave him to die in the street like a dog. Philip was out of his senses with grief and rage. He did not like whisky, but he drank to stupefy himself. He went to bed drunk on the Tuesday and on the Wednesday night.

On Thursday morning he got up very late and dragged himself, blear-eyed and sallow, into his sitting-room to see if there were any letters. A curious feeling shot through his heart when he recognized the handwriting of Griffiths.

Dear old man,

I hardly know how to write to you and yet I feel I must write. I hope you're not awfully angry with me. I know I oughtn't to have gone away with Milly, but I simply couldn't help myself. She simply carried me off my feet and I would have done anything to get her. When she told me you had offered us the money to go I simply couldn't resist. And now it's all over I'm awfully ashamed of myself and I wish I hadn't been such a fool. I wish you'd write and say you're not angry with me, and I want you to let me come and see you. I was awfully hurt at your telling Milly you didn't want to see me. Do write me a line, there's a good chap, and tell me you forgive me. It'll ease my conscience. I thought you wouldn't mind or you wouldn't have offered the money. But I know I oughtn't to have taken it. I came home on Monday and Milly wanted to stay a couple of days at Oxford by herself. She's going back to London on Wednesday, so by the time you receive this letter you will have seen her and I hope everything will go off all right. Do write and say you forgive me. Please write at once.

Yours ever,

Harry.

Philip tore up the letter furiously. He did not mean to answer it. He despised Griffiths for his apologies, he had no patience with his prickings of conscience: one could do a dastardly thing if one chose, but it was contemptible to regret it afterwards. He thought the letter cowardly and hypocritical. He was disgusted at its sentimentality.

"It would be very easy if you could do a beastly thing," he muttered to himself, "and then say you were sorry, and that put it all right again."

He hoped with all his heart he would have the chance one day to do Griffiths a bad turn.

But at all events he knew that Mildred was in town. He dressed hurriedly, not waiting to shave, drank a cup of tea, and took a cab to her rooms. The cab seemed to crawl. He was painfully anxious to see her, and unconsciously he uttered a prayer to the God he did not believe in to make her receive him kindly. He only wanted to forget. With beating heart he rang the bell. He forgot all his suffering in the passionate desire to enfold her once more in his arms.

"Is Mrs. Miller in?" he asked joyously.

"She's gone," the maid answered.

He looked at her blankly.

"She came about an hour ago and took away her things."

For a moment he did not know what to say.

"Did you give her my letter? Did she say where she was going?"

Then he understood that Mildred had deceived him again.

She was not coming back to him. He made an effort to save his face.

"Oh, well, I daresay I shall hear from her. She may have sent a letter to another address."

He turned away and went back hopeless to his rooms. He might have known that she would do this; she had never cared for him, she had made a fool of him from the beginning; she had no pity, she had no kindness, she had no charity. The only thing was to accept the inevitable. The pain he was suffering was horrible, he would sooner be dead than endure it; and the thought came to him that it would be better to finish with the whole thing: he might throw himself in the river or put his neck on a railway line; but he had no sooner set the thought into words than he rebelled against it. His reason told him that he would get over his unhappiness in time; if he tried with all his might he could forget her; and it would be grotesque to kill himself on account of a vulgar slut. He had only one life, and it was madness to fling it away. He *felt* that he would never overcome his passion, but he *knew* that after all it was only a matter of time.

He would not stay in London. There everything reminded him of his unhappiness. He telegraphed to his uncle that he was coming to Blackstable, and, hurrying to pack, took the first train he could. He wanted to get away from the sordid rooms in which he had endured so much suffering. He wanted to breathe clean air. He was disgusted with himself. He felt that he was a little mad.

Since he was grown up Philip had been given the best spare room at the vicarage. It was a corner-room and in front of one window was an old tree which blocked the view, but from the other you saw, beyond the garden and the vicarage field, broad meadows. Philip remembered the wall-paper from his earliest years. On the walls were quaint water colours of the early Victorian period by a friend of the Vicar's youth. They had a faded charm. The dressing-table was surrounded by stiff muslin. There was an old tallboy to put your clothes in. Philip gave a sigh of pleasure; he had never realized that all those things meant anything to him at all. At the vicarage life went on as it had always done. No piece of furniture had been moved from one place to another; the Vicar ate the same things, said the same things, went for the same walk every day; he had grown a little fatter, a little more silent, a little more narrow. He had become accustomed to living without his wife and missed her very little. He bickered still with Josiah Graves. Philip went to see the churchwarden. He was a little thinner, a little whiter, a little more austere; he was autocratic still and still disapproved of candles on the altar. The shops had still a pleasant quaintness; and Philip stood in front of that in which things useful to seamen were sold, sea-boots and tarpaulins and tackle, and remembered that he had felt there in his childhood the thrill of the sea and the adventurous magic of the unknown.

He could not help his heart beating at each double knock of the postman in case there might be a letter from Mildred sent on by his landlady in London; but he knew that there would be none. Now that he could think it out more calmly he understood that in trying to force Mildred to love him he had been attempting the impossible. He did not know what it was that passed from a man to a woman, from a woman to a man, and made one of them a slave: it was convenient to call it the sexual instinct; but if it was no more than that, he did not understand why it should occasion so vehement an attraction to one person rather than another. It was irresistible: the mind could not battle with it; friendship, gratitude, interest, had no power beside it. Because he had not attracted Mildred sexually, nothing that he did had any effect upon her. The idea revolted him; it made human nature beastly; and he felt suddenly that the hearts of men were full of dark places. Because Mildred was indifferent to him he had thought her sexless; her anaemic appearance and thin lips, the body with its narrow hips and flat chest, the languor of her manner, carried out his supposition; and yet she was capable of sudden passions which made her willing to risk everything to gratify them. He had never understood her adventure with Emil Miller: it had seemed so unlike her, and she had never been able to explain it; but now that he had seen her with Griffiths he knew that just the same thing had happened then: she had been carried off her feet by an ungovernable desire. He tried to think out what those two men had which so strangely attracted her. They both had a vulgar facetiousness which tickled her simple sense of humour, and a certain coarseness of nature; but what took her perhaps was the blatant sexuality which was their most marked characteristic. She had a genteel refinement which shuddered at the facts of life, she looked upon the bodily functions as indecent, she had all sorts of euphemisms for common objects, she always chose an elaborate word as more becoming than a simple one: the brutality of these men was like a whip on her thin white shoulders, and she shuddered with voluptuous pain.

One thing Philip had made up his mind about. He would not go back to the lodgings in which he had suffered. He wrote to his landlady and gave her notice. He wanted to have his own things about him. He determined to take unfurnished rooms: it would be pleasant and cheaper; and this was an urgent consideration, for during the last year and a half he had spent nearly seven hundred pounds. He must make up for it now by the most rigid economy. Now and then he thought of the future with panic; he had been a fool to spend so much money on Mildred; but he knew that if it were to come again he would act in the same way. It amused him sometimes to consider that his friends, because he had a face which did not express his feelings very vividly and a rather slow way of moving, looked upon him as strong-minded, deliberate, and cool. They thought him reasonable and praised his common sense; but he knew that his placid expression was no more than a mask, assumed unconsciously, which acted like the protective colouring of butterflies; and himself was astonished at the weakness of his will. It seemed to him that he was swayed by every light emotion, as though he were a leaf in the wind, and when passion seized him he was powerless. He had no self-control. He merely seemed to possess it because he was indifferent to many of the things which moved other people.

He considered with some irony the philosophy which he had developed for himself, for it had not been of much use to him in the conjuncture he had passed through; and he wondered whether thought really helped a man in any of the critical affairs of life: it seemed to him rather that he was swayed by some power alien to and yet within himself, which urged him like that great wind of Hell which drove Paolo and Francesca ceaselessly on. He thought of what he was going to do and, when the time came to act, he was powerless in the grasp of instincts, emotions, he knew not what. He acted as though he were a machine driven by the two forces of his environment and his personality; his reason was someone looking on, observing the facts but powerless to interfere: it was like those gods of Epicurus, who saw the doings of men from their empyrean heights and had no might to alter one smallest particle of what occurred.

Chapter 79

Philip went up to London a couple of days before the session began in order to find himself rooms. He hunted about the streets that led out of the Westminster Bridge Road, but their dinginess was distasteful to him; and at last he found one in Kennington which had a quiet and old-world air. It reminded one a little of the London which Thackeray knew on that side of the river, and in the Kennington Road, through which the great barouche of the Newcomes must have passed as it drove the family to the West of London, the plane-trees were bursting into leaf. The houses in the street which Philip fixed upon were two-storeyed, and in most of the windows was a notice to state that lodgings were to let. He knocked at one which announced that the lodgings were unfurnished, and was shown by an austere, silent woman four very small rooms, in one of which there was a kitchen range and a sink. The rent was nine shillings a week. Philip did not want so many rooms, but the rent was low and he wished to settle down at once. He asked the landlady if she could keep the place clean for him and cook his breakfast, but she replied that she had enough work to do without that; and he was pleased rather than otherwise because she intimated that she wished to have nothing more to do with him than to receive his rent. She told him that, if he inquired at the grocer's round the corner, which was also a post office, he might hear of a woman who would "do" for him.

Philip had a little furniture which he had gathered as he went along, an armchair that he had bought in Paris, and a table, a few drawings, and the small Persian rug which Cronshaw had given him. His uncle had offered a fold-up bed for which, now that he no longer let his house in August, he had no further use; and by spending another ten pounds Philip bought himself whatever else was essential. He spent ten shillings on putting a corn-coloured paper in the room he was making his parlour; and he hung on the walls a sketch which Lawson had given him of the Quai des Grands Augustins, and the photograph of the *Odalisque* by Ingres and Manet's *Olympia* which in Paris had been the objects of his contemplation while he shaved. To remind himself that he too had once been engaged in the practice of art, he put up a charcoal drawing of the young Spaniard Miguel Ajuria: it was the best thing he had ever done, a nude standing with clenched hands, his feet gripping the floor with a peculiar force, and on his face that air of determination which had been so impressive; and though Philip after the long interval saw very well the defects of his work its associations made him look upon it with tolerance. He wondered what had happened to Miguel. There is nothing so terrible as the pursuit of art by those who have no talent. Perhaps, worn out by exposure, starvation, disease, he had found an end in some hospital, or in an access of despair had sought death in the turbid

Seine; but perhaps with his Southern instability he had given up the struggle of his own accord, and now, a clerk in some office in Madrid, turned his fervent rhetoric to politics and bull-fighting.

Philip asked Lawson and Hayward to come and see his new rooms, and they came, one with a bottle of whisky, the other with a *pâté de foie gras*, and he was delighted when they praised his taste. He would have invited the Scotch stockbroker too, but he had only three chairs, and thus could entertain only a definite number of guests. Lawson was aware that through him Philip had become very friendly with Norah Nesbit and now remarked that he had run across her a few days before.

"She was asking how you were."

Philip flushed at the mention of her name (he could not get himself out of the awkward habit of reddening when he was embarrassed), and Lawson looked at him quizzically. Lawson, who now spent most of the year in London, had so far surrendered to his environment as to wear his hair short and to dress himself in a neat serge suit and a bowler hat.

"I gather that all is over between you," he said.

"I've not seen her for months."

"She was looking rather nice. She had a very smart hat on with a lot of white ostrich feathers on it. She must be doing pretty well."

Philip changed the conversation, but he kept thinking of her, and after an interval, when the three of them were talking of something else, he asked suddenly:

"Did you gather that Norah was angry with me?"

"Not a bit. She talked very nicely of you."

"I've got half a mind to go and see her."

"She won't eat you."

Philip had thought of Norah often. When Mildred left him his first thought was of her, and he told himself bitterly that she would never have treated him so. His impulse was to go to her; he could depend on her pity; but he was ashamed; she had been good to him always, and he had treated her abominably.

"If I'd only had the sense to stick to her!" he said to himself, afterwards, when Lawson and Hayward had gone and he was smoking a last pipe before going to bed.

He remembered the pleasant hours they had spent together in the cosy sitting-room in Vincent Square, their visits to galleries and to the play, and the charming evenings of intimate conversation. He recollected her solicitude for his welfare and her interest in all that concerned him. She had loved him with a love that was kind and lasting, there was more than sensuality in it, it was almost maternal; he had always known that it was a precious thing for which with all his soul he should thank the gods. He made up his mind to throw himself on her mercy. She must have suffered horribly, but he felt she had the greatness of heart to forgive him; she was incapable of malice. Should he write to her? No. He would break in on her suddenly and cast himself at her feet—he knew that when the time came he would feel too shy to perform such a dramatic gesture, but that was how he liked to think of it—and tell her that if she would take him back she might rely on him for ever. He was cured of the hateful disease from which he had suffered, he knew her worth, and now she might trust him. His imagination leaped forward to the future.

He pictured himself rowing with her on the river on Sundays; he would take her to Greenwich, he had never forgotten that delightful excursion with Hayward, and the beauty of the Port of London remained a permanent treasure in his recollection; and on the warm summer afternoons they would sit in the Park together and talk: he laughed to himself as he remembered her gay chatter, which poured out like a brook bubbling over little stones, amusing, flippant, and full of character. The agony he had suffered would pass from his mind like a bad dream.

But when next day, about tea-time, an hour at which he was pretty certain to find Norah at home, he knocked at her door his courage suddenly failed him. Was it possible for her to forgive him? It would be abominable of him to force himself on her presence. The door was opened by a maid new since he had been in the habit of calling every day, and he inquired if Mrs. Nesbit was in.

"Will you ask her if she could see Mr. Carey?" he said. "I'll wait here."

The maid ran upstairs and in a moment clattered down again.

"Will you step up, please, sir? Second floor front."

"I know," said Philip, with a slight smile.

He went with a fluttering heart. He knocked at the door.

"Come in," said the well-known, cheerful voice.

It seemed to say come in to a new life of peace and happiness. When he entered Norah stepped forward to greet him. She shook hands with him as if they had parted the day before. A man stood up.

"Mr. Carey—Mr. Kingsford."

Philip, bitterly disappointed at not finding her alone, sat down and took stock of the stranger. He had never heard her mention his name, but he seemed to Philip to occupy his chair as though he were very much at home. He was a man of forty, clean-shaven, with long fair hair very neatly plastered down, and the reddish skin and pale, tired eyes which fair men get when their youth is passed. He had a large nose, a large mouth; the bones of his face were prominent, and he was heavily made; he was a man of more than average height, and broad-shouldered.

"I was wondering what had become of you," said Norah, in her sprightly manner. "I met Mr. Lawson the other day—did he tell you? —and I informed him that it was really high time you came to see me again."

Philip could see no shadow of embarrassment in her countenance, and he admired the ease with which she carried off an encounter of which himself felt the intense awkwardness. She gave him tea. She was about to put sugar in it when he stopped her.

"How stupid of me!" she cried. "I forgot."

He did not believe that. She must remember quite well that he never took sugar in his tea. He accepted the incident as a sign that her nonchalance was affected.

The conversation which Philip had interrupted went on, and presently he began to feel a little in the way. Kingsford took no particular notice of him. He talked fluently and well, not without humour, but with a slightly dogmatic manner: he was a journalist, it appeared, and had something amusing to say on every topic that was touched upon; but it exasperated Philip to find himself edged out of the conversation. He was determined to stay the visitor out. He wondered if he admired Norah. In the old days they had often talked of the men who wanted to flirt with her and had laughed at them together. Philip tried to bring back the conversation to matters which only he and Norah knew about, but each time the journalist broke in and succeeded in drawing it away to a subject upon which Philip was forced to be silent. He grew faintly angry with Norah, for she must see he was being made ridiculous; but perhaps she was inflicting this upon him as a punishment, and with this thought he regained his good humour. At last, however, the clock struck six, and Kingsford got up.

"I must go," he said.

Norah shook hands with him, and accompanied him to the landing. She shut the door behind her and stood outside for a couple of minutes. Philip wondered what they were talking about.

"Who is Mr. Kingsford?" he asked cheerfully, when she returned.

"Oh, he's the editor of one of Harmsworth's magazines. He's been taking a good deal of my work lately."

"I thought he was never going."

"I'm glad you stayed. I wanted to have a talk with you." She curled herself into the large armchair, feet and all, in a way her small size made possible, and lit a cigarette. He smiled when he saw her assume the attitude which had always amused him.

"You look just like a cat."

She gave him a flash of her dark, fine eyes.

"I really ought to break myself of the habit. It's absurd to behave like a child when you're my age, but I'm comfortable with my legs under me."

"It's awfully jolly to be sitting in this room again," said Philip happily. "You don't know how I've missed it."

"Why on earth didn't you come before?" she asked gaily.

"I was afraid to," he said, reddening.

She gave him a look full of kindness. Her lips outlined a charming smile.

"You needn't have been."

He hesitated for a moment. His heart beat quickly.

"D'you remember the last time we met? I treated you awfully badly—I'm dreadfully ashamed of myself."

She looked at him steadily. She did not answer. He was losing his head; he seemed to have come on an errand of which he was only now realizing the outrageousness. She did not help him, and he could only blurt out bluntly:

"Can you ever forgive me?"

Then impetuously he told her that Mildred had left him and that his unhappiness had been so great that he almost killed himself. He told her of all that had happened between them, of the birth of the child, and of the meeting with Griffiths, of his folly and his trust and his immense deception. He told her how often he had thought of her kindness and of her love, and how bitterly he had regretted throwing it away: he had only been happy when he was with her, and he knew now how great was her worth. His voice was hoarse with emotion. Sometimes he was so ashamed of what he was saying that he spoke with his eyes fixed on the ground. His face was distorted with pain, and yet he felt it a strange relief to speak. At last he finished. He flung himself back in his chair, exhausted, and waited. He had concealed nothing, and even, in his self-abasement, he had striven to make himself more despicable than he had really been. He was surprised that she did not speak, and at last he raised his eyes. She was not looking at him. Her face was quite white, and she seemed to be lost in thought.

"Haven't you got anything to say to me?"

She started and reddened.

"I'm afraid you've had a rotten time," she said. "I'm dreadfully sorry."

She seemed about to go on, but she stopped, and again he waited. At length she seemed to force herself to speak.

"I'm engaged to be married to Mr. Kingsford."

"Why didn't you tell me at once?" he cried. "You needn't have allowed me to humiliate myself before you."

"I'm sorry, I couldn't stop you…. I met him soon after you" —she seemed to search for an expression that should not wound him— "told me your friend had come back. I was very wretched for a bit, he was extremely kind to me. He knew someone had made me suffer, of course he doesn't know it was you, and I don't know what I should have done without him. And suddenly I felt I couldn't go on working, working, working; I was so tired, I felt so ill. I told him about my husband. He offered to give me the money to get my divorce if I would marry him as soon as I could. He had a very good job, and it wouldn't be necessary for me to do anything unless I wanted to. He was so fond of me and so anxious to take care of me. I was awfully touched. And now I'm very, very fond of him."

"Have you got your divorce then?" asked Philip.

"I've got the decree *nisi*. It'll be made absolute in July, and then we are going to be married at once."

For some time Philip did not say anything.

"I wish I hadn't made such a fool of myself," he muttered at length.

He was thinking of his long, humiliating confession. She looked at him curiously.

"You were never really in love with me," she said.

"It's not very pleasant being in love."

But he was always able to recover himself quickly, and, getting up now and holding out his hand, he said:

"I hope you'll be very happy. After all, it's the best thing that could have happened to you."

She looked a little wistfully at him as she took his hand and held it.

"You'll come and see me again, won't you?" she asked.

"No," he said, shaking his head. "It would make me too envious to see you happy."

He walked slowly away from her house. After all she was right when she said he had never loved her. He was disappointed, irritated even, but his vanity was more affected than his heart. He knew that himself. And presently he grew conscious that the gods had played a very good practical joke on him, and he laughed at himself mirthlessly. It is not very comfortable to have the gift of being amused at one's own absurdity.

Chapter 80

For the next three months Philip worked on subjects which were new to him. The unwieldy crowd which had entered the Medical School nearly two years before had thinned out: some had left the hospital, finding the examinations more difficult to pass than they expected, some had been taken away by parents who had not foreseen the expense of life in London, and some had drifted away to other callings. One youth whom Philip knew had devised an ingenious plan to make money; he had bought things at sales and pawned them, but presently found it more profitable to pawn goods bought on credit; and it had caused a little excitement at the hospital when someone pointed out his name in police-court proceedings. There had been a remand, then assurances on the part of a harassed father, and the young man had gone out to bear the White Man's Burden overseas. The imagination of another, a lad who had never before been in a town at all, fell to the glamour of music halls and bar parlours; he spent his time among racing-men, tipsters, and trainers, and now was become a bookmaker's clerk. Philip had seen him once in a bar near Piccadilly Circus in a tight-waisted coat and a brown hat with a broad, flat brim. A third, with a gift for singing and mimicry, who had achieved success at the smoking concerts of the Medical School by his imitation of notorious comedians, had abandoned the hospital for the chorus of a musical comedy. Still another, and he interested Philip because his uncouth manner and interjectional speech did not suggest that he was capable of any deep emotion, had felt himself stifle among the houses of London. He grew haggard in shut-in spaces, and the soul he knew not he possessed struggled like a sparrow held in the hand, with little frightened gasps and a quick palpitation of the heart: he yearned for the broad skies and the open, desolate places among which his childhood had been spent; and he walked off one day, without a word to anybody, between one lecture and another; and the next thing his friends heard was that he had thrown up medicine and was working on a farm.

Philip attended now lectures on medicine and on surgery. On certain mornings in the weeks he practised bandaging on out-patients, glad to earn a little money, and he was taught auscultation and how to use the stethoscope. He learned dispensing. He was taking the examination in *Materia Medica* in July, and it amused him to play with various drugs, concocting mixtures, rolling pills, and making ointments. He seized avidly upon anything from which he could extract a suggestion of human interest.

He saw Griffiths once in the distance, but, not to have the pain of cutting him dead, avoided him. Philip had felt a certain self-consciousness with Griffiths's friends, some of whom were now friends of his, when he realized they knew of his quarrel with

Griffiths and surmised they were aware of the reason. One of them, a very tall fellow, with a small head and a languid air, a youth called Ramsden, who was one of Griffiths's most faithful admirers, copied his ties, his boots, his manner of talking, and his gestures, told Philip that Griffiths was very much hurt because Philip had not answered his letter. He wanted to be reconciled with him.

"Has he asked you to give me the message?" asked Philip.

"Oh, no. I'm saying this entirely on my own," said Ramsden. "He's awfully sorry for what he did, and he says you always behaved like a perfect brick to him. I know he'd be glad to make it up. He doesn't come to the hospital because he's afraid of meeting you, and he thinks you'd cut him."

"I should."

"It makes him feel rather wretched, you know."

"I can bear the trifling inconvenience that he feels with a good deal of fortitude," said Philip.

"He'll do anything he can to make it up."

"How childish and hysterical! Why should he care? I'm a very insignificant person, and he can do very well without my company. I'm not interested in him any more."

Ramsden thought Philip hard and cold. He paused for a moment or two, looking about him in a perplexed way.

"Harry wishes to God he'd never had anything to do with the woman."

"Does he?" asked Philip.

He spoke with an indifference which he was satisfied with. No one could have guessed how violently his heart was beating. He waited impatiently for Ramsden to go on.

"I suppose you've quite got over it now, haven't you?"

"I?" said Philip. "Quite."

Little by little he discovered the history of Mildred's relations with Griffiths. He listened with a smile on his lips, feigning an equanimity which quite deceived the dull-witted boy who talked to him. The weekend she spent with Griffiths at Oxford inflamed rather than extinguished her sudden passion; and when Griffiths went home, with a feeling that was unexpected in her, she determined to stay in Oxford by herself for a couple of days, because she had been so happy in it. She felt that nothing could induce her to go back to Philip. He revolted her. Griffiths was taken aback at the fire he had aroused, for he had found his two days with her in the country somewhat tedious; and he had no desire to turn an amusing epis into a tiresome affair. She made him promise to write to her, and, being an honest, decent fellow, with natural politeness and a desire to make himself pleasant to everybody, when he got home he wrote her a long and charming letter. She answered it with reams of passion, clumsy, for she had no gift of expression, ill-written and vulgar; the letter bored him, and when it was followed next day by another, and the day after by a third, he began to think her love no longer flattering but alarming. He did not answer; and she bombarded him with telegrams, asking him if he were ill and had received her letters; she said his silence made her dreadfully anxious. He was forced to write, but he sought to make his reply as casual as was possible without being offensive: he begged her not to wire, since it was difficult to explain telegrams to his mother, an old-fashioned person for whom a telegram was still an event to excite tremor. She answered by return of post that she must see him and announced her intention to pawn things (she had the dressing-case which Philip had given her as a wedding-present and could raise eight pounds on that) in order to come up and stay at the market town four miles from which was the village in which his father practised. This frightened Griffiths; and he, this time, made use of the telegraph wires to tell her that she must do nothing of the kind. He promised to let her know the moment he came up to London, and, when he did, found that she had already been asking for him at the hospital at which he had an appointment. He did not like this, and, on seeing her, told Mildred that she was not to come there on any pretext; and now, after an absence of three weeks, he found that she bored him quite decidedly; he wondered why he had ever troubled about her, and made up his mind to break with her as soon as he could. He was a person who dreaded quarrels, nor did he want to give pain; but at the same time he had other things to do, and he was quite determined not to let Mildred bother him. When he met her he was pleasant, cheerful, amusing, affectionate; he invented convincing excuses for the interval since last he had seen her; but he did everything he could to avoid her. When she forced him to make appointments he sent telegrams to her at the last moment to put himself off; and his landlady (the first three months of his appointment he was spending in rooms) had orders to say he was out when Mildred called. She would waylay him in the street and, knowing she had been waiting about for him to come out of the hospital for a couple of hours, he would give her a few charming, friendly words and bolt off with the excuse that he had a business engagement. He grew very skilful in slipping out of the hospital unseen. Once, when he went back to his lodgings at midnight, he saw a woman standing at the area railings and suspecting who it was went to beg a shake-down in Ramsden's rooms; next day the landlady told him that Mildred had sat crying on the doorsteps for hours, and she had been obliged to tell her at last that if she did not go away she would send for a policeman.

"I tell you, my boy," said Ramsden, "you're jolly well out of it. Harry says that if he'd suspected for half a second she was going to make such a blooming nuisance of herself he'd have seen himself damned before he had anything to do with her."

Philip thought of her sitting on that doorstep through the long hours of the night. He saw her face as she looked up dully at the landlady who sent her away.

"I wonder what she's doing now."

"Oh, she's got a job somewhere, thank God. That keeps her busy all day."

The last thing he heard, just before the end of the summer session, was that Griffiths's urbanity had given way at length under the exasperation of the constant persecution. He had told Mildred that he was sick of being pestered, and she had better take herself off and not bother him again.

"It was the only thing he could do," said Ramsden. "It was getting a bit too thick."

"Is it all over then?" asked Philip.

"Oh, he hasn't seen her for ten days. You know, Harry's wonderful at dropping people. This is about the toughest nut he's ever had to crack, but he's cracked it all right."

Then Philip heard nothing more of her at all. She vanished into the vast anonymous mass of the population of London.

Chapter 81

At the beginning of the winter session Philip became an out-patients' clerk. There were three assistant-physicians who took out-patients, two days a week each, and Philip put his name down for Dr. Tyrell. He was popular with the students, and there was some competition to be his clerk. Dr. Tyrell was a tall, thin man of thirty-five, with a very small head, red hair cut short, and prominent blue eyes: his face was bright scarlet. He talked well in a pleasant voice, was fond of a little joke, and treated the world lightly. He was a successful man, with a large consulting practice and a knighthood in prospect. From commerce with students and poor people he had the patronizing air, and from dealing always with the sick he had the healthy man's jovial condescension, which some consultants achieve as the professional manner. He made the patient feel like a boy confronted by a jolly schoolmaster; his illness was an absurd piece of naughtiness which amused rather than irritated.

The student was supposed to attend in the out-patients' room every day, see cases, and pick up what information he could; but on the days on which he clerked his duties were a little more definite. At that time the out-patients' department at St. Luke's consisted of three rooms, leading into one another, and a large, dark waiting-room with massive pillars of masonry and long benches. Here the patients waited after having been given their "letters" at midday; and the long rows of them, bottles and gallipots in hand, some tattered and dirty, others decent enough, sitting in the dimness, men and women of all ages, children, gave one an impression which was weird and horrible. They suggested the grim drawings of Daumier. All the rooms were painted alike, in salmon-colour with a high dado of maroon; and there was in them an odour of disinfectants, mingling as the afternoon wore on with the crude stench of humanity. The first room was the largest, and in the middle of it were a table and an office chair for the physician; on each side of this were two smaller tables, a little lower: at one of these sat the house-physician and at the other the clerk who took the "book" for the day. This was a large volume in which were written down the name, age, sex, profession of the patient, and the diagnosis of his disease.

At half past one the house-physician came in, rang the bell, and told the porter to send in the old patients. There were always a good many of these, and it was necessary to get through as many of them as possible before Dr. Tyrell came at two. The H. P. with whom Philip came in contact was a dapper little man, excessively conscious of his importance: he treated the clerks with condescension and patently resented the familiarity of older students who had been his contemporaries and did not use him with the respect he felt his present position demanded. He set about the cases. A clerk helped him. The patients streamed in. The men came first. Chronic bronchitis, "a nasty 'acking cough," was what they chiefly suffered from; one went to the H. P. and the other to the clerk, handing in their letters: if they were going on well the words *Rep 14* were written on them, and they went to the dispensary with their bottles or gallipots in order to have medicine given them for fourteen days more. Some old stagers held back so that they might be seen by the physician himself, but they seldom succeeded in this; and only three or four, whose condition seemed to demand his attention, were kept.

Dr. Tyrell came in with quick movements and a breezy manner. He reminded one slightly of a clown leaping into the arena of a circus with the cry: Here we are again. His air seemed to indicate: What's all this nonsense about being ill? I'll soon put that right. He took his seat, asked if there were any old patients for him to see, rapidly passed them in review, looking at them with shrewd eyes as he discussed their symptoms, cracked a joke (at which all the clerks laughed heartily) with the H. P., who laughed heartily too, but with an air as if he thought it was rather impudent for the clerks to laugh, remarked that it was a fine day or a hot one, and rang the bell for the porter to show in the new patients.

They came in one by one and walked up to the table at which sat Dr. Tyrell. They were old men and young men and middle-aged men, mostly of the labouring class, dock labourers, draymen, factory hands, barmen; but some, neatly dressed, were of a station which was obviously superior, shop-assistants, clerks, and the like. Dr. Tyrell looked at these with suspicion. Sometimes they put on shabby clothes in order to pretend they were poor; but he had a keen eye to prevent what he regarded as fraud and sometimes refused to see people who, he thought, could well pay for medical attendance. Women were the worst offenders and they managed the thing more clumsily. They would wear a cloak and a skirt which were almost in rags, and neglect to take the rings off their fingers.

"If you can afford to wear jewellery you can afford a doctor. A hospital is a charitable institution," said Dr. Tyrell.

He handed back the letter and called for the next case.

"But I've got my letter."

"I don't care a hang about your letter; you get out. You've got no business to come and steal the time which is wanted by the really poor."

The patient retired sulkily, with an angry scowl.

"She'll probably write a letter to the papers on the gross mismanagement of the London hospitals," said Dr. Tyrell, with a smile, as he took the next paper and gave the patient one of his shrewd glances.

Most of them were under the impression that the hospital was an institution of the state, for which they paid out of the rates, and took the attendance they received as a right they could claim. They imagined the physician who gave them his time was heavily paid.

Dr. Tyrell gave each of his clerks a case to examine. The clerk took the patient into one of the inner rooms; they were smaller, and each had a couch in it covered with black horse-hair: he asked his patient a variety of questions, examined his lungs, his heart, and his liver, made notes of fact on the hospital letter, formed in his own mind some idea of the diagnosis, and then waited for Dr. Tyrell to come in. This he did, followed by a small crowd of students, when he had finished the men, and the clerk read out what he had learned. The physician asked him one or two questions, and examined the patient himself. If there was anything interesting to hear students applied their stethoscope: you would see a man with two or three to the chest, and two perhaps to his back, while others waited impatiently to listen. The patient stood among them a little embarrassed, but not altogether displeased to find himself the centre of attention: he listened confusedly while Dr. Tyrell discoursed glibly on the case. Two or three students listened again to recognize the murmur or the crepitation which the physician described, and then the man was told to put on his clothes.

When the various cases had been examined Dr. Tyrell went back into the large room and sat down again at his desk. He asked any student who happened to be standing near him what he would prescribe for a patient he had just seen. The student mentioned one or two drugs.

"Would you?" said Dr. Tyrell. "Well, that's original at all events. I don't think we'll be rash."

This always made the students laugh, and with a twinkle of amusement at his own bright humour the physician prescribed some other drug than that which the student had suggested. When there were two cases of exactly the same sort and the student proposed the treatment which the physician had ordered for the first, Dr. Tyrell exercised considerable ingenuity in thinking of something else. Sometimes, knowing that in the dispensary they were worked off their legs and preferred to give the medicines which they had all ready, the good hospital mixtures which had been found by the experience of years to answer their purpose so well, he amused himself by writing an elaborate prescription.

"We'll give the dispenser something to do. If we go on prescribing *mist: alb:* he'll lose his cunning."

The students laughed, and the doctor gave them a circular glance of enjoyment in his joke. Then he touched the bell and, when the porter poked his head in, said:

"Old women, please."

He leaned back in his chair, chatting with the H. P. while the porter herded along the old patients. They came in, strings of anaemic girls, with large fringes and pallid lips, who could not digest their bad, insufficient food; old ladies, fat and thin, aged prematurely by frequent confinements, with winter coughs; women with this, that, and the other, the matter with them. Dr. Tyrell and his house-physician got through them quickly. Time was getting on, and the air in the small room was growing more sickly. The physician looked at his watch.

"Are there many new women today?" he asked.

"A good few, I think," said the H. P.

"We'd better have them in. You can go on with the old ones."

They entered. With the men the most common ailments were due to the excessive use of alcohol, but with the women they were due to defective nourishment. By about six o'clock they were finished. Philip, exhausted by standing all the time, by the bad air, and by the attention he had given, strolled over with his fellow-clerks to the Medical School to have tea.

He found the work of absorbing interest. There was humanity there in the rough, the materials the artist worked on; and Philip felt a curious thrill when it occurred to him that he was in the position of the artist and the patients were like clay in his hands. He remembered with an amused shrug of the shoulders his life in Paris, absorbed in colour, tone, values, Heaven knows what, with the aim of producing beautiful things: the directness of contact with men and women gave a thrill of power which he had never known. He found an endless excitement in looking at their faces and hearing them speak; they came in each with his peculiarity, some shuffling uncouthly, some with a little trip, others with heavy, slow tread, some shyly. Often you could guess their trades by the look of them. You learnt in what way to put your questions so that they should be understood, you discovered on what subjects nearly all lied, and by what inquiries you could extort the truth notwithstanding. You saw the different way people took the same things. The diagnosis of dangerous illness would be accepted by one with a laugh and a joke, by another with dumb despair. Philip found that he was less shy with these people than he had ever been with others; he felt not exactly sympathy, for sympathy suggests condescension; but he felt at home with them. He found that he was able to put them at their ease, and, when he had been given a case to find out what he could about it, it seemed to him that the patient delivered himself into his hands with a peculiar confidence.

"Perhaps," he thought to himself, with a smile, "perhaps I'm cut out to be a doctor. It would be rather a lark if I'd hit upon the one thing I'm fit for."

It seemed to Philip that he alone of the clerks saw the dramatic interest of those afternoons. To the others men and women were only cases, good if they were complicated, tiresome if obvious; they heard murmurs and were astonished at abnormal livers; an unexpected sound in the lungs gave them something to talk about. But to Philip there was much more. He found an interest in just looking at them, in the shape of their heads and their hands, in the look of their eyes and the length of their noses. You saw in that room human nature taken by surprise, and often the mask of custom was torn off rudely, showing you the soul all raw. Sometimes you saw an untaught stoicism which was profoundly moving. Once Philip saw a man, rough and illiterate, told his case was hopeless; and, self-controlled himself, he wondered at the splendid instinct which forced the fellow to keep a stiff upper-lip before strangers. But was it possible for him to be brave when he was by himself, face to face with his soul, or would he then surrender to despair? Sometimes there was tragedy. Once a young woman brought her sister to be examined, a girl of eighteen, with delicate features and large blue eyes, fair hair that sparkled with gold when a ray of autumn sunshine touched it for a moment, and a skin of amazing beauty. The students' eyes went to her with little smiles. They did not often see a pretty girl in these dingy rooms. The elder woman gave the family history, father and mother had died of phthisis, a brother and a sister, these two were the only ones left. The girl had been coughing lately and losing weight. She took off her blouse and the skin of her neck was like milk. Dr. Tyrell examined her quietly, with his usual rapid method; he told two or three of his clerks to apply their stethoscopes to a place he indicated with his finger; and then she was allowed to dress. The sister was standing a little apart and she spoke to him in a low voice, so that the girl should not hear. Her voice trembled with fear.

"She hasn't got it, doctor, has she?"

"I'm afraid there's no doubt about it."

"She was the last one. When she goes I shan't have anybody."

She began to cry, while the doctor looked at her gravely; he thought she too had the type; she would not make old bones either. The girl turned round and saw her sister's tears. She understood what they meant. The colour fled from her lovely face and tears fell down her cheeks. The two stood for a minute or two, crying silently, and then the older, forgetting the indifferent crowd that watched them, went up to her, took her in her arms, and rocked her gently to and fro as if she were a baby.

When they were gone a student asked:

"How long d'you think she'll last, sir?"

Dr. Tyrell shrugged his shoulders.

"Her brother and sister died within three months of the first symptoms. She'll do the same. If they were rich one might do something. You can't tell these people to go to St. Moritz. Nothing can be done for them."

Once a man who was strong and in all the power of his manhood came because a persistent aching troubled him and his club-doctor did not seem to do him any good; and the verdict for him too was death, not the inevitable death that horrified and yet was tolerable because science was helpless before it, but the death which was inevitable because the man was a little wheel in the great machine of a complex civilization, and had as little power of changing the circumstances as an automaton. Complete rest was his only chance. The physician did not ask impossibilities.

"You ought to get some very much lighter job."

"There ain't no light jobs in my business."

"Well, if you go on like this you'll kill yourself. You're very ill."

"D'you mean to say I'm going to die?"

"I shouldn't like to say that, but you're certainly unfit for hard work."

"If I don't work who's to keep the wife and the kids?"

Dr. Tyrell shrugged his shoulders. The dilemma had been presented to him a hundred times. Time was pressing and there were many patients to be seen.

"Well, I'll give you some medicine and you can come back in a week and tell me how you're getting on."

The man took his letter with the useless prescription written upon it and walked out. The doctor might say what he liked. He did not feel so bad that he could not go on working. He had a good job and he could not afford to throw it away.

"I give him a year," said Dr. Tyrell.

Sometimes there was comedy. Now and then came a flash of cockney humour, now and then some old lady, a character such as Charles Dickens might have drawn, would amuse them by her garrulous oddities. Once a woman came who was a member of the ballet at a famous music hall. She looked fifty, but gave her age as twenty-eight. She was outrageously painted and ogled the students impudently with large black eyes; her smiles were grossly alluring. She had abundant self-confidence and treated Dr. Tyrell, vastly amused, with the easy familiarity with which she might have used an intoxicated admirer. She had chronic bronchitis, and told him it hindered her in the exercise of her profession.

"I don't know why I should 'ave such a thing, upon my word I don't. I've never 'ad a day's illness in my life. You've only got to look at me to know that."

She rolled her eyes round the young men, with a long sweep of her painted eyelashes, and flashed her yellow teeth at them. She spoke with a cockney accent, but with an affectation of refinement which made every word a feast of fun.

"It's what they call a winter cough," answered Dr. Tyrell gravely. "A great many middle-aged women have it."

"Well, I never! That is a nice thing to say to a lady. No one ever called me middle-aged before."

She opened her eyes very wide and cocked her head on one side, looking at him with indescribable archness.

"That is the disadvantage of our profession," said he. "It forces us sometimes to be ungallant."

She took the prescription and gave him one last, luscious smile.

"You will come and see me dance, dearie, won't you?"

"I will indeed."

He rang the bell for the next case.

"I am glad you gentlemen were here to protect me."

But on the whole the impression was neither of tragedy

nor of comedy. There was no describing it. It was manifold and various; there were tears and laughter, happiness and woe; it was tedious and interesting and indifferent; it was as you saw it: it was tumultuous and passionate; it was grave; it was sad and comic; it was trivial; it was simple and complex; joy was there and despair; the love of mothers for their children, and of men for women; lust trailed itself through the rooms with leaden feet, punishing the guilty and the innocent, helpless wives and wretched children; drink seized men and women and cost its inevitable price; death sighed in these rooms; and the beginning of life, filling some poor girl with terror and shame, was diagnosed there. There was neither good nor bad there. There were just facts. It was life.

Chapter 82

Towards the end of the year, when Philip was bringing to a close his three months as clerk in the out-patients' department, he received a letter from Lawson, who was in Paris.

Dear Philip,

Cronshaw is in London and would be glad to see you. He is living at 43 Hyde Street, Soho. I don't know where it is, but I daresay you will be able to find out. Be a brick and look after him a bit. He is very down on his luck. He will tell you what he is doing. Things are going on here very much as usual. Nothing seems to have changed since you were here. Clutton is back, but he has become quite impossible. He has quarrelled with everybody. As far as I can make out he hasn't got a cent, he lives in a little studio right away beyond the Jardin des Plantes, but he won't let anybody see his work. He doesn't show anywhere, so one doesn't know what he is doing. He may be a genius, but on the other hand he may be off his head. By the way, I ran against Flanagan the other day. He was showing Mrs. Flanagan round the Quarter. He has chucked art and is now in popper's business. He seems to be rolling. Mrs. Flanagan is very pretty and I'm trying to work a portrait. How much would you ask if you were me? I don't want to frighten them, and then on the other hand I don't want to be such an ass as to ask £150 if they're quite willing to give £ 300.

Yours ever,

Frederick Lawson.

Philip wrote to Cronshaw and received in reply the following letter. It was written on a half-sheet of common note-paper, and the flimsy envelope was dirtier than was justified by its passage through the post.

Dear Carey,

Of course I remember you very well. I have an idea that I had some part in rescuing you from the Slough of Despond in which myself am hopelessly immersed. I shall be glad to see you. I am a stranger in a strange city and I am buffeted by the philistines. It will be pleasant to talk of Paris. I do not ask you to come and see me, since my lodging is not of a magnificence fit for the reception of an eminent member of Monsieur Purgon's profession, but you will find me eating modestly any evening between seven and eight at a restaurant yclept Au Bon Plaisir in Dean Street.

Your sincere

J. Cronshaw.

Philip went the day he received this letter. The restaurant, consisting of one small room, was of the poorest class, and Cronshaw seemed to be its only customer. He was sitting in the corner, well away from draughts, wearing the same shabby great-coat which Philip had never seen him without, with his old bowler on his head.

"I eat here because I can be alone," he said. "They are not doing well; the only people who come are a few trollops and one or two waiters out of a job; they are giving up business, and the food is execrable. But the ruin of their fortunes is my advantage."

Cronshaw had before him a glass of absinthe. It was nearly three years since they had met, and Philip was shocked by the change in his appearance. He had been rather corpulent, but now he had a dried-up, yellow look: the skin of his neck was loose and winkled; his clothes hung about him as though they had been bought for someone else; and his collar, three or four sizes too large, added to the slatternliness of his appearance. His hands trembled continually. Philip remembered the handwriting which scrawled over the page with shapeless, haphazard letters. Cronshaw was evidently very ill.

"I eat little these days," he said. "I'm very sick in the morning. I'm just having some soup for my dinner, and then I shall have a bit of cheese."

Philip's glance unconsciously went to the absinthe, and Cronshaw, seeing it, gave him the quizzical look with which he reproved the admonitions of common sense.

"You have diagnosed my case, and you think it's very wrong of me to drink absinthe."

"You've evidently got cirrhosis of the liver," said Philip.

"Evidently."

He looked at Philip in the way which had formerly had the power of making him feel incredibly narrow. It seemed to point out that what he was thinking was distressingly obvious; and when you have agreed with the obvious what more is there to say? Philip changed the topic.

"When are you going back to Paris?"

"I'm not going back to Paris. I'm going to die."

The very naturalness with which he said this startled Philip. He thought of half a dozen things to say, but they seemed futile. He knew that Cronshaw was a dying man.

"Are you going to settle in London then?" he asked lamely.

"What is London to me? I am a fish out of water. I walk through the crowded streets, men jostle me, and I seem to walk in a dead city. I felt that I couldn't die in Paris. I wanted to die among my own people. I don't know what hidden instinct drew me back at the last."

Philip knew of the woman Cronshaw had lived with and the two draggle-tailed children, but Cronshaw had never mentioned them to him, and he did not like to speak of them. He wondered what had happened to them.

"I don't know why you talk of dying," he said.

"I had pneumonia a couple of winters ago, and they told me then it was a miracle that I came through. It appears I'm extremely liable to it, and another bout will kill me."

"Oh, what nonsense! You're not so bad as all that. You've only got to take precautions. Why don't you give up drinking?"

"Because I don't choose. It doesn't matter what a man does if he's ready to take the consequences. Well, I'm ready to take the consequences. You talk glibly of giving up drinking, but it's the only thing I've got left now. What do you think life would be to me without it? Can you understand the happiness I get out of my absinthe? I yearn for it; and when I drink it I savour every drop, and afterwards I feel my soul swimming in ineffable happiness. It disgusts you. You are a puritan and in your heart you despise sensual pleasures. Sensual pleasures are the most violent and the most exquisite. I am a man blessed with vivid senses, and I have indulged them with all my soul. I have to pay the penalty now, and I am ready to pay."

Philip looked at him for a while steadily.

"Aren't you afraid?"

For a moment Cronshaw did not answer. He seemed to consider his reply.

"Sometimes, when I'm alone." He looked at Philip. "You think that's a condemnation? You're wrong. I'm not afraid of my fear. It's folly, the Christian argument that you should live always in view of your death. The only way to live is to forget that you're going to die. Death is unimportant. The fear of it should never influence a single action of the wise man. I know that I shall die struggling for breath, and I know that I shall be horribly afraid. I know that I shall not be able to keep myself from regretting bitterly the life that has brought me to such a pass; but I disown that regret. I now, weak, old, diseased, poor, dying, hold still my soul in my hands, and I regret nothing."

"D'you remember that Persian carpet you gave me?" asked

Philip.

Cronshaw smiled his old, slow smile of past days.

"I told you that it would give you an answer to your question when you asked me what was the meaning of life. Well, have you discovered the answer?"

"No," smiled Philip. "Won't you tell it me?"

"No, no, I can't do that. The answer is meaningless unless you discover it for yourself."

Chapter 83

Cronshaw was publishing his poems. His friends had been urging him to do this for years, but his laziness made it impossible for him to take the necessary steps. He had always answered their exhortations by telling them that the love of poetry was dead in England. You brought out a book which had cost you years of thought and labour; it was given two or three contemptuous lines among a batch of similar volumes, twenty or thirty copies were sold, and the rest of the edition was pulped. He had long since worn out the desire for fame. That was an illusion like all else. But one of his friends had taken the matter into his own hands. This was a man of letters, named Leonard Upjohn, whom Philip had met once or twice with Cronshaw in the cafés of the Quarter. He had a considerable reputation in England as a critic and was the accredited exponent in this country of modern French literature. He had lived a good deal in France among the men who made the *Mercure de France* the liveliest review of the day, and by the simple process of expressing in English their point of view he had acquired in England a reputation for originality. Philip had read some of his articles. He had formed a style for himself by a close imitation of Sir Thomas Browne; he used elaborate sentences, carefully balanced, and obsolete, resplendent words; it gave his writing an appearance of individuality. Leonard Upjohn had induced Cronshaw to give him all his poems and found that there were enough to make a volume of reasonable size. He promised to use his influence with publishers. Cronshaw was in want of money. Since his illness he had found it more difficult than ever to work steadily; he made barely enough to keep himself in liquor; and when Upjohn wrote to him that this publisher and the other, though admiring the poems, thought it not worth while to publish them, Cronshaw began to grow interested. He wrote impressing upon Upjohn his great need and urging him to make more strenuous efforts. Now that he was going to die he wanted to leave behind him a published book, and at the back of his mind was the feeling that he had produced great poetry. He expected to burst upon the world like a new star. There was something fine in keeping to himself these treasures of beauty all his life and giving them to the world disdainfully when, he and the world parting company, he had no further use for them.

His decision to come to England was caused directly by an announcement from Leonard Upjohn that a publisher had consented to print the poems. By a miracle of persuasion Upjohn had persuaded him to give ten pounds in advance of royalties.

"In advance of royalties, mind you," said Cronshaw to Philip. "Milton only got ten pounds down."

Upjohn had promised to write a signed article about them, and he would ask his friends who reviewed to do their best.

Cronshaw pretended to treat the matter with detachment, but it was easy to see that he was delighted with the thought of the stir he would make.

One day Philip went to dine by arrangement at the wretched eating-house at which Cronshaw insisted on taking his meals, but Cronshaw did not appear. Philip learned that he had not been there for three days. He got himself something to eat and went round to the address from which Cronshaw had first written to him. He had some difficulty in finding Hyde Street. It was a street of dingy houses huddled together; many of the windows had been broken and were clumsily repaired with strips of French newspaper; the doors had not been painted for years; there were shabby little shops on the ground floor, laundries, cobblers, stationers. Ragged children played in the road, and an old barrel-organ was grinding out a vulgar tune. Philip knocked at the door of Cronshaw's house (there was a shop of cheap sweetstuffs at the bottom), and it was opened by an elderly Frenchwoman in a dirty apron. Philip asked her if Cronshaw was in.

"Ah, yes, there is an Englishman who lives at the top, at the back. I don't know if he's in. If you want him you had better go up and see."

The staircase was lit by one jet of gas. There was a revolting odour in the house. When Philip was passing up a woman came out of a room on the first floor, looked at him suspiciously, but made no remark. There were three doors on the top landing. Philip knocked at one, and knocked again; there was no reply; he tried the handle, but the door was locked. He knocked at another door, got no answer, and tried the door again. It opened. The room was dark.

"Who's that?"

He recognized Cronshaw's voice.

"Carey. Can I come in?"

He received no answer. He walked in. The window was closed and the stink was overpowering. There was a certain amount of light from the arc-lamp in the street, and he saw that it was a small room with two beds in it, end to end; there was a washing-stand and one chair, but they left little space for anyone to move in. Cronshaw was in the bed nearest the window. He made no movement, but gave a low chuckle.

"Why don't you light the candle?" he said then.

Philip struck a match and discovered that there was a candlestick on the floor beside the bed. He lit it and put it on the washing-stand. Cronshaw was lying on his back immobile; he looked very odd in his nightshirt; and his baldness was disconcerting. His face was earthy and deathlike.

"I say, old man, you look awfully ill. Is there anyone to look after you here?"

"George brings me in a bottle of milk in the morning before he goes to his work."

"Who's George?"

"I call him George because his name is Adolphe. He shares this palatial apartment with me."

Philip noticed then that the second bed had not been made since it was slept in. The pillow was black where the head had rested.

"You don't mean to say you're sharing this room with

somebody else?" he cried.

"Why not? Lodging costs money in Soho. George is a waiter. He goes out at eight in the morning and does not come in till closing time, so he isn't in my way at all. We neither of us sleep well, and he helps to pass away the hours of the night by telling me stories of his life. He's a Swiss, and I've always had a taste for waiters. They see life from an entertaining angle."

"How long have you been in bed?"

"Three days."

"D'you mean to say you've had nothing but a bottle of milk for the last three days? Why on earth didn't you send me a line? I can't bear to think of you lying here all day long without a soul to attend to you."

Cronshaw gave a little laugh.

"Look at your face. Why, dear boy, I really believe you're distressed. You nice fellow."

Philip blushed. He had not suspected that his face showed the dismay he felt at the sight of that horrible room and the wretched circumstances of the poor poet. Cronshaw, watching Philip, went on with a gentle smile.

"I've been quite happy. Look, here are my proofs. Remember that I am indifferent to discomforts which would harass other folk. What do the circumstances of life matter if your dreams make you lord paramount of time and space."

The proofs were lying on his bed, and as he lay in the darkness he had been able to place his hands on them. He showed them to Philip and his eyes glowed. He turned over the pages, rejoicing in the clear type; he read out a stanza.

"They don't look bad, do they?"

Philip had an idea. It would involve him in a little expense and he could not afford even the smallest increase of expenditure; but on the other hand this was a case where it revolted him to think of economy.

"I say, I can't bear the thought of your remaining here. I've got an extra room, it's empty at present, but I can easily get someone to lend me a bed. Won't you come and live with me for a while? It'll save you the rent of this."

"Oh, my dear boy, you'd insist on my keeping my window open."

"You shall have every window in the place sealed if you like."

"I shall be all right tomorrow. I could have got up today, only I felt lazy."

"Then you can very easily make the move. And then if you don't feel well at any time you can just go to bed, and I shall be there to look after you."

"If it'll please you I'll come," said Cronshaw, with his torpid not unpleasant smile.

"That'll be ripping."

They settled that Philip should fetch Cronshaw next day, and Philip snatched an hour from his busy morning to arrange the change. He found Cronshaw dressed, sitting in his hat and greatcoat on the bed, with a small, shabby portmanteau, containing his clothes and books, already packed: it was on the floor by his feet, and he looked as if he were sitting in the waiting-room of a station. Philip laughed at the sight of him. They went over to Kennington in a four-wheeler, of which the windows were carefully closed, and Philip installed his guest in his own room. He had gone out early in the morning and bought for himself a second-hand bedstead, a cheap chest of drawers, and a looking-glass. Cronshaw settled down at once to correct his proofs. He was much better.

Philip found him, except for the irritability which was a symptom of his disease, an easy guest. He had a lecture at nine in the morning, so did not see Cronshaw till the night. Once or twice Philip persuaded him to share the scrappy meal he prepared for himself in the evening, but Cronshaw was too restless to stay in, and preferred generally to get himself something to eat in one or other of the cheapest restaurants in Soho. Philip asked him to see Dr. Tyrell, but he stoutly refused; he knew a doctor would tell him to stop drinking, and this he was resolved not to do. He always felt horribly ill in the morning, but his absinthe at midday put him on his feet again, and by the time he came home, at midnight, he was able to talk with the brilliancy which had astonished Philip when first he made his acquaintance. His proofs were corrected; and the volume was to come out among the publications of the early spring, when the public might be supposed to have recovered from the avalanche of Christmas books.

Chapter 84

At the new year Philip became dresser in the surgical out-patients' department. The work was of the same character as that which he had just been engaged on, but with the greater directness which surgery has than medicine; and a larger proportion of the patients suffered from those two diseases which a supine public allows, in its prudishness, to be spread broadcast. The assistant-surgeon for whom Philip dressed was called Jacobs. He was a short, fat man, with an exuberant joviality, a bald head, and a loud voice; he had a cockney accent, and was generally described by the students as an "awful bounder"; but his cleverness, both as a surgeon and as a teacher, caused some of them to overlook this. He had also a considerable facetiousness, which he exercised impartially on the patients and on the students. He took a great pleasure in making his dressers look foolish. Since they were ignorant, nervous, and could not answer as if he were their equal, this was not very difficult. He enjoyed his afternoons, with the home truths he permitted himself, much more than the students who had to put up with them with a smile. One day a case came up of a boy with a club-foot. His parents wanted to know whether anything could be done. Mr. Jacobs turned to Philip.

"You'd better take this case, Carey. It's a subject you ought to know something about."

Philip flushed, all the more because the surgeon spoke obviously with a humorous intention, and his brow-beaten dressers laughed obsequiously. It was in point of fact a subject which Philip, since coming to the hospital, had studied with anxious attention. He had read everything in the library which treated of talipes in its various forms. He made the boy take off his boot and stocking. He was fourteen, with a snub nose, blue eyes, and a freckled face. His father explained that they wanted something done if possible, it was such a hindrance to the kid in earning his living. Philip looked at him curiously. He was a jolly boy, not at all shy, but talkative and with a cheekiness which his father reproved. He was much interested in his foot.

"It's only for the looks of the thing, you know," he said to Philip. "I don't find it no trouble."

"Be quiet, Ernie," said his father. "There's too much gas about you."

Philip examined the foot and passed his hand slowly over the shapelessness of it. He could not understand why the boy felt none of the humiliation which always oppressed himself. He wondered why he could not take his deformity with that philosophic indifference. Presently Mr. Jacobs came up to him. The boy was sitting on the edge of a couch, the surgeon and Philip stood on each side of him; and in a semi-circle, crowding round, were students. With accustomed brilliancy Jacobs gave a graphic little discourse upon the club-foot: he spoke of its varieties and of the forms which followed upon different anatomical conditions.

"I suppose you've got talipes equinus?" he said, turning suddenly to Philip.

"Yes."

Philip felt the eyes of his fellow-students rest on him, and he cursed himself because he could not help blushing. He felt the sweat start up in the palms of his hands. The surgeon spoke with the fluency due to long practice and with the admirable perspicacity which distinguished him. He was tremendously interested in his profession. But Philip did not listen. He was only wishing that the fellow would get done quickly. Suddenly he realized that Jacobs was addressing him.

"You don't mind taking off your sock for a moment, Carey?"

Philip felt a shudder pass through him. He had an impulse to tell the surgeon to go to hell, but he had not the courage to make a scene. He feared his brutal ridicule. He forced himself to appear indifferent.

"Not a bit," he said.

He sat down and unlaced his boot. His fingers were trembling, and he thought he should never untie the knot. He remembered how they had forced him at school to show his foot, and the misery which had eaten into his soul.

"He keeps his feet nice and clean, doesn't he?" said Jacobs, in his rasping, cockney voice.

The attendant students giggled. Philip noticed that the boy whom they were examining looked down at his foot with eager curiosity. Jacobs took the foot in his hands and said:

"Yes, that's what I thought. I see you've had an operation. When you were a child, I suppose?"

He went on with his fluent explanations. The students leaned over and looked at the foot. Two or three examined it minutely when Jacobs let it go.

"When you've quite done," said Philip, with a smile, ironically.

He could have killed them all. He thought how jolly it would be to jab a chisel (he didn't know why that particular instrument came into his mind) into their necks. What beasts men were! He wished he could believe in hell so as to comfort himself with the thought of the horrible tortures which would be theirs. Mr. Jacobs turned his attention to treatment. He talked partly to the boy's father and partly to the students. Philip put on his sock and laced his boot. At last the surgeon finished. But he seemed to have an afterthought and turned to Philip.

"You know, I think it might be worth your while to have an operation. Of course I couldn't give you a normal foot, but I think I can do something. You might think about it, and when you want a holiday you can just come into the hospital for a bit."

Philip had often asked himself whether anything could be done, but his distaste for any reference to the subject had prevented him from consulting any of the surgeons at the hospital. His reading told him that, whatever might have been done when he was a small boy—and then treatment of talipes was not as skilful as in the present day—there was small chance now of any great benefit. Still it would be worth while if an operation made it possible for him to wear a more ordinary boot and to limp less. He remembered how passionately he had prayed for the miracle which his uncle had assured him was possible to omnipotence. He smiled ruefully.

"I was rather a simple soul in those days," he thought.

Towards the end of February it was clear that Cronshaw was growing much worse. He was no longer able to get up. He lay in bed, insisting that the window should be closed always, and refused to see a doctor; he would take little nourishment, but demanded whisky and cigarettes: Philip knew that he should have neither, but Cronshaw's argument was unanswerable.

"I daresay they are killing me. I don't care. You've warned me, you've done all that was necessary: I ignore your warning. Give me something to drink and be damned to you."

Leonard Upjohn blew in two or three times a week, and there was something of the dead leaf in his appearance which made the word exactly descriptive of the manner of his appearance. He was a weedy-looking fellow of five-and-thirty, with long pale hair and a white face; he had the look of a man who lived too little in the open air. He wore a hat like a dissenting minister's. Philip disliked him for his patronizing manner and was bored by his fluent conversation. Leonard Upjohn liked to hear himself talk. He was not sensitive to the interest of his listeners, which is the first requisite of the good talker; and he never realized that he was telling people what they knew already. With measured words he told Philip what to think of Rodin, Albert Samain, and César Franck. Philip's charwoman only came in for an hour in the morning, and since Philip was obliged to be at the hospital all day Cronshaw was left much alone. Upjohn told Philip that he thought someone should remain with him, but did not offer to make it possible.

"It's dreadful to think of that great poet alone. Why, he might die without a soul at hand."

"I think he very probably will," said Philip.

"How can you be so callous!"

"Why don't you come and do your work here every day, and then you'd be near if he wanted anything?" asked Philip drily.

"I? My dear fellow, I can only work in the surroundings I'm used to, and besides I go out so much."

Upjohn was also a little put out because Philip had brought Cronshaw to his own rooms.

"I wish you had left him in Soho," he said, with a wave of his long, thin hands. "There was a touch of romance in that sordid attic. I could even bear it if it were Wapping or Shoreditch, but the respectability of Kennington! What a place for a poet to die!"

Cronshaw was often so ill-humoured that Philip could only keep his temper by remembering all the time that this irritability was a symptom of the disease. Upjohn came sometimes before Philip was in, and then Cronshaw would complain of him bitterly. Upjohn listened with complacency.

"The fact is that Carey has no sense of beauty," he smiled. "He has a middle-class mind."

He was very sarcastic to Philip, and Philip exercised a good deal of self-control in his dealings with him. But one evening he could not contain himself. He had had a hard day at the hospital and was tired out. Leonard Upjohn came to him, while he was making himself a cup of tea in the kitchen, and said that Cronshaw was complaining of Philip's insistence that he should have a doctor.

"Don't you realize that you're enjoying a very rare, a very exquisite privilege? You ought to do everything in your power, surely, to show your sense of the greatness of your trust."

"It's a rare and exquisite privilege which I can ill afford," said Philip.

Whenever there was any question of money, Leonard Upjohn assumed a slightly disdainful expression. His sensitive temperament was offended by the reference.

"There's something fine in Cronshaw's attitude, and you disturb it by your importunity. You should make allowances for the delicate imaginings which you cannot feel."

Philip's face darkened.

"Let us go in to Cronshaw," he said frigidly.

The poet was lying on his back, reading a book, with a pipe in his mouth. The air was musty; and the room, notwithstanding Philip's tidying up, had the bedraggled look which seemed to accompany Cronshaw wherever he went. He took off his spectacles as they came in. Philip was in a towering rage.

"Upjohn tells me you've been complaining to him because I've urged you to have a doctor," he said. "I want you to have a doctor, because you may die any day, and if you hadn't been seen by anyone I shouldn't be able to get a certificate. There'd have to be an inquest and I should be blamed for not calling a doctor in."

"I hadn't thought of that. I thought you wanted me to see a doctor for my sake and not for your own. I'll see a doctor whenever you like."

Philip did not answer, but gave an almost imperceptible shrug of the shoulders. Cronshaw, watching him, gave a little chuckle.

"Don't look so angry, my dear. I know very well you want to do everything you can for me. Let's see your doctor, perhaps he can do something for me, and at any rate it'll comfort you." He turned his eyes to Upjohn. "You're a damned fool, Leonard. Why d'you want to worry the boy? He has quite enough to do to put up with me. You'll do nothing more for me than write a pretty article about me after my death. I know you."

Next day Philip went to Dr. Tyrell. He felt that he was the sort of man to be interested by the story, and as soon as Tyrell was free of his day's work he accompanied Philip to Kennington. He could only agree with what Philip had told him. The case was hopeless.

"I'll take him into the hospital if you like," he said. "He can have a small ward."

"Nothing would induce him to come."

"You know, he may die any minute, or else he may get another attack of pneumonia."

Philip nodded. Dr. Tyrell made one or two suggestions, and promised to come again whenever Philip wanted him to. He left his address. When Philip went back to Cronshaw he found him quietly reading. He did not trouble to enquire what the doctor had said.

"Are you satisfied now, dear boy?" he asked.

"I suppose nothing will induce you to do any of the things Tyrell advised?"

"Nothing," smiled Cronshaw.

Chapter 85

About a fortnight after this Philip, going home one evening after his day's work at the hospital, knocked at the door of Cronshaw's room. He got no answer and walked in. Cronshaw was lying huddled up on one side, and Philip went up to the bed. He did not know whether Cronshaw was asleep or merely lay there in one of his uncontrollable fits of irritability. He was surprised to see that his mouth was open. He touched his shoulder. Philip gave a cry of dismay. He slipped his hand under Cronshaw's shirt and felt his heart; he did not know what to do; helplessly, because he had heard of this being done, he held a looking-glass in front of his mouth. It startled him to be alone with Cronshaw. He had his hat and coat still on, and he ran down the stairs into the street; he hailed a cab and drove to Harley Street. Dr. Tyrell was in.

"I say, would you mind coming at once? I think Cronshaw's dead."

"If he is it's not much good my coming, is it?"

"I should be awfully grateful if you would. I've got a cab at the door. It'll only take half an hour."

Tyrell put on his hat. In the cab he asked him one or two questions.

"He seemed no worse than usual when I left this morning," said Philip. "It gave me an awful shock when I went in just now. And the thought of his dying all alone... D'you think he knew he was going to die?"

Philip remembered what Cronshaw had said. He wondered whether at that last moment he had been seized with the terror of death. Philip imagined himself in such a plight, knowing it was inevitable and with no one, not a soul, to give an encouraging word when the fear seized him.

"You're rather upset," said Dr. Tyrell.

He looked at him with his bright blue eyes. They were not unsympathetic. When he saw Cronshaw, he said:

"He must have been dead for some hours. I should think he died in his sleep. They do sometimes."

The body looked shrunk and ignoble. It was not like anything human. Dr. Tyrell looked at it dispassionately. With a mechanical gesture he took out his watch.

"Well, I must be getting along. I'll send the certificate round. I suppose you'll communicate with the relatives."

"I don't think there are any," said Philip.

"How about the funeral?"

"Oh, I'll see to that."

Dr. Tyrell gave Philip a glance. He wondered whether he ought to offer a couple of sovereigns towards it. He knew nothing of Philip's circumstances; perhaps he could well afford the expense; Philip might think it impertinent if he made any suggestion.

"Well, let me know if there's anything I can do," he said.

Philip and he went out together, parting on the doorstep, and Philip went to a telegraph office in order to send a message to Leonard Upjohn. Then he went to an undertaker whose shop he passed every day on his way to the hospital. His attention had been drawn to it often by the three words in silver lettering on a black cloth, which, with two model coffins, adorned the window: Economy, Celerity, Propriety. They had always diverted him. The undertaker was a little fat Jew with curly black hair, long and greasy, in black, with a large diamond ring on a podgy finger. He received Philip with a peculiar manner formed by the mingling of his natural blatancy with the subdued air proper to his calling. He quickly saw that Philip was very helpless and promised to send round a woman at once to perform the needful offices. His suggestions for the funeral were very magnificent; and Philip felt ashamed of himself when the undertaker seemed to think his objections mean. It was horrible to haggle on such a matter, and finally Philip consented to an expensiveness which he could ill afford.

"I quite understand, sir," said the undertaker, "you don't want any show and that—I'm not a believer in ostentation myself, mind you—but you want it done gentlemanly-like. You leave it to me, I'll do it as cheap as it can be done, 'aving regard to what's right and proper. I can't say more than that, can I?"

Philip went home to eat his supper, and while he ate the woman came along to lay out the corpse. Presently a telegram arrived from Leonard Upjohn:

Shocked and grieved beyond measure. Regret cannot
come tonight. Dining out. With you early tomorrow.

Deepest sympathy.

Upjohn.

In a little while the woman knocked at the door of the sitting-room.

"I've done now, sir. Will you come and look at 'im and see it's all right?"

Philip followed her. Cronshaw was lying on his back, with his eyes closed and his hands folded piously across his chest.

"You ought by rights to 'ave a few flowers, sir."

"I'll get some tomorrow."

She gave the body a glance of satisfaction. She had performed her job, and now she rolled down her sleeves, took off her apron, and put on her bonnet. Philip asked her how much he owed her.

"Well, sir, some give me two and sixpence and some give me five shillings."

Philip was ashamed to give her less than the larger sum. She thanked him with just so much effusiveness as was seemly in presence of the grief he might be supposed to feel, and left him. Philip went back into his sitting-room, cleared away the remains of his supper, and sat down to read Walsham's *Surgery*. He found it difficult. He felt singularly nervous. When there was a sound on the stairs he jumped, and his heart beat violently. That thing in the adjoining room, which had been a man and now was nothing, frightened him. The silence seemed alive, as if some mysterious movement were taking place within it; the presence of death weighed upon these rooms, unearthly and terrifying: Philip felt a sudden horror for what had once been his friend. He tried to force himself to read, but presently pushed away his book in despair. What troubled him was the absolute futility of the life which had just ended. It did not matter if Cronshaw was alive or dead. It would have been just as well if he had never lived. Philip thought of Cronshaw young; and it needed an effort of imagination to picture him slender, with a springing step, and with hair on his head, buoyant and hopeful. Philip's rule of life, to follow one's instincts with due regard to the policeman round the corner, had not acted very well there: it was because Cronshaw had done this that he had made such a lamentable failure of existence. It seemed that the instincts could not be trusted. Philip was puzzled, and he asked himself what rule of life was there, if that one was useless, and why people acted in one way rather than in another. They acted according to their emotions, but their emotions might be good or bad; it seemed just a chance whether they led to triumph or disaster. Life seemed an inextricable confusion. Men hurried hither and thither, urged by forces they knew not; and the purpose of it all escaped them; they seemed to hurry just for hurrying's sake.

Next morning Leonard Upjohn appeared with a small wreath of laurel. He was pleased with his idea of crowning the dead poet with this; and attempted, notwithstanding Philip's disapproving silence, to fix it on the bald head; but the wreath fitted grotesquely. It looked like the brim of a hat worn by a low comedian in a music hall.

"I'll put it over his heart instead," said Upjohn.

"You've put it on his stomach," remarked Philip.

Upjohn gave a thin smile.

"Only a poet knows where lies a poet's heart," he answered.

They went back into the sitting-room, and Philip told him what arrangements he had made for the funeral.

"I hoped you've spared no expense. I should like the hearse to be followed by a long string of empty coaches, and I should like the horses to wear tall nodding plumes, and there should be a vast number of mutes with long streamers on their hats. I like the thought of all those empty coaches."

"As the cost of the funeral will apparently fall on me and I'm not over-flush just now, I've tried to make it as moderate as possible."

"But, my dear fellow, in that case, why didn't you get him a pauper's funeral? There would have been something poetic in that. You have an unerring instinct for mediocrity."

Philip flushed a little, but did not answer; and next day he and Upjohn followed the hearse in the one carriage which Philip had ordered. Lawson, unable to come, had sent a wreath; and Philip, so that the coffin should not seem too neglected, had bought a couple. On the way back the coachman whipped up his horses. Philip was dog-tired and presently went to sleep. He was awakened by Upjohn's voice.

"It's rather lucky the poems haven't come out yet. I think we'd better hold them back a bit and I'll write a preface. I began thinking of it during the drive to the cemetery. I believe I can do something rather good. Anyhow I'll start with an article in *The Saturday*."

Philip did not reply, and there was silence between them. At last Upjohn said:

"I daresay I'd be wiser not to whittle away my copy. I think I'll do an article for one of the reviews, and then I can just print it afterwards as a preface."

Philip kept his eye on the monthlies, and a few weeks later it appeared. The article made something of a stir, and extracts from it were printed in many of the papers. It was a very good article, vaguely biographical, for no one knew much of Cronshaw's early life, but delicate, tender, and picturesque. Leonard Upjohn in his intricate style drew graceful little pictures of Cronshaw in the Latin Quarter, talking, writing poetry: Cronshaw became a picturesque figure, an English Verlaine; and Leonard Upjohn's coloured phrases took on a tremulous dignity, a more pathetic grandiloquence, as he described the sordid end, the shabby little room in Soho; and, with a reticence which was wholly charming and suggested a much greater generosity than modesty allowed him to state, the efforts he made to transport the poet to some cottage embowered with honeysuckle amid a flowering orchard. And the lack of sympathy, well-meaning but so tactless, which had taken the poet instead to the vulgar respectability of Kennington! Leonard Upjohn described Kennington with that restrained humour which a strict adherence to the vocabulary of Sir Thomas Browne necessitated. With delicate sarcasm he narrated the last weeks, the patience with which Cronshaw bore the well-meaning clumsiness of the young student who had appointed himself his nurse, and the pitifulness of that divine vagabond in those hopelessly middle-class surroundings. Beauty from ashes, he quoted from Isaiah. It was a triumph of irony for that outcast poet to die amid the trappings of vulgar respectability; it reminded Leonard Upjohn of Christ among the Pharisees, and the analogy gave him opportunity for an exquisite passage. And then he told how a friend—his good taste did not suffer him more than to hint subtly who the friend was with such gracious fancies—had laid a laurel wreath on the dead poet's heart; and the beautiful dead hands had seemed to rest with a voluptuous passion upon Apollo's leaves, fragrant with the fragrance of art, and more green than jade brought by swart mariners from the manifold, inexplicable China. And, an admirable contrast, the article ended with a description of the middle-class, ordinary, prosaic funeral of him who should have been buried like a prince or like a pauper. It was the crowning buffet, the final victory of Philistia over art, beauty, and immaterial things.

Leonard Upjohn had never written anything better. It was a miracle of charm, grace, and pity. He printed all Cronshaw's best poems in the course of the article, so that when the volume appeared much of its point was gone; but he advanced his own position a good deal. He was thenceforth a critic to be reckoned with. He had seemed before a little aloof; but there was a warm humanity about this article which was infinitely attractive.

Chapter 86

In the spring Philip, having finished his dressing in the out-patients' department, became an in-patients' clerk. This appointment lasted six months. The clerk spent every morning in the wards, first in the men's, then in the women's, with the house-physician; he wrote up cases, made tests, and passed the time of day with the nurses. On two afternoons a week the physician in charge went round with a little knot of students, examined the cases, and dispensed information. The work had not the excitement, the constant change, the intimate contact with reality, of the work in the out-patients' department; but Philip picked up a good deal of knowledge. He got on very well with the patients, and he was a little flattered at the pleasure they showed in his attendance on them. He was not conscious of any deep sympathy in their sufferings, but he liked them; and because he put on no airs he was more popular with them than others of the clerks. He was pleasant, encouraging, and friendly. Like everyone connected with hospitals he found that male patients were more easy to get on with than female. The women were often querulous and ill-tempered. They complained bitterly of the hard-worked nurses, who did not show them the attention they thought their right; and they were troublesome, ungrateful, and rude.

Presently Philip was fortunate enough to make a friend. One morning the house-physician gave him a new case, a man; and, seating himself at the bedside, Philip proceeded to write down particulars on the "letter." He noticed on looking at this that the patient was described as a journalist: his name was Thorpe Athelny, an unusual one for a hospital patient, and his age was forty-eight. He was suffering from a sharp attack of jaundice, and had been taken into the ward on account of obscure symptoms which it seemed necessary to watch. He answered the various questions which it was Philip's duty to ask him in a pleasant, educated voice. Since he was lying in bed it was difficult to tell if he was short or tall, but his small head and small hands suggested that he was a man of less than average height. Philip had the habit of looking at people's hands, and Athelny's astonished him: they were very small, with long, tapering fingers and beautiful, rosy finger-nails; they were very smooth and except for the jaundice would have been of a surprising whiteness. The patient kept them outside the bed-clothes, one of them slightly spread out, the second and third fingers together, and, while he spoke to Philip, seemed to contemplate them with satisfaction. With a twinkle in his eyes Philip glanced at the man's face. Notwithstanding the yellowness it was distinguished; he had blue eyes, a nose of an imposing boldness, hooked, aggressive, but not clumsy, and a small beard, pointed and grey: he was rather bald, but his hair had evidently been quite fine, curling prettily, and he still wore it long.

"I see you're a journalist," said Philip. "What papers d'you write for?"

"I write for all the papers. You cannot open a paper without seeing some of my writing."

There was one by the side of the bed and reaching for it he pointed out an advertisement. In large letters was the name of a firm well known to Philip: Lynn and Sedley, Regent Street, London; and below, in type smaller but still of some magnitude, was the dogmatic statement: Procrastination is the Thief of Time. Then a question, startling because of its reasonableness: Why not order today? There was a repetition, in large letters, like the hammering of conscience on a murderer's heart: Why not? Then, boldly: Thousands of pairs of gloves from the leading markets of the world at astounding prices. Thousands of pairs of stockings from the most reliable manufacturers of the universe at sensational reductions. Finally the question recurred, but flung now like a challenging gauntlet in the lists: Why not order today?

"I'm the press representative of Lynn and Sedley." He gave a little wave of his beautiful hand. "To what base uses…"

Philip went on asking the regulation questions, some a mere matter of routine, others artfully devised to lead the patient to discover things which he might be expected to desire to conceal.

"Have you ever lived abroad?" asked Philip.

"I was in Spain for eleven years."

"What were you doing there?"

"I was secretary of the English water company at Toledo."

Philip remembered that Clutton had spent some months in Toledo, and the journalist's answer made him look at him with more interest; but he felt it would be improper to show this: it was necessary to preserve the distance between the hospital patient and the staff. When he had finished his examination he went on to other beds.

Thorpe Athelny's illness was not grave, and, though remaining very yellow, he soon felt much better: he stayed in bed only because the physician thought he should be kept under observation till certain reactions became normal. One day, on entering the ward, Philip noticed that Athelny, pencil in hand, was reading a book. He put it down when Philip came to his bed.

"May I see what you're reading?" asked Philip, who could never pass a book without looking at it.

Philip took it up and saw that it was a volume of Spanish verse, the poems of San Juan de la Cruz, and as he opened it a sheet of paper fell out. Philip picked it up and noticed that verse was written upon it.

"You're not going to tell me you've been occupying your leisure in writing poetry? That's a most improper proceeding in a hospital patient."

"I was trying to do some translations. D'you know Spanish?"

"No."

"Well, you know all about San Juan de la Cruz, don't you?"

"I don't indeed."

"He was one of the Spanish mystics. He's one of the best poets they've ever had. I thought it would be worth while translating him into English."

"May I look at your translation?"

"It's very rough," said Athelny, but he gave it to Philip with an alacrity which suggested that he was eager for him to read it.

It was written in pencil, in a fine but very peculiar handwriting, which was hard to read: it was just like black letter.

"Doesn't it take you an awful time to write like that? It's wonderful."

"I don't know why handwriting shouldn't be beautiful."

Philip read the first verse:

> *In an obscure night*
> *With anxious love inflamed,*
> *O happy lot!*
> *Forth unobserved I went,*
> *My house being now at rest...*

Philip looked curiously at Thorpe Athelny. He did not know whether he felt a little shy with him or was attracted by him. He was conscious that his manner had been slightly patronizing, and he flushed as it struck him that Athelny might have thought him ridiculous.

"What an unusual name you've got," he remarked, for something to say.

"It's a very old Yorkshire name. Once it took the head of my family a day's hard riding to make the circuit of his estates, but the mighty are fallen. Fast women and slow horses."

He was short-sighted and when he spoke looked at you with a peculiar intensity. He took up his volume of poetry.

"You should read Spanish," he said. "It is a noble tongue. It has not the mellifluousness of Italian—Italian is the language of tenors and organ-grinders—but it has grandeur: it does not ripple like a brook in a garden, but it surges tumultuous like a mighty river in flood."

His grandiloquence amused Philip, but he was sensitive to rhetoric; and he listened with pleasure while Athelny, with picturesque expressions and the fire of a real enthusiasm, described to him the rich delight of reading *Don Quixote* in the original and the music, romantic, limpid, passionate, of the enchanting *Calderón*.

"I must get on with my work," said Philip presently.

"Oh, forgive me, I forgot. I will tell my wife to bring me a photo-graph of Toledo, and I will show it you. Come and talk to me when you have the chance. You don't know what a pleasure it gives me."

During the next few days, in moments snatched whenever there was opportunity, Philip's acquaintance with the journalist increased. Thorpe Athelny was a good talker. He did not say brilliant things but he talked inspiringly, with an eager vividness which fired the imagination; Philip, living so much in a world of make-believe, found his fancy teeming with new pictures. Athelny had very good manners. He knew much more than Philip, both of the world and of books; he was a much older man; and the readiness of his conversation gave him a certain superiority; but he was in the hospital a recipient of charity, subject to strict rules; and he held himself between the two positions with ease and humour. Once Philip asked him why he had come to the hospital.

"Oh, my principle is to profit by all the benefits that society provides. I take advantage of the age I live in. When I'm ill I get myself patched up in a hospital, and I have no false shame, and I send my children to be educated at the board-school."

"Do you really?" said Philip.

"And a capital education they get too, much better than I got at Winchester. How else do you think I could educate them at all? I've got nine. You must come and see them all when I get home again. Will you?"

"I'd like to very much," said Philip.

Chapter 87

Ten days later Thorpe Athelny was well enough to leave the hospital. He gave Philip his address, and Philip promised to dine with him at one o'clock on the following Sunday. Athelny had told him that he lived in a house built by Inigo Jones; he had raved, as he raved over everything, over the balustrade of old oak; and when he came down to open the door for Philip he made him at once admire the elegant carving of the lintel. It was a shabby house, badly needing a coat of paint, but with the dignity of its period, in a little street between Chancery Lane and Holborn, which had once been fashionable but was now little better than a slum: there was a plan to pull it down in order to put up handsome offices; meanwhile the rents were small, and Athelny was able to get the two upper floors at a price which suited his income. Philip had not seen him up before and was surprised at his small size; he was not more than five feet and five inches high. He was dressed fantastically in blue linen trousers of the sort worn by working men in France, and a very old brown velvet coat; he wore a bright red sash round his waist, a low collar, and for tie a flowing bow of the kind used by the comic Frenchman in the pages of *Punch*. He greeted Philip with enthusiasm. He began talking at once of the house and passed his hand lovingly over the balusters.

"Look at it, feel it, it's like silk. What a miracle of grace! And in five years the house-breaker will sell it for firewood."

He insisted on taking Philip into a room on the first floor, where a man in shirt-sleeves, a blousy woman, and three children were having their Sunday dinner.

"I've just brought this gentleman in to show him your ceiling. Did you ever see anything so wonderful? How are you, Mrs. Hodgson? This is Mr. Carey, who looked after me when I was in the hospital."

"Come in, sir," said the man. "Any friend of Mr. Athelny's is welcome. Mr. Athelny shows the ceiling to all his friends. And it don't matter what we're doing, if we're in bed or if I'm 'aving a wash, in 'e comes."

Philip could see that they looked upon Athelny as a little queer; but they liked him none the less; and they listened openmouthed while he discoursed with his impetuous fluency on the beauty of the seventeenth-century ceiling.

"What a crime to pull this down, eh, Hodgson? You're an influential citizen, why don't you write to the papers and protest?"

The man in shirt-sleeves gave a laugh and said to Philip:

"Mr. Athelny will 'ave his little joke. They do say these 'ouses are that insanitary, it's not safe to live in them."

"Sanitation be damned, give me art," cried Athelny. "I've got nine children and they thrive on bad drains. No, no, I'm not going to take any risk. None of your new-fangled notions for me! When I move from here I'm going to make sure the drains are bad before I take anything."

There was a knock at the door, and a little fair-haired girl opened it.

"Daddy, mummy says, do stop talking and come and eat your dinner."

"This is my third daughter," said Athelny, pointing to her with a dramatic forefinger. "She is called *María del Pilar*, but she answers more willingly to the name of Jane. Jane, your nose wants blowing."

"I haven't got a hanky, daddy."

"Tut, tut, child," he answered, as he produced a vast, brilliant bandanna, "what do you suppose the Almighty gave you fingers for?"

They went upstairs, and Philip was taken into a room with walls panelled in dark oak. In the middle was a narrow table of teak on trestle legs, with two supporting bars of iron, of the kind called in Spain *mesa de bieraje*. They were to dine there, for two places were laid, and there were two large armchairs, with broad flat arms of oak and leathern backs, and leathern seats. They were severe, elegant, and uncomfortable. The only other piece of furniture was a *bargueno*, elaborately ornamented with gilt iron-work, on a stand of ecclesiastical design roughly but very finely carved. There stood on this two or three lustre plates, much broken but rich in colour; and on the walls were old masters of the Spanish school in beautiful though dilapidated frames: though gruesome in subject, ruined by age and bad treatment, and second-rate in their conception, they had a glow of passion. There was nothing in the room of any value, but the effect was lovely. It was magnificent and yet austere. Philip felt that it offered the very spirit of old Spain. Athelny was in the middle of showing him the inside of the *bargueno*, with its beautiful ornamentation and secret drawers, when a tall girl, with two plaits of bright brown hair hanging down her back, came in.

"Mother says dinner's ready and waiting and I'm to bring it in as soon as you sit down."

"Come and shake hands with Mr. Carey, Sally." He turned to Philip. "Isn't she enormous? She's my eldest. How old are you, Sally?"

"Fifteen, father, come next June."

"I christened her María del Sol, because she was my first child and I dedicated her to the glorious sun of Castile; but her mother calls her Sally and her brother Pudding-Face."

The girl smiled shyly, she had even, white teeth, and blushed. She was well set-up, tall for her age, with pleasant grey eyes and a broad forehead. She had red cheeks.

"Go and tell your mother to come in and shake hands with Mr. Carey before he sits down."

"Mother says she'll come in after dinner. She hasn't washed herself yet."

"Then we'll go in and see her ourselves. He mustn't eat the Yorkshire pudding till he's shaken the hand that made it."

Philip followed his host into the kitchen. It was small and much overcrowded. There had been a lot of noise, but it stopped as soon as the stranger entered. There was a large table in the middle and round it, eager for dinner, were seated Athelny's children. A woman was standing at the oven, taking out baked potatoes one by one.

"Here's Mr. Carey, Betty," said Athelny.

"Fancy bringing him in here. What will he think?"

She wore a dirty apron, and the sleeves of her cotton dress were turned up above her elbows; she had curling pins in her hair. Mrs. Athelny was a large woman, a good three inches taller than her husband, fair, with blue eyes and a kindly expression; she had been a handsome creature, but advancing years and the bearing of many children had made her fat and blousy; her blue eyes had become pale, her skin was coarse and red, the colour had gone out of her hair. She straightened herself, wiped her hand on her apron, and held it out.

"You're welcome, sir," she said, in a slow voice, with an accent that seemed oddly familiar to Philip. "Athelny said you was very kind to him in the 'orspital."

"Now you must be introduced to the live stock," said Athelny. "That is Thorpe," he pointed to a chubby boy with curly hair, "he is my eldest son, heir to the title, estates, and responsibilities of the family. There is Athelstan, Harold, Edward." He pointed with his forefinger to three smaller boys, all rosy, healthy, and smiling, though when they felt Philip's smiling eyes upon them they looked shyly down at their plates. "Now the girls in order: María del Sol…"

"Pudding-face," said one of the small boys.

"Your sense of humour is rudimentary, my son. María de los Mercedes, María del Pilar, María de la Concepción, María del

685

Rosario."

"I call them Sally, Molly, Connie, Rosie, and Jane," said Mrs. Athelny. "Now, Athelny, you go into your own room and I'll send you your dinner. I'll let the children come in afterwards for a bit when I've washed them."

"My dear, if I'd had the naming of you I should have called you María of the Soapsuds. You're always torturing these wretched brats with soap."

"You go first, Mr. Carey, or I shall never get him to sit down and eat his dinner."

Athelny and Philip installed themselves in the great monkish chairs, and Sally brought them in two plates of beef, Yorkshire pudding, baked potatoes, and cabbage. Athelny took sixpence out of his pocket and sent her for a jug of beer.

"I hope you didn't have the table laid here on my account," said Philip. "I should have been quite happy to eat with the children."

"Oh no, I always have my meals by myself. I like these antique customs. I don't think that women ought to sit down at table with men. It ruins conversation and I'm sure it's very bad for them. It puts ideas in their heads, and women are never at ease with themselves when they have ideas."

Both host and guest ate with a hearty appetite.

"Did you ever taste such Yorkshire pudding? No one can make it like my wife. That's the advantage of not marrying a lady. You noticed she wasn't a lady, didn't you?"

It was an awkward question, and Philip did not know how to answer it.

"I never thought about it," he said lamely.

Athelny laughed. He had a peculiarly joyous laugh.

"No, she's not a lady, nor anything like it. Her father was a farmer, and she's never bothered about aitches in her life. We've had twelve children and nine of them are alive. I tell her it's about time she stopped, but she's an obstinate woman, she's got into the habit of it now, and I don't believe she'll be satisfied till she's had twenty."

At that moment Sally came in with the beer, and, having poured out a glass for Philip, went to the other side of the table to pour some out for her father. He put his hand round her waist.

"Did you ever see such a handsome, strapping girl? Only fifteen and she might be twenty. Look at her cheeks. She's never had a day's illness in her life. It'll be a lucky man who marries her, won't it, Sally?"

Sally listened to all this with a slight, slow smile, not much embarrassed, for she was accustomed to her father's outbursts, but with an easy modesty which was very attractive.

"Don't let your dinner get cold, father," she said, drawing herself away from his arm. "You'll call when you're ready for your pudding, won't you?"

They were left alone, and Athelny lifted the pewter tankard to his lips. He drank long and deep.

"My word, is there anything better than English beer?" he said. "Let us thank God for simple pleasures, roast beef and rice pudding, a good appetite and beer. I was married to a lady once. My God! Don't marry a lady, my boy."

Philip laughed. He was exhilarated by the scene, the funny

little man in his odd clothes, the panelled room and the Spanish furniture, the English fare: the whole thing had an exquisite incongruity.

"You laugh, my boy, you can't imagine marrying beneath you. You want a wife who's an intellectual equal. Your head is crammed full of ideas of comradeship. Stuff and nonsense, my boy! A man doesn't want to talk politics to his wife, and what do you think I care for Betty's views upon the Differential Calculus? A man wants a wife who can cook his dinner and look after his children. I've tried both and I know. Let's have the pudding in."

He clapped his hands and presently Sally came. When she took away the plates, Philip wanted to get up and help her, but Athelny stopped him.

"Let her alone, my boy. She doesn't want you to fuss about, do you, Sally? And she won't think it rude of you to sit still while she waits upon you. She don't care a damn for chivalry, do you, Sally?"

"No, father," answered Sally demurely.

"Do you know what I'm talking about, Sally?"

"No, father. But you know mother doesn't like you to swear."

Athelny laughed boisterously. Sally brought them plates of rice pudding, rich, creamy, and luscious. Athelny attacked his with gusto.

"One of the rules of this house is that Sunday dinner should never alter. It is a ritual. Roast beef and rice pudding for fifty Sundays in the year. On Easter Sunday lamb and green peas, and at Michaelmas roast goose and apple sauce. Thus we preserve the traditions of our people. When Sally marries she will forget many of the wise things I have taught her, but she will never forget that if you want to be good and happy you must eat on Sundays roast beef and rice pudding."

"You'll call when you're ready for cheese," said Sally impassively.

"D'you know the legend of the halcyon?" said Athelny. Philip was growing used to his rapid leaping from one subject to another. "When the kingfisher, flying over the sea, is exhausted, his mate places herself beneath him and bears him along upon her stronger wings. That is what a man wants in a wife, the halcyon. I lived with my first wife for three years. She was a lady, she had fifteen hundred a year, and we used to give nice little dinner parties in our little red-brick house in Kensington. She was a charming woman; they all said so, the barristers and their wives who dined with us, and the literary stockbrokers, and the budding politicians; oh, she was a charming woman. She made me go to church in a silk hat and a frockcoat, she took me to classical concerts, and she was very fond of lectures on Sunday afternoon; and she sat down to breakfast every morning at eight-thirty, and if I was late breakfast was cold; and she read the right books, admired the right pictures, and adored the right music. My God, how that woman bored me! She is charming still, and she lives in the little red-brick house in Kensington, with Morris's papers and Whistler's etchings on the walls, and gives the same nice little dinner parties, with veal creams and ices from Gunter's, as she did twenty years ago."

Philip did not ask by what means the ill-matched couple had separated, but Athelny told him.

"Betty's not my wife, you know; my wife wouldn't divorce

me. The children are bastards, every jack one of them, and are they any the worse for that? Betty was one of the maids in the little red-brick house in Kensington. Four or five years ago I was on my uppers, and I had seven children, and I went to my wife and asked her to help me. She said she'd make me an allowance if I'd give Betty up and go abroad. Can you see me giving Betty up? We starved for a while instead. My wife said I loved the gutter. I've degenerated; I've come down in the world; I earn three pounds a week as press agent to a linendraper, and every day I thank God that I'm not in the little red-brick house in Kensington."

Sally brought in Cheddar cheese, and Athelny went on with his fluent conversation.

"It's the greatest mistake in the world to think that one needs money to bring up a family. You need money to make them gentlemen and ladies, but I don't want my children to be ladies and gentlemen. Sally's going to earn her living in another year. She's to be apprenticed to a dressmaker, aren't you, Sally? And the boys are going to serve their country. I want them all to go into the Navy; it's a jolly life and a healthy life, good food, good pay, and a pension to end their days on."

Philip lit his pipe. Athelny smoked cigarettes of Havana tobacco, which he rolled himself. Sally cleared away. Philip was reserved, and it embarrassed him to be the recipient of so many confidences. Athelny, with his powerful voice in the diminutive body, with his bombast, with his foreign look, with his emphasis, was an astonishing creature. He reminded Philip a good deal of Cronshaw. He appeared to have the same independence of thought, the same bohemianism, but he had an infinitely more vivacious temperament; his mind was coarser, and he had not that interest in the abstract which made Cronshaw's conversation so captivating. Athelny was very proud of the county family to which he belonged; he showed Philip photographs of an Elizabethan mansion, and told him:

"The Athelnys have lived there for seven centuries, my boy. Ah, if you saw the chimney-pieces and the ceilings!"

There was a cupboard in the wainscoting and from this he took a family tree. He showed it to Philip with childlike satisfaction. It was indeed imposing.

"You see how the family names recur, Thorpe, Athelstan, Harold, Edward; I've used the family names for my sons. And the girls, you see, I've given Spanish names to."

An uneasy feeling came to Philip that possibly the whole story was an elaborate imposture, not told with any base motive, but merely from a wish to impress, startle, and amaze. Athelny had told him that he was at Winchester; but Philip, sensitive to differences of manner, did not feel that his host had the characteristics of a man educated at a great public school. While he pointed out the great alliances which his ancestors had formed, Philip amused himself by wondering whether Athelny was not the son of some tradesman in Winchester, auctioneer or coal-merchant, and whether a similarity of surname was not his only connection with the ancient family whose tree he was displaying.

Chapter 88

There was a knock at the door and a troop of children came in. They were clean and tidy now; their faces shone with soap, and their hair was plastered down; they were going to Sunday school under Sally's charge. Athelny joked with them in his dramatic, exuberant fashion, and you could see that he was devoted to them all. His pride in their good health and their good looks was touching. Philip felt that they were a little shy in his presence, and when their father sent them off they fled from the room in evident relief. In a few minutes Mrs. Athelny appeared. She had taken her hair out of the curling pins and now wore an elaborate fringe. She had on a plain black dress, a hat with cheap flowers, and was forcing her hands, red and coarse from much work, into black kid gloves.

"I'm going to church, Athelny," she said. "There's nothing you'll be wanting, is there?"

"Only your prayers, my Betty."

"They won't do you much good, you're too far gone for that," she smiled. Then, turning to Philip, she drawled: "I can't get him to go to church. He's no better than an atheist."

"Doesn't she look like Rubens's second wife?" cried Athelny. "Wouldn't she look splendid in a seventeenth-century costume? That's the sort of wife to marry, my boy. Look at her."

"I believe you'd talk the hind leg off a donkey, Athelny," she answered calmly.

She succeeded in buttoning her gloves, but before she went she turned to Philip with a kindly, slightly embarrassed smile.

"You'll stay to tea, won't you? Athelny likes someone to talk to, and it's not often he gets anybody who's clever enough."

"Of course he'll stay to tea," said Athelny. Then when his wife had gone: "I make a point of the children going to Sunday school, and I like Betty to go to church. I think women ought to be religious. I don't believe myself, but I like women and children to."

Philip, strait-laced in matters of truth, was a little shocked by this airy attitude.

"But how can you look on while your children are being taught things which you don't think are true?"

"If they're beautiful I don't much mind if they're not true. It's asking a great deal that things should appeal to your reason as well as to your sense of the aesthetic. I wanted Betty to become a Roman Catholic, I should have liked to see her converted in a crown of paper flowers, but she's hopelessly Protestant. Besides, religion is a matter of temperament; you will believe anything if you have the religious turn of mind, and if you haven't it doesn't matter what beliefs were instilled into you, you will grow out of them. Perhaps religion is the best school of morality. It is like one of those drugs you gentlemen use in medicine which carries another in solution: it is of no efficacy in itself, but enables the other to be absorbed. You take your morality because it is combined with religion; you lose the religion and the morality stays behind. A man is more likely to be a good man if he has learned goodness through the love of God than through a perusal of Herbert Spencer."

This was contrary to all Philip's ideas. He still looked upon Christianity as a degrading bondage that must be cast away at any cost; it was connected subconsciously in his mind with the dreary services in the cathedral at Tercanbury, and the long hours of boredom in the cold church at Blackstable; and the morality of which Athelny spoke was to him no more than a part of the religion which a halting intelligence preserved, when it had laid aside the beliefs which alone made it reasonable. But while he was meditating a reply Athelny, more interested in hearing himself speak than in discussion, broke into a tirade upon Roman Catholicism. For him it was an essential part of Spain; and Spain meant much to him, because he had escaped to it from the conventionality which during his married life he had found so irksome. With large gestures and in the emphatic tone which made what he said so striking, Athelny described to Philip the Spanish cathedrals with their vast dark spaces, the massive gold of the altar-pieces, and the sumptuous iron-work, gilt and faded, the air laden with incense, the silence: Philip almost saw the Canons in their short surplices of lawn, the acolytes in red, passing from the sacristy to the choir; he almost heard the monotonous chanting of vespers. The names which Athelny mentioned, Avila, Tarragona, Saragossa, Segovia, Cordova, were like trumpets in his heart. He seemed to see the great grey piles of granite set in old Spanish towns amid a landscape tawny, wild, and windswept.

"I've always thought I should love to go to Seville," he said casually, when Athelny, with one hand dramatically uplifted, paused for a moment.

"Seville!" cried Athelny. "No, no, don't go there. Seville: it brings to the mind girls dancing with castanets, singing in gardens by the Guadalquivir, bull-fights, orange-blossom, mantillas, *mantones de Manila*. It is the Spain of comic opera and Montmartre. Its facile charm can offer permanent entertainment only to an intelligence which is superficial. Théophile Gautier got out of Seville all that it has to offer. We who come after him can only repeat his sensations. He put large fat hands on the obvious and there is nothing but the obvious there; and it is all finger-marked and frayed. Murillo is its painter."

Athelny got up from his chair, walked over to the Spanish cabinet, let down the front with its great gilt hinges and gorgeous lock, and displayed a series of little drawers. He took out a bundle of photographs.

"Do you know El Greco?" he asked.

"Oh, I remember one of the men in Paris was awfully impressed by him."

"El Greco was the painter of Toledo. Betty couldn't find the photograph I wanted to show you. It's a picture that El Greco painted of the city he loved, and it's truer than any photograph. Come and sit at the table."

Philip dragged his chair forward, and Athelny set the photograph before him. He looked at it curiously, for a long time, in silence. He stretched out his hand for other photographs, and Athelny passed them to him. He had never before seen the work of that enigmatic master; and at the first glance he was bothered by the arbitrary drawing: the figures were extraordinarily elongated; the heads were very small; the attitudes were extravagant. This was not realism, and yet, and yet even in the photographs you had the impression of a troubling reality. Athelny was describing eagerly, with vivid phrases, but Philip only heard vaguely what he said. He was puzzled. He was curiously moved. These pictures seemed to offer some meaning to him, but he did not know what the meaning was. There were portraits of men with large, melancholy eyes which seemed to say you knew not what; there were long monks in the Franciscan habit or in the Dominican, with distraught faces, making gestures whose sense escaped you; there was an Assumption of the Virgin; there was a Crucifixion in which the painter by some magic of feeling had been able to suggest that the flesh of Christ's dead body was not human flesh only but divine; and there was an Ascension in which the Saviour seemed to surge up towards the empyrean and yet to stand upon the air as steadily as though it were solid ground: the uplifted arms of the Apostles, the sweep of their draperies, their ecstatic gestures, gave an impression of exultation and of holy joy. The background of nearly all was the sky by night, the dark night of the soul, with wild clouds swept by strange winds of Hell and lit luridly by an uneasy moon.

"I've seen that sky in Toledo over and over again," said Athelny. "I have an idea that when first El Greco came to the city it was by such a night, and it made so vehement an impression upon him that he could never get away from it."

Philip remembered how Clutton had been affected by this strange master, whose work he now saw for the first time. He thought that Clutton was the most interesting of all the people he had known in Paris. His sardonic manner, his hostile aloofness, had made it difficult to know him; but it seemed to Philip, looking back, that there had been in him a tragic force, which sought vainly to express itself in painting. He was a man of unusual character, mystical after the fashion of a time that had no leaning to mysticism, who was impatient with life because he found himself unable to say the things which the obscure impulses of his heart suggested. His intellect was not fashioned to the uses of the spirit. It was not surprising that he felt a deep sympathy with the Greek who had devised a new technique to express the yearnings of his soul. Philip looked again at the series of portraits of Spanish gentlemen, with ruffles and pointed beards, their faces pale against the sober black of their clothes and the darkness of the background. El Greco was the painter of the soul; and these gentlemen, wan and wasted, not by exhaustion but by restraint, with their tortured minds, seem to walk unaware of the beauty of the world; for their eyes look only in their hearts, and they are dazzled by the glory of the unseen. No painter has shown more pitilessly that the world is but a place of passage. The souls of the men he painted speak their strange longings through their eyes; their senses are miraculously acute, not for sounds and odours and colour, but for the very subtle sensations of the soul. The noble walks with the monkish heart within him, and his eyes see things which saints in their cells see too, and he is unastounded. His lips are not lips that smile.

Philip, silent still, returned to the photograph of Toledo, which seemed to him the most arresting picture of them all. He could not take his eyes off it. He felt strangely that he was on the threshold of some new discovery in life. He was tremulous with a sense of adventure. He thought for an instant of the love that had consumed him: love seemed very trivial beside the excitement which now leaped in his heart. The picture he looked at was a long one, with houses crowded upon a hill; in one corner a boy was holding a large map of the town; in another was a classical figure representing the river Tagus; and in the sky was the Virgin surrounded by angels. It was a landscape alien to all Philip's notion, for he had lived in circles that worshipped exact realism; and yet here again, strangely to himself, he felt a reality greater than any achieved by the masters in whose steps humbly he had sought to walk. He heard Athelny say that the representation was so precise that when the citizens of Toledo came to look at the picture they recognized their houses. The painter had painted exactly what he saw, but he had seen with the eyes of the spirit. There was something unearthly in that city of pale grey. It was a city of the soul seen by a wan light that was neither that of night nor day. It stood on a green hill, but of a green not of this world, and it was surrounded by massive walls and bastions to be stormed by no machines or engines of man's invention, but by prayer and fasting, by contrite sighs and by mortifications of the flesh. It was a stronghold of God. Those grey houses were made of no stone known to masons, there was something terrifying in their aspect, and you did not know what men might live in them. You might walk through the streets and be unamazed to find them all deserted, and yet not empty; for you felt a presence invisible and yet manifest to every inner sense. It was a mystical city in which the imagination faltered like one who steps out of the light into darkness; the soul walked naked to and fro, knowing the unknowable, and conscious strangely of experience, intimate but inexpressible, of the absolute. And without surprise, in that blue sky, real with a reality that not the eye but the soul confesses, with its rack of light clouds driven by strange breezes, like the cries and the sighs of lost souls, you saw the Blessed Virgin with a gown of red and a cloak of blue, surrounded by winged angels. Philip felt that the inhabitants of that city would have seen the apparition without astonishment, reverent and thankful, and have gone their ways.

Athelny spoke of the mystical writers of Spain, of Teresa de Avila, San Juan de la Cruz, Fray Diego de León; in all of them was that passion for the unseen which Philip felt in the pictures of El Greco: they seemed to have the power to touch the incorporeal and see the invisible. They were Spaniards of their age, in whom were tremulous all the mighty exploits of a great nation: their fancies were rich with the glories of America and the green islands of the Caribbean Sea; in their veins was the power that had come from age-long battling with the Moor; they were proud, for they were masters of the world; and they felt in themselves the wide distances, the tawny wastes, the snow-capped mountains of Castile, the sunshine and the blue sky, and the flowering plains of Andalusia. Life was passionate and manifold, and because it offered so much they felt a restless yearning for something more; because they were human they were unsatisfied; and they threw this eager vitality of theirs into a vehement striving after the ineffable. Athelny was not displeased to find someone to whom he could read the translations with which for some time he had amused his leisure; and in his fine, vibrating voice he recited the canticle of the Soul and Christ her lover, the lovely poem which begins with the words *en una noche oscura,* and the *noche serena* of Fray Luis de León. He had translated them quite simply, not without skill, and he had found words which at all events suggested the rough-hewn grandeur of the original. The pictures of El Greco explained them, and they explained the pictures.

Philip had cultivated a certain disdain for idealism. He had always had a passion for life, and the idealism he had come across seemed to him for the most part a cowardly shrinking from it. The idealist withdrew himself, because he could not suffer the jostling of the human crowd; he had not the strength to fight and so called the battle vulgar; he was vain, and since his fellows would not take him at his own estimate, consoled himself with despising his fellows. For Philip his type was Hayward, fair, languid, too fat now and rather bald, still cherishing the remains of his good looks and still delicately proposing to do exquisite things in the uncertain future; and at the back of this were whisky and vulgar *amours* of the street. It was in reaction from what Hayward represented that Philip clamoured for life as it stood; sordidness, vice, deformity, did not offend him; he declared that he wanted man in his nakedness; and he rubbed his hands when an instance came before him of meanness, cruelty, selfishness, or lust: that was the real thing. In Paris he had learned that there was neither ugliness nor beauty, but only truth: the search after beauty was sentimental. Had he not painted an advertisement of *chocolat Menier* in a landscape in order to escape from the tyranny of prettiness?

But here he seemed to divine something new. He had been coming to it, all hesitating, for some time, but only now was conscious of the fact; he felt himself on the brink of a discovery. He felt vaguely that here was something better than the realism which he had adored; but certainly it was not the bloodless idealism which stepped aside from life in weakness; it was too strong; it was virile; it accepted life in all its vivacity, ugliness and beauty, squalor and heroism; it was realism still; but it was realism carried to some higher pitch, in which facts were transformed by the more vivid light in which they were seen. He seemed to see things more profoundly through the grave eyes of those dead noblemen of Castile; and the gestures of the saints, which at first had seemed wild and distorted, appeared to have some mysterious significance. But he could not tell what that significance was. It was like a message which it was very important for him to receive, but it was given him in an unknown tongue, and he could not understand. He was always seeking for a meaning in life, and here it seemed to him that a meaning was offered; but it was obscure and vague. He was profoundly troubled. He saw what looked like the truth as by flashes of lightning on a dark, stormy night you might see a mountain range. He seemed to see that a man need not leave his life to chance, but that his will was powerful; he seemed to see that self-control might be as passionate and as active as the surrender to passion; he seemed to see that the inward life might be as manifold, as varied, as rich with experience, as the life of one who conquered realms and explored unknown lands.

Chapter 89

The conversation between Philip and Athelny was broken into by a clatter up the stairs. Athelny opened the door for the children coming back from Sunday school, and with laughter and shouting they came in. Gaily he asked them what they had learned. Sally appeared for a moment, with instructions from her mother that father was to amuse the children while she got tea ready; and Athelny began to tell them one of Hans Andersen's stories. They were not shy children, and they quickly came to the conclusion that Philip was not formidable. Jane came and stood by him and presently settled herself on his knees. It was the first time that Philip in his lonely life had been present in a family circle: his eyes smiled as they rested on the fair children engrossed in the fairy tale. The life of his new friend, eccentric as it appeared at first glance, seemed now to have the beauty of perfect naturalness. Sally came in once more.

"Now then, children, tea's ready," she said.

Jane slipped off Philip's knees, and they all went back to the kitchen. Sally began to lay the cloth on the long Spanish table.

"Mother says, shall she come and have tea with you?" she asked. "I can give the children their tea."

"Tell your mother that we shall be proud and honoured if she will favour us with her company," said Athelny.

It seemed to Philip that he could never say anything without an oratorical flourish.

"Then I'll lay for her," said Sally.

She came back again in a moment with a tray on which were a cottage loaf, a slab of butter, and a jar of strawberry jam. While she placed the things on the table her father chaffed her. He said it was quite time she was walking out; he told Philip that she was very proud, and would have nothing to do with aspirants to that honour who lined up at the door, two by two, outside the Sunday school and craved the honour of escorting her home.

"You do talk, father," said Sally, with her slow, good-natured smile.

"You wouldn't think to look at her that a tailor's assistant has enlisted in the army because she would not say how d'you do to him, and an electrical engineer, an electrical engineer, mind you, has taken to drink because she refused to share her hymn-book with him in church. I shudder to think what will happen when she puts her hair up."

"Mother'll bring the tea along herself," said Sally.

"Sally never pays any attention to me," laughed Athelny, looking at her with fond, proud eyes. "She goes about her business indifferent to wars, revolutions, and cataclysms. What a wife she'll make to an honest man!"

Mrs. Athelny brought in the tea. She sat down and proceeded

to cut bread and butter. It amused Philip to see that she treated her husband as though he were a child. She spread jam for him and cut up the bread and butter into convenient slices for him to eat. She had taken off her hat; and in her Sunday dress, which seemed a little tight for her, she looked like one of the farmer's wives whom Philip used to call on sometimes with his uncle when he was a small boy. Then he knew why the sound of her voice was familiar to him. She spoke just like the people round Blackstable.

"What part of the country d'you come from?" he asked her.

"I'm a Kentish woman. I come from Ferne."

"I thought as much. My uncle's Vicar of Blackstable."

"That's a funny thing now," she said. "I was wondering in church just now whether you was any connection of Mr. Carey. Many's the time I've seen 'im. A cousin of mine married Mr. Barker of Roxley Farm, over by Blackstable Church, and I used to go and stay there often when I was a girl. Isn't that a funny thing now?"

She looked at him with a new interest, and a brightness came into her faded eyes. She asked him whether he knew Ferne. It was a pretty village about ten miles across country from Blackstable, and the Vicar had come over sometimes to Blackstable for the harvest thanksgiving. She mentioned names of various farmers in the neighbourhood. She was delighted to talk again of the country in which her youth was spent, and it was a pleasure to her to recall scenes and people that had remained in her memory with the tenacity peculiar to her class. It gave Philip a queer sensation too. A breath of the countryside seemed to be wafted into that panelled room in the middle of London. He seemed to see the fat Kentish fields with their stately elms; and his nostrils dilated with the scent of the air; it is laden with the salt of the North Sea, and that makes it keen and sharp.

Philip did not leave the Athelnys' till ten o'clock. The children came in to say good night at eight and quite naturally put up their faces for Philip to kiss. His heart went out to them. Sally only held out her hand.

"Sally never kisses gentlemen till she's seen them twice," said her father.

"You must ask me again then," said Philip.

"You mustn't take any notice of what father says," remarked Sally, with a smile.

"She's a most self-possessed young woman," added her parent.

They had supper of bread and cheese and beer while Mrs. Athelny was putting the children to bed; and when Philip went into the kitchen to bid her good night (she had been sitting there, resting herself and reading *The Weekly Dispatch*) she invited him cordially to come again.

"There's always a good dinner on Sundays so long as Athelny's in work," she said, "and it's a charity to come and talk to him."

On the following Saturday Philip received a postcard from Athelny saying that they were expecting him to dinner next day; but fearing their means were not such that Mr. Athelny would desire him to accept, Philip wrote back that he would only come to tea. He bought a large plum cake so that his entertainment should cost nothing. He found the whole family glad to see him, and the cake completed his conquest of the children. He insisted that they should all have tea together in the kitchen, and the meal was noisy and hilarious.

Soon Philip got into the habit of going to Athelny's every Sunday. He became a great favourite with the children, because he was simple and unaffected and because it was so plain that he was fond of them. As soon as they heard his ring at the door one of them popped a head out of window to make sure it was he, and then they all rushed downstairs tumultuously to let him in. They flung themselves into his arms. At tea they fought for the privilege of sitting next to him. Soon they began to call him Uncle Philip.

Athelny was very communicative, and little by little Philip learned the various stages of his life. He had followed many occupations, and it occurred to Philip that he managed to make a mess of everything he attempted. He had been on a tea plantation in Ceylon and a traveller in America for Italian wines; his secretaryship of the water company in Toledo had lasted longer than any of his employments; he had been a journalist and for some time had worked as police-court reporter for an evening paper; he had been sub-editor of a paper in the Midlands and editor of another on the Riviera. From all his occupations he had gathered amusing anecdotes, which he told with a keen pleasure in his own powers of entertainment. He had read a great deal, chiefly delighting in books which were unusual; and he poured forth his stores of abstruse knowledge with childlike enjoyment of the amazement of his hearers. Three or four years before, abject poverty had driven him to take the job of press-representative to a large firm of drapers; and though he felt the work unworthy his abilities, which he rated highly, the firmness of his wife and the needs of his family had made him stick to it.

Chapter 90

When he left the Athelnys' Philip walked down Chancery Lane and along the Strand to get a bus at the top of Parliament Street. One Sunday, when he had known them about six weeks, he did this as usual, but he found the Kennington bus full. It was June, but it had rained during the day and the night was raw and cold. He walked up to Piccadilly Circus in order to get a seat; the bus waited at the fountain, and when it arrived there seldom had more than two or three people in it. This service ran every quarter of an hour, and he had some time to wait. He looked idly at the crowd. The public-houses were closing, and there were many people about. His mind was busy with the ideas Athelny had the charming gift of suggesting.

Suddenly his heart stood still. He saw Mildred. He had not thought of her for weeks. She was crossing over from the corner of Shaftesbury Avenue and stopped at the shelter till a string of cabs passed by. She was watching her opportunity and had no eyes for anything else. She wore a large black straw hat with a mass of feathers on it and a black silk dress; at that time it was fashionable for women to wear trains; the road was clear, and Mildred crossed, her skirt trailing on the ground, and walked down Piccadilly. Philip, his heart beating excitedly, followed her. He did not wish to speak to her, but he wondered where she was going at that hour; he wanted to get a look at her face. She walked slowly along and turned down Air Street and so got through into Regent Street. She walked up again towards the Circus. Philip was puzzled. He could not make out what she was doing. Perhaps she was waiting for somebody, and he felt a great curiosity to know who it was. She overtook a short man in a bowler hat, who was strolling very slowly in the same direction as herself; she gave him a sidelong glance as she passed. She walked a few steps more till she came to Swan and Edgar's, then stopped and waited, facing the road. When the man came up she smiled. The man stared at her for a moment, turned away his head, and sauntered on. Then Philip understood.

He was overwhelmed with horror. For a moment he felt such a weakness in his legs that he could hardly stand; then he walked after her quickly; he touched her on the arm.

"Mildred."

She turned round with a violent start. He thought that she reddened, but in the obscurity he could not see very well. For a while they stood and looked at one another without speaking. At last she said:

"Fancy seeing you!"

He did not know what to answer; he was horribly shaken; and the phrases that chased one another through his brain seemed incredibly melodramatic.

"It's awful," he gasped, almost to himself.

She did not say anything more, she turned away from him, and looked down at the pavement. He felt that his face was distorted with misery.

"Isn't there anywhere we can go and talk?"

"I don't want to talk," she said sullenly. "Leave me alone, can't you?"

The thought struck him that perhaps she was in urgent need of money and could not afford to go away at that hour.

"I've got a couple of sovereigns on me if you're hard up," he blurted out.

"I don't know what you mean. I was just walking along here on my way back to my lodgings. I expected to meet one of the girls from where I work."

"For God's sake don't lie now," he said.

Then he saw that she was crying, and he repeated his question.

"Can't we go and talk somewhere? Can't I come back to your rooms?"

"No, you can't do that," she sobbed. "I'm not allowed to take gentlemen in there. If you like I'll meet you tomorrow."

He felt certain that she would not keep an appointment. He was not going to let her go.

"No. You must take me somewhere now."

"Well, there is a room I know, but they'll charge six shillings for it."

"I don't mind that. Where is it?"

She gave him the address, and he called a cab. They drove to a shabby street beyond the British Museum in the neighbourhood of the Gray's Inn Road, and she stopped the cab at the corner.

"They don't like you to drive up to the door," she said.

They were the first words either of them had spoken since getting into the cab. They walked a few yards and Mildred knocked three times, sharply, at a door. Philip noticed in the fanlight a cardboard on which was an announcement that apartments were to let. The door was opened quietly, and an elderly tall woman let them in. She gave Philip a stare and then spoke to Mildred in an undertone. Mildred led Philip along a passage to a room at the back. It was quite dark; she asked him for a match, and lit the gas; there was no globe, and the gas flared shrilly. Philip saw that he was in a dingy little bedroom with a suite of furniture painted to look like pine much too large for it; the lace curtains were very dirty; the grate was hidden by a large paper fan. Mildred sank on the chair which stood by the side of the chimney-piece. Philip sat on the edge of the bed. He felt ashamed. He saw now that Mildred's cheeks were thick with rouge, her eyebrows were blackened; but she looked thin and ill, and the red on her cheeks exaggerated the greenish pallor of her skin. She stared at the paper fan in a listless fashion. Philip could not think what to say, and he had a choking in his throat as if he were going to cry. He covered his eyes with his hands.

"My God, it is awful," he groaned.

"I don't know what you've got to fuss about. I should have thought you'd have been rather pleased."

Philip did not answer, and in a moment she broke into a sob.

"You don't think I do it because I like it, do you?"

"Oh, my dear," he cried. "I'm so sorry, I'm so awfully sorry."

"That'll do me a fat lot of good."

Again Philip found nothing to say. He was desperately afraid of saying anything which she might take for a reproach or a sneer.

"Where's the baby?" he asked at last.

"I've got her with me in London. I hadn't got the money to keep her on at Brighton, so I had to take her. I've got a room up Highbury way. I told them I was on the stage. It's a long way to have to come down to the West End every day, but it's a rare job to find anyone who'll let to ladies at all."

"Wouldn't they take you back at the shop?"

"I couldn't get any work to do anywhere. I walked my legs off looking for work. I did get a job once, but I was off for a week because I was queer, and when I went back they said they didn't want me any more. You can't blame them either, can you? Them places, they can't afford to have girls that aren't strong."

"You don't look very well now," said Philip.

"I wasn't fit to come out tonight, but I couldn't help myself, I wanted the money. I wrote to Emil and told him I was broke, but he never even answered the letter."

"You might have written to me."

"I didn't like to, not after what happened, and I didn't want you to know I was in difficulties. I shouldn't have been surprised if you'd just told me I'd only got what I deserved."

"You don't know me very well, do you, even now?"

For a moment he remembered all the anguish he had suffered on her account, and he was sick with the recollection of his pain. But it was no more than recollection. When he looked at her he knew that he no longer loved her. He was very sorry for her, but he was glad to be free. Watching her gravely, he asked himself why he had been so besotted with passion for her.

"You're a gentleman in every sense of the word," she said. "You're the only one I've ever met." She paused for a minute and then flushed. "I hate asking you, Philip, but can you spare me anything?"

"It's lucky I've got some money on me. I'm afraid I've only got two pounds."

He gave her the sovereigns.

"I'll pay you back, Philip."

"Oh, that's all right," he smiled. "You needn't worry."

He had said nothing that he wanted to say. They had talked as if the whole thing were natural; and it looked as though she would go now, back to the horror of her life, and he would be able to do nothing to prevent it. She had got up to take the money, and they were both standing.

"Am I keeping you?" she asked. "I suppose you want to be getting home."

"No, I'm in no hurry," he answered.

"I'm glad to have a chance of sitting down."

Those words, with all they implied, tore his heart, and it was dreadfully painful to see the weary way in which she sank back into the chair. The silence lasted so long that Philip in his embarrassment lit a cigarette.

"It's very good of you not to have said anything disagreeable to me, Philip. I thought you might say I didn't know what all."

He saw that she was crying again. He remembered how she

had come to him when Emil Miller had deserted her and how she had wept. The recollection of her suffering and of his own humiliation seemed to render more overwhelming the compassion he felt now.

"If I could only get out of it!" she moaned. "I hate it so. I'm unfit for the life, I'm not the sort of girl for that. I'd do anything to get away from it, I'd be a servant if I could. Oh, I wish I was dead."

And in pity for herself she broke down now completely. She sobbed hysterically, and her thin body was shaken.

"Oh, you don't know what it is. Nobody knows till they've done it."

Philip could not bear to see her cry. He was tortured by the horror of her position.

"Poor child," he whispered. "Poor child."

He was deeply moved. Suddenly he had an inspiration. It filled him with a perfect ecstasy of happiness.

"Look here, if you want to get away from it, I've got an idea. I'm frightfully hard up just now, I've got to be as economical as I can; but I've got a sort of little flat in Kennington and I've got a spare room. If you like you and the baby can come and live there. I pay a woman three and sixpence a week to keep the place clean and to do a little cooking for me. You could do that and your food wouldn't come to much more than the money I should save on her. It doesn't cost any more to feed two than one, and I don't suppose the baby eats much."

She stopped crying and looked at him.

"D'you mean to say that you could take me back after all

that's happened?"

Philip flushed a little in embarrassment at what he had to say.

"I don't want you to mistake me. I'm just giving you a room which doesn't cost me anything and your food. I don't expect anything more from you than that you should do exactly the same as the woman I have in does. Except for that I don't want anything from you at all. I daresay you can cook well enough for that."

She sprang to her feet and was about to come towards him.

"You are good to me, Philip."

"No, please stop where you are," he said hurriedly, putting out his hand as though to push her away.

He did not know why it was, but he could not bear the thought that she should touch him.

"I don't want to be anything more than a friend to you."

"You are good to me," she repeated. "You are good to me."

"Does that mean you'll come?"

"Oh, yes, I'd do anything to get away from this. You'll never regret what you've done, Philip, never. When can I come, Philip?"

"You'd better come tomorrow."

Suddenly she burst into tears again.

"What on earth are you crying for now?" he smiled.

"I'm so grateful to you. I don't know how I can ever make it up to you?"

"Oh, that's all right. You'd better go home now."

He wrote out the address and told her that if she came at half past five he would be ready for her. It was so late that he had to walk home, but it did not seem a long way, for he was intoxicated with delight; he seemed to walk on air.

Chapter 91

Next day he got up early to make the room ready for Mildred. He told the woman who had looked after him that he would not want her any more. Mildred came about six, and Philip, who was watching from the window, went down to let her in and help her to bring up the luggage: it consisted now of no more than three large parcels wrapped in brown paper, for she had been obliged to sell everything that was not absolutely needful. She wore the same black silk dress she had worn the night before, and, though she had now no rouge on her cheeks, there was still about her eyes the black which remained after a perfunctory wash in the morning: it made her look very ill. She was a pathetic figure as she stepped out of the cab with the baby in her arms. She seemed a little shy, and they found nothing but commonplace things to say to one another.

"So you've got here all right."

"I've never lived in this part of London before."

Philip showed her the room. It was that in which Cronshaw had died. Philip, though he thought it absurd, had never liked the idea of going back to it; and since Cronshaw's death he had remained in the little room, sleeping on a fold-up bed, into which he had first moved in order to make his friend comfortable. The baby was sleeping placidly.

"You don't recognize her, I expect," said Mildred.

"I've not seen her since we took her down to Brighton."

"Where shall I put her? She's so heavy I can't carry her very long."

"I'm afraid I haven't got a cradle," said Philip, with a nervous laugh.

"Oh, she'll sleep with me. She always does."

Mildred put the baby in an armchair and looked round the room. She recognized most of the things which she had known in his old diggings. Only one thing was new, a head and shoulders of Philip which Lawson had painted at the end of the preceding summer; it hung over the chimney-piece; Mildred looked at it critically.

"In some ways I like it and in some ways I don't. I think you're better, looking than that."

"Things are looking up," laughed Philip. "You've never told me I was good-looking before."

"I'm not one to worry myself about a man's looks. I don't like good-looking men. They're too conceited for me."

Her eyes travelled round the room in an instinctive search for a looking-glass, but there was none; she put up her hand and patted her large fringe.

"What'll the other people in the house say to my being here?" she asked suddenly.

"Oh, there's only a man and his wife living here. He's out all day, and I never see her except on Saturday to pay my rent. They keep entirely to themselves. I've not spoken two words to either of them since I came."

Mildred went into the bedroom to undo her things and put them away. Philip tried to read, but his spirits were too high: he leaned back in his chair, smoking a cigarette, and with smiling eyes looked at the sleeping child. He felt very happy. He was quite sure that he was not at all in love with Mildred. He was surprised that the old feeling had left him so completely; he discerned in himself a faint physical repulsion from her; and he thought that if he touched her it would give him goose-flesh. He could not understand himself. Presently, knocking at the door, she came in again.

"I say, you needn't knock," he said. "Have you made the tour of the mansion?"

"It's the smallest kitchen I've ever seen."

"You'll find it large enough to cook our sumptuous repasts," he retorted lightly.

"I see there's nothing in. I'd better go out and get something."

"Yes, but I venture to remind you that we must be devilish economical."

"What shall I get for supper?"

"You'd better get what you think you can cook," laughed Philip.

He gave her some money and she went out. She came in half an hour later and put her purchases on the table. She was out of breath from climbing the stairs.

"I say, you are anaemic," said Philip. "I'll have to dose you with Blaud's Pills."

"It took me some time to find the shops. I bought some liver. That's tasty, isn't it? And you can't eat much of it, so it's more economical than butcher's meat."

There was a gas stove in the kitchen, and when she had put the liver on, Mildred came into the sitting-room to lay the cloth.

"Why are you only laying one place?" asked Philip. "Aren't you going to eat anything?"

Mildred flushed.

"I thought you mightn't like me to have my meals with you."

"Why on earth not?"

"Well, I'm only a servant, aren't I?"

"Don't be an ass. How can you be so silly?"

He smiled, but her humility gave him a curious twist in his heart. Poor thing! He remembered what she had been when first he knew her. He hesitated for an instant.

"Don't think I'm conferring any benefit on you," he said. "It's simply a business arrangement; I'm giving you board and lodging in return for your work. You don't owe me anything. And there's nothing humiliating to you in it."

She did not answer, but tears rolled heavily down her cheeks. Philip knew from his experience at the hospital that women of her class looked upon service as degrading: he could not help feeling a little impatient with her; but he blamed himself, for it was clear that she was tired and ill. He got up and helped her to lay another place at the table. The baby was awake now, and Mildred had prepared some Mellin's Food for it. The liver and bacon were ready and they sat down. For economy's sake Philip had given up drinking anything but water, but he had in the house a half bottle of whisky, and he thought a little would do Mildred good. He did his best to make the supper pass cheerfully, but Mildred was subdued and exhausted. When they had finished she got up to put the baby to bed.

"I think you'll do well to turn in early yourself," said Philip. "You look absolute done up."

"I think I will after I've washed up."

Philip lit his pipe and began to read. It was pleasant to hear somebody moving about in the next room. Sometimes his loneliness had oppressed him. Mildred came in to clear the table, and he heard the clatter of plates as she washed up. Philip smiled as he thought how characteristic it was of her that she should do all that in a black silk dress. But he had work to do, and he brought his book up to the table. He was reading Osler's *Medicine*, which had recently taken the place in the students' favour of Taylor's work, for many years the textbook most in use. Presently Mildred came in, rolling down her sleeves. Philip gave her a casual glance, but did not move; the occasion was curious, and he felt a little nervous. He feared that Mildred might imagine he was going to make a nuisance of himself, and he did not quite know how without brutality to reassure her.

"By the way, I've got a lecture at nine, so I should want breakfast at a quarter past eight. Can you manage that?"

"Oh, yes. Why, when I was in Parliament Street I used to catch the eight-twelve from Herne Hill every morning."

"I hope you'll find your room comfortable. You'll be a different woman tomorrow after a long night in bed."

"I suppose you work till late?"

"I generally work till about eleven or half past."

"I'll say good night then."

"Good night."

The table was between them. He did not offer to shake hands with her. She shut the door quietly. He heard her moving about in the bed-room, and in a little while he heard the creaking of the bed as she got in.

Chapter 92

The following day was Tuesday. Philip as usual hurried through his breakfast and dashed off to get to his lecture at nine. He had only time to exchange a few words with Mildred. When he came back in the evening he found her seated at the window, darning his socks.

"I say, you are industrious," he smiled. "What have you been doing with yourself all day?"

"Oh, I gave the place a good cleaning and then I took baby out for a little."

She was wearing an old black dress, the same as she had worn as uniform when she served in the tea-shop; it was shabby, but she looked better in it than in the silk of the day before. The baby was sitting on the floor. She looked up at Philip with large, mysterious eyes and broke into a laugh when he sat down beside her and began playing with her bare toes. The afternoon sun came into the room and shed a mellow light.

"It's rather jolly to come back and find someone about the place. A woman and a baby make very good decoration in a room."

He had gone to the hospital dispensary and got a bottle of Blaud's Pills. He gave them to Mildred and told her she must take them after each meal. It was a remedy she was used to, for she had taken it off and on ever since she was sixteen.

"I'm sure Lawson would love that green skin of yours," said Philip. "He'd say it was so paintable, but I'm terribly matter-of-fact nowadays, and I shan't be happy till you're as pink and white as a milkmaid."

"I feel better already."

After a frugal supper Philip filled his pouch with tobacco and put on his hat. It was on Tuesdays that he generally went to the tavern in Beak Street, and he was glad that this day came so soon after Mildred's arrival, for he wanted to make his relations with her perfectly clear.

"Are you going out?" she said.

"Yes, on Tuesdays I give myself a night off. I shall see you tomorrow. Good night."

Philip always went to the tavern with a sense of pleasure. Macalister, the philosophic stockbroker, was generally there and glad to argue upon any subject under the sun; Hayward came regularly when he was in London; and though he and Macalister disliked one another they continued out of habit to meet on that one evening in the week. Macalister thought Hayward a poor creature, and sneered at his delicacies of sentiment: he asked satirically about Hayward's literary work and received with scornful smiles his vague suggestions of future masterpieces; their arguments were often heated; but the punch was good, and they were both fond of it; towards the end of the evening they generally composed their differences and thought each other capital fellows. This evening Philip found them both there, and Lawson also; Lawson came more seldom now that he was beginning to know people in London and went out to dinner a good deal. They were all on excellent terms with themselves, for Macalister had given them a good thing on the Stock Exchange, and Hayward and Lawson had made fifty pounds apiece. It was a great thing for Lawson, who was extravagant and earned little money: he had arrived at that stage of the portrait-painter's career when he was noticed a good deal by the critics and found a number of aristocratic ladies who were willing to allow him to paint them for nothing (it advertised them both, and gave the great ladies quite an air of patronesses of the arts); but he very seldom got hold of the solid philistine who was ready to pay good money for a portrait of his wife. Lawson was brimming over with satisfaction.

"It's the most ripping way of making money that I've ever struck," he cried. "I didn't have to put my hand in my pocket for sixpence."

"You lost something by not being here last Tuesday, young man," said Macalister to Philip.

"My God, why didn't you write to me?" said Philip. "If you only knew how useful a hundred pounds would be to me."

"Oh, there wasn't time for that. One has to be on the spot. I heard of a good thing last Tuesday, and I asked these fellows if they'd like to have a flutter, I bought them a thousand shares on Wednesday morning, and there was a rise in the afternoon, so I sold them at once. I made fifty pounds for each of them and a couple of hundred for myself."

Philip was sick with envy. He had recently sold the last mortgage in which his small fortune had been invested and now had only six hundred pounds left. He was panic-stricken sometimes when he thought of the future. He had still to keep himself for two years before he could be qualified, and then he meant to try for hospital appointments, so that he could not expect to earn anything for three years at least. With the most rigid economy he would not have more than a hundred pounds left then. It was very little to have as a stand-by in case he was ill and could not earn money or found himself at any time without work. A lucky gamble would make all the difference to him.

"Oh, well, it doesn't matter," said Macalister. "Something is sure to turn up soon. There'll be a boom in South Africans again one of these days, and then I'll see what I can do for you."

Macalister was in the Kaffir market and often told them stories of the sudden fortunes that had been made in the great boom of a year or two back.

"Well, don't forget next time."

They sat on talking till nearly midnight, and Philip, who lived furthest off, was the first to go. If he did not catch the last tram he had to walk, and that made him very late. As it was he did not reach home till nearly half past twelve. When he got upstairs he was surprised to find Mildred still sitting in his armchair.

"Why on earth aren't you in bed?" he cried.

"I wasn't sleepy."

"You ought to go to bed all the same. It would rest you."

She did not move. He noticed that since supper she had changed into her black silk dress.

"I thought I'd rather wait up for you in case you wanted anything."

She looked at him, and the shadow of a smile played upon her thin pale lips. Philip was not sure whether he understood or not. He was slightly embarrassed, but assumed a cheerful matter-of-fact air.

"It's very nice of you, but it's very naughty also. Run off to bed as fast as you can, or you won't be able to get up tomorrow morning."

"I don't feel like going to bed."

"Nonsense," he said coldly.

She got up, a little sulkily, and went into her room. He smiled when he heard her lock the door loudly.

The next few days passed without incident. Mildred settled down in her new surroundings. When Philip hurried off after breakfast she had the whole morning to do the housework. They ate very simply, but she liked to take a long time to buy the few things they needed; she could not be bothered to cook anything for her dinner, but made herself some cocoa and ate bread and butter; then she took the baby out in the go-cart, and when she came in spent the rest of the afternoon in idleness. She was tired out, and it suited her to do so little. She made friends with Philip's forbidding landlady over the rent, which he left with Mildred to pay, and within a week was able to tell him more about his neighbours than he had learned in a year.

"She's a very nice woman," said Mildred. "Quite the lady. I

told her we was married."

"D'you think that was necessary?"

"Well, I had to tell her something. It looks so funny me being here and not married to you. I didn't know what she'd think of me."

"I don't suppose she believed you for a moment."

"That she did, I lay. I told her we'd been married two years—I had to say that, you know, because of baby—only your people wouldn't hear of it, because you was only a student" — she pronounced it stoodent— "and so we had to keep it a secret, but they'd given way now and we were all going down to stay with them in the summer."

"You're a past-mistress of the cock-and-bull story," said Philip.

He was vaguely irritated that Mildred still had this passion for telling fibs. In the last two years she had learnt nothing. But he shrugged his shoulders.

"When all's said and done," he reflected, "she hasn't had much chance."

It was a beautiful evening, warm and cloudless, and the people of South London seemed to have poured out into the streets. There was that restlessness in the air which seizes the cockney sometimes when a turn in the weather calls him into the open. After Mildred had cleared away the supper she went and stood at the window. The street noises came up to them, noises of people calling to one another, of the passing traffic, of a barrel-organ in the distance.

"I suppose you must work tonight, Philip?" she asked him,

with a wistful expression.

"I ought, but I don't know that I must. Why, d'you want me to do anything else?"

"I'd like to go out for a bit. Couldn't we take a ride on the top of a tram?"

"If you like."

"I'll just go and put on my hat," she said joyfully.

The night made it almost impossible to stay indoors. The baby was asleep and could be safely left; Mildred said she had always left it alone at night when she went out; it never woke. She was in high spirits when she came back with her hat on. She had taken the opportunity to put on a little rouge. Philip thought it was excitement which had brought a faint colour to her pale cheeks; he was touched by her childlike delight, and reproached himself for the austerity with which he had treated her. She laughed when she got out into the air. The first tram they saw was going towards Westminster Bridge and they got on it. Philip smoked his pipe, and they looked at the crowded street. The shops were open, gaily lit, and people were doing their shopping for the next day. They passed a music hall called the Canterbury and Mildred cried out:

"Oh, Philip, do let's go there. I haven't been to a music hall for months."

"We can't afford stalls, you know."

"Oh, I don't mind, I shall be quite happy in the gallery."

They got down and walked back a hundred yards till they came to the doors. They got capital seats for sixpence each, high up but not in the gallery, and the night was so fine that there was plenty of room. Mildred's eyes glistened. She enjoyed herself thoroughly. There was a simple-mindedness in her which touched Philip. She was a puzzle to him. Certain things in her still pleased him, and he thought that there was a lot in her which was very good: she had been badly brought up, and her life was hard; he had blamed her for much that she could not help; and it was his own fault if he had asked virtues from her which it was not in her power to give. Under different circumstances she might have been a charming girl. She was extraordinarily unfit for the battle of life. As he watched her now in profile, her mouth slightly open and that delicate flush on her cheeks, he thought she looked strangely virginal. He felt an overwhelming compassion for her, and with all his heart he forgave her for the misery she had caused him. The smoky atmosphere made Philip's eyes ache, but when he suggested going she turned to him with beseeching face and asked him to stay till the end. He smiled and consented. She took his hand and held it for the rest of the performance. When they streamed out with the audience into the crowded street she did not want to go home; they wandered up the Westminster Bridge Road, looking at the people.

"I've not had such a good time as this for months," she said.

Philip's heart was full, and he was thankful to the fates because he had carried out his sudden impulse to take Mildred and her baby into his flat. It was very pleasant to see her happy gratitude. At last she grew tired and they jumped on a tram to go home; it was late now, and when they got down and turned into their own street there was no one about. Mildred slipped her arm through his.

"It's just like old times, Phil," she said.

She had never called him Phil before, that was what Griffiths called him; and even now it gave him a curious pang. He remembered how much he had wanted to die then; his pain had been so great that he had thought quite seriously of committing suicide. It all seemed very long ago. He smiled at his past self. Now he felt nothing for Mildred but infinite pity. They reached the house, and when they got into the sitting-room Philip lit the gas.

"Is the baby all right?" he asked.

"I'll just go in and see."

When she came back it was to say that it had not stirred since she left it. It was a wonderful child. Philip held out his hand.

"Well, good night."

"D'you want to go to bed already?"

"It's nearly one. I'm not used to late hours these days," said Philip.

She took his hand, and holding it looked into his eyes with a little smile.

"Phil, the other night in that room, when you asked me to come and stay here, I didn't mean what you thought I meant, when you said you didn't want me to be anything to you except just to cook and that sort of thing."

"Didn't you?" answered Philip, withdrawing his hand. "I did."

"Don't be such an old silly," she laughed.

He shook his head.

"I meant it quite seriously. I shouldn't have asked you to stay here on any other condition."

"Why not?"

"I feel I couldn't. I can't explain it, but it would spoil it all."

She shrugged her shoulders.

"Oh, very well, it's just as you choose. I'm not one to go down on my hands and knees for that, and chance it."

She went out, slamming the door behind her.

Chapter 93

Next morning Mildred was sulky and taciturn. She remained in her room till it was time to get the dinner ready. She was a bad cook and could do little more than chops and steaks; and she did not know how to use up odds and ends, so that Philip was obliged to spend more money than he had expected. When she served up she sat down opposite Philip, but would eat nothing; he remarked on it; she said she had a bad headache and was not hungry. He was glad that he had somewhere to spend the rest of the day; the Athelnys were cheerful and friendly: it was a delightful and an unexpected thing to realize that everyone in that household looked forward with pleasure to his visit. Mildred had gone to bed when he came back, but next day she was still silent. At supper she sat with a haughty expression on her face and a little frown between her eyes. It made Philip impatient, but he told himself that he must be considerate to her; he was bound to make allowance.

"You're very silent," he said, with a pleasant smile.

"I'm paid to cook and clean, I didn't know I was expected to talk as well."

He thought it an ungracious answer, but if they were going to live together he must do all he could to make things go easily.

"I'm afraid you're cross with me about the other night," he said.

It was an awkward thing to speak about, but apparently it was necessary to discuss it.

"I don't know what you mean," she answered.

"Please don't be angry with me. I should never have asked you to come and live here if I'd not meant our relations to be merely friendly. I suggested it because I thought you wanted a home and you would have a chance of looking about for something to do."

"Oh, don't think I care."

"I don't for a moment," he hastened to say. "You mustn't think I'm ungrateful. I realize that you only proposed it for my sake. It's just a feeling I have, and I can't help it, it would make the whole thing ugly and horrid."

"You are funny," she said, looking at him curiously. "I can't make you out."

She was not angry with him now, but puzzled; she had no idea what he meant: she accepted the situation, she had indeed a vague feeling that he was behaving in a very noble fashion and that she ought to admire it; but also she felt inclined to laugh at him and perhaps even to despise him a little.

"He's a rum customer," she thought.

Life went smoothly enough with them. Philip spent all day at the hospital and worked at home in the evening except when he went to the Athelnys' or to the tavern in Beak Street. Once the physician for whom he clerked asked him to a solemn dinner, and two or three times he went to parties given by fellow-students. Mildred accepted the monotony of her life. If she minded that Philip left her sometimes by herself in the evening she never mentioned it. Occasionally he took her to a music hall. He carried out his intention that the only tie between them should be the domestic service she did in return for board and lodging. She had made up her mind that it was no use trying to get work that summer, and with Philip's approval determined to stay where she was till the autumn. She thought it would be easy to get something to do then.

"As far as I'm concerned you can stay on here when you've got a job if it's convenient. The room's there, and the woman who did for me before can come in to look after the baby."

He grew very much attached to Mildred's child. He had a naturally affectionate disposition, which had had little opportunity to display itself. Mildred was not unkind to the little girl. She looked after her very well and once when she had a bad cold proved herself a devoted nurse; but the child bored her, and she spoke to her sharply when she bothered; she was fond of her, but had not the maternal passion which might have induced her to forget herself. Mildred had no demonstrativeness, and she found the manifestations of affection ridiculous. When Philip sat with the baby on his knees, playing with it and kissing it, she laughed at him.

"You couldn't make more fuss of her if you was her father," she said. "You're perfectly silly with the child."

Philip flushed, for he hated to be laughed at. It was absurd to be so devoted to another man's baby, and he was a little ashamed of the overflowing of his heart. But the child, feeling Philip's attachment, would put her face against his or nestle in his arms.

"It's all very fine for you," said Mildred. "You don't have any of the disagreeable part of it. How would you like being kept awake for an hour in the middle of the night because her ladyship wouldn't go to sleep?"

Philip remembered all sorts of things of his childhood which he thought he had long forgotten. He took hold of the baby's toes.

"This little pig went to market, this little pig stayed at home."

When he came home in the evening and entered the sitting-room his first glance was for the baby sprawling on the floor, and it gave him a little thrill of delight to hear the child's crow of pleasure at seeing him. Mildred taught her to call him daddy, and when the child did this for the first time of her own accord, laughed immoderately.

"I wonder if you're that stuck on baby because she's mine," asked Mildred, "or if you'd be the same with anybody's baby."

"I've never known anybody else's baby, so I can't say," said Philip.

Towards the end of his second term as in-patients' clerk a piece of good fortune befell Philip. It was the middle of July. He went one Tuesday evening to the tavern in Beak Street and found nobody there but Macalister. They sat together, chatting about their absent friends, and after a while Macalister said to him:

"Oh, by the way, I heard of a rather good thing today, New Kleinfonteins; it's a gold mine in Rhodesia. If you'd like to have a flutter you might make a bit."

Philip had been waiting anxiously for such an opportunity, but now that it came he hesitated. He was desperately afraid of losing money. He had little of the gambler's spirit.

"I'd love to, but I don't know if I dare risk it. How much could I lose if things went wrong?"

"I shouldn't have spoken of it, only you seemed so keen about it," Macalister answered coldly.

Philip felt that Macalister looked upon him as rather a donkey.

"I'm awfully keen on making a bit," he laughed.

"You can't make money unless you're prepared to risk money."

Macalister began to talk of other things and Philip, while he was answering him, kept thinking that if the venture turned out well the stockbroker would be very facetious at his expense next time they met. Macalister had a sarcastic tongue.

"I think I will have a flutter if you don't mind," said Philip anxiously.

"All right. I'll buy you two hundred and fifty shares and if I see a half-crown rise I'll sell them at once."

Philip quickly reckoned out how much that would amount to, and his mouth watered; thirty pounds would be a godsend just then, and he thought the fates owed him something. He told Mildred what he had done when he saw her at breakfast next morning. She thought him very silly.

"I never knew anyone who made money on the Stock Exchange," she said. "That's what Emil always said; you can't expect to make money on the Stock Exchange, he said."

Philip bought an evening paper on his way home and turned at once to the money columns. He knew nothing about these things and had difficulty in finding the stock which Macalister had spoken of. He saw they had advanced a quarter. His heart leaped, and then he felt sick with apprehension in case Macalister had forgotten or for some reason had not bought. Macalister had promised to telegraph. Philip could not wait to take a tram home. He jumped into a cab. It was an unwonted extravagance.

"Is there a telegram for me?" he said, as he burst in.

"No," said Mildred.

His face fell, and in bitter disappointment he sank heavily into a chair.

"Then he didn't buy them for me after all. Curse him," he added violently. "What cruel luck! And I've been thinking all day of what I'd do with the money."

"Why, what were you going to do?" she asked.

"What's the good of thinking about that now? Oh, I wanted the money so badly."

She gave a laugh and handed him a telegram.

"I was only having a joke with you. I opened it."

He tore it out of her hands. Macalister had bought him two hundred and fifty shares and sold them at the half-crown profit he had suggested. The commission note was to follow next day. For one moment Philip was furious with Mildred for her cruel jest, but then he could only think of his joy.

"It makes such a difference to me," he cried. "I'll stand you a new dress if you like."

"I want it badly enough," she answered.

"I'll tell you what I'm going to do. I'm going to be operated upon at the end of July."

"Why, have you got something the matter with you?" she interrupted.

It struck her that an illness she did not know might explain what had so much puzzled her. He flushed, for he hated to refer to his deformity.

"No, but they think they can do something to my foot. I couldn't spare the time before, but now it doesn't matter so much. I shall start my dressing in October instead of next month. I shall only be in hospital a few weeks and then we can go away to the seaside for the rest of the summer. It'll do us all good, you and the baby and me."

"Oh, let's go to Brighton, Philip, I like Brighton, you get such a nice class of people there."

Philip had vaguely thought of some little fishing village in Cornwall, but as she spoke it occurred to him that Mildred would be bored to death there.

"I don't mind where we go as long as I get the sea."

He did not know why, but he had suddenly an irresistible longing for the sea. He wanted to bathe, and he thought with delight of splashing about in the salt water. He was a good swimmer, and nothing exhilarated him like a rough sea.

"I say, it will be jolly," he cried.

"It'll be like a honeymoon, won't it?" she said. "How much can I have for my new dress, Phil?"

Chapter 94

Philip asked Mr. Jacobs, the assistant-surgeon for whom he had dressed, to do the operation. Jacobs accepted with pleasure, since he was interested just then in neglected talipes and was getting together materials for a paper. He warned Philip that he could not make his foot like the other, but he thought he could do a good deal; and though he would always limp he would be able to wear a boot less unsightly than that which he had been accustomed to. Philip remembered how he had prayed to a God who was able to remove mountains for him who had faith, and he smiled bitterly.

"I don't expect a miracle," he answered.

"I think you're wise to let me try what I can do. You'll find a club-foot rather a handicap in practice. The layman is full of fads, and he doesn't like his doctor to have anything the matter with him."

Philip went into a "small ward," which was a room on the landing, outside each ward, reserved for special cases. He remained there a month, for the surgeon would not let him go till he could walk; and, bearing the operation very well, he had a pleasant enough time. Lawson and Athelny came to see him, and one day Mrs. Athelny brought two of her children; students whom he knew looked in now and again to have a chat; Mildred came twice a week. Everyone was very kind to him, and Philip, always surprised when anyone took trouble with him, was touched and grateful. He enjoyed the relief from care; he need not worry there about the future, neither whether his money would last out nor whether he would pass his final examinations; and he could read to his heart's content. He had not been able to read much of late, since Mildred disturbed him: she would make an aimless remark when he was trying to concentrate his attention, and would not be satisfied unless he answered; whenever he was comfortably settled down with a book she would want something done and would come to him with a cork she could not draw or a hammer to drive in a nail.

They settled to go to Brighton in August. Philip wanted to take lodgings, but Mildred said that she would have to do housekeeping, and it would only be a holiday for her if they went to a boarding-house.

"I have to see about the food every day at home; I get that sick of it I want a thorough change."

Philip agreed, and it happened that Mildred knew of a boarding-house at Kemp Town where they would not be charged more than twenty-five shillings a week each. She arranged with Philip to write about rooms, but when he got back to Kennington he found that she had done nothing. He was irritated.

"I shouldn't have thought you had so much to do as all that," he said.

"Well, I can't think of everything. It's not my fault if I forget, is it?"

Philip was so anxious to get to the sea that he would not wait to communicate with the mistress of the boarding-house.

"We'll leave the luggage at the station and go to the house and see if they've got rooms, and if they have we can just send an outside porter for our traps."

"You can please yourself," said Mildred stiffly.

She did not like being reproached, and, retiring huffily into a haughty silence, she sat by listlessly while Philip made the preparations for their departure. The little flat was hot and stuffy under the August sun, and from the road beat up a malodorous sultriness. As he lay in his bed in the small ward with its red, distempered walls he had longed for fresh air and the splashing of the sea against his breast. He felt he would go mad if he had to spend another night in London. Mildred recovered her good temper when she saw the streets of Brighton crowded with people making holiday, and they were both in high spirits as they drove out to Kemp Town. Philip stroked the baby's cheek.

"We shall get a very different colour into them when we've been down here a few days," he said, smiling.

They arrived at the boarding-house and dismissed the cab. An untidy maid opened the door and, when Philip asked if they had rooms, said she would inquire. She fetched her mistress. A middle-aged woman, stout and businesslike, came downstairs, gave them the scrutinizing glance of her profession, and asked what accommodation they required.

"Two single rooms, and if you've got such a thing, we'd rather like a cot in one of them."

"I'm afraid I haven't got that. I've got one nice large double room, and I could let you have a cot."

"I don't think that would do," said Philip.

"I could give you another room next week. Brighton's very full just now, and people have to take what they can get."

"If it were only for a few days, Philip, I think we might be able to manage," said Mildred.

"I think two rooms would be more convenient. Can you recommend any other place where they take boarders?"

"I can, but I don't suppose they'd have room any more than I have."

"Perhaps you wouldn't mind giving me the address."

The house the stout woman suggested was in the next street, and they walked towards it. Philip could walk quite well, though he had to lean on a stick, and he was rather weak. Mildred carried the baby. They went for a little in silence, and then he saw she was crying. It annoyed him, and he took no notice, but she forced his attention.

"Lend me a hanky, will you? I can't get at mine with baby," she said in a voice strangled with sobs, turning her head away from him.

He gave her his handkerchief, but said nothing. She dried her eyes, and as he did not speak, went on:

"I might be poisonous."

"Please don't make a scene in the street," he said.

"It'll look so funny insisting on separate rooms like that.

What'll they think of us?"

"If they knew the circumstances I imagine they'd think us surprisingly moral," said Philip.

She gave him a sidelong glance.

"You're not going to give it away that we're not married?" she asked quickly.

"No."

"Why won't you live with me as if we were married then?"

"My dear, I can't explain. I don't want to humiliate you, but I simply can't. I daresay it's very silly and unreasonable, but it's stronger than I am. I loved you so much that now…" he broke off. "After all, there's no accounting for that sort of thing."

"A fat lot you must have loved me!" she exclaimed.

The boarding-house to which they had been directed was kept by a bustling maiden lady, with shrewd eyes and voluble speech. They could have one double room for twenty-five shillings a week each, and five shillings extra for the baby, or they could have two single rooms for a pound a week more.

"I have to charge that much more," the woman explained apologetically, "because if I'm pushed to it I can put two beds even in the single rooms."

"I daresay that won't ruin us. What do you think, Mildred?"

"Oh, I don't mind. Anything's good enough for me," she answered.

Philip passed off her sulky reply with a laugh, and, the landlady having arranged to send for their luggage, they sat down to rest themselves. Philip's foot was hurting him a little, and he was glad to put it up on a chair.

"I suppose you don't mind my sitting in the same room with you," said Mildred aggressively.

"Don't let's quarrel, Mildred," he said gently.

"I didn't know you was so well off you could afford to throw away a pound a week."

"Don't be angry with me. I assure you it's the only way we can live together at all."

"I suppose you despise me, that's it."

"Of course I don't. Why should I?"

"It's so unnatural."

"Is it? You're not in love with me, are you?"

"Me? Who d'you take me for?"

"It's not as if you were a very passionate woman, you're not that."

"It's so humiliating," she said sulkily.

"Oh, I wouldn't fuss about that if I were you."

There were about a dozen people in the boarding-house. They ate in a narrow, dark room at a long table, at the head of which the landlady sat and carved. The food was bad. The landlady called it French cooking, by which she meant that the poor quality of the materials was disguised by ill-made sauces: plaice masqueraded as sole and New Zealand mutton as lamb. The kitchen was small and inconvenient, so that everything was served up lukewarm. The people were dull and pretentious; old ladies with elderly maiden daughters; funny old bachelors with mincing ways; pale-faced, middle-aged clerks with wives, who talked of their married daughters and their sons who were in a very good position in the Colonies. At table they discussed Miss

Corelli's latest novel; some of them liked Lord Leighton better than Mr. Alma-Tadema, and some of them liked Mr. Alma-Tadema better than Lord Leighton. Mildred soon told the ladies of her romantic marriage with Philip; and he found himself an object of interest because his family, county people in a very good position, had cut him off with a shilling because he married while he was only a stoodent; and Mildred's father, who had a large place down Devonshire way, wouldn't do anything for them because she had married Philip. That was why they had come to a boarding-house and had not a nurse for the baby; but they had to have two rooms because they were both used to a good deal of accommodation and they didn't care to be cramped. The other visitors also had explanations of their presence: one of the single gentlemen generally went to the Metropole for his holiday, but he liked cheerful company and you couldn't get that at one of those expensive hotels; and the old lady with the middle-aged daughter was having her beautiful house in London done up and she said to her daughter: "Gwennie, my dear, we must have a cheap holiday this year," and so they had come there, though of course it wasn't at all the kind of thing they were used to. Mildred found them all very superior, and she hated a lot of common, rough people. She liked gentlemen to be gentlemen in every sense of the word.

"When people are gentlemen and ladies," she said, "I like them to be gentlemen and ladies."

The remark seemed cryptic to Philip, but when he heard her say it two or three times to different persons, and found that it aroused hearty agreement, he came to the conclusion that it was only obscure to his own intelligence. It was the first time that

Philip and Mildred had been thrown entirely together. In London he did not see her all day, and when he came home the household affairs, the baby, the neighbours, gave them something to talk about till he settled down to work. Now he spent the whole day with her. After breakfast they went down to the beach; the morning went easily enough with a bathe and a stroll along the front; the evening, which they spent on the pier, having put the baby to bed, was tolerable, for there was music to listen to and a constant stream of people to look at (Philip amused himself by imagining who they were and weaving little stories about them; he had got into the habit of answering Mildred's remarks with his mouth only so that his thoughts remained undisturbed); but the afternoons were long and dreary. They sat on the beach. Mildred said they must get all the benefit they could out of Doctor Brighton, and he could not read because Mildred made observations frequently about things in general. If he paid no attention she complained.

"Oh, leave that silly old book alone. It can't be good for you always reading. You'll addle your brain, that's what you'll do, Philip."

"Oh, rot!" he answered.

"Besides, it's so unsociable."

He discovered that it was difficult to talk to her. She had not even the power of attending to what she was herself saying, so that a dog running in front of her or the passing of a man in a loud blazer would call forth a remark and then she would forget what she had been speaking of. She had a bad memory for names, and it irritated her not to be able to think of them, so that she would pause in the middle of some story to rack her brains. Sometimes she had to give it up, but it often occurred to her afterwards, and when Philip was talking of something she would interrupt him.

"Collins, that was it. I knew it would come back to me some time. Collins, that's the name I couldn't remember."

It exasperated him because it showed that she was not listening to anything he said, and yet, if he was silent, she reproached him for sulkiness. Her mind was of an order that could not deal for five minutes with the abstract, and when Philip gave way to his taste for generalizing she very quickly showed that she was bored. Mildred dreamt a great deal, and she had an accurate memory for her dreams, which she would relate every day with prolixity.

One morning he received a long letter from Thorpe Athelny. He was taking his holiday in the theatrical way, in which there was much sound sense, which characterized him. He had done the same thing for ten years. He took his whole family to a hop-field in Kent, not far from Mrs. Athelny's home, and they spent three weeks hopping. It kept them in the open air, earned them money, much to Mrs. Athelny's satisfaction, and renewed their contact with mother earth. It was upon this that Athelny laid stress. The sojourn in the fields gave them a new strength; it was like a magic ceremony, by which they renewed their youth and the power of their limbs and the sweetness of the spirit: Philip had heard him say many fantastic, rhetorical, and picturesque things on the subject. Now Athelny invited him to come over for a day, he had certain meditations on Shakespeare and the musical glasses which he desired to impart, and the children were clamouring for a sight of Uncle Philip. Philip read the letter again in the afternoon when he was sitting with Mildred on the beach. He thought of Mrs. Athelny, cheerful mother of many children, with her kindly hospitality and her good humour; of Sally, grave for her years, with funny little maternal ways and an air of authority, with her long plait of fair hair and her broad forehead; and then in a bunch of all the others, merry, boisterous, healthy, and handsome. His heart went out to them. There was one quality which they had that he did not remember to have noticed in people before, and that was goodness. It had not occurred to him till now, but it was evidently the beauty of their goodness which attracted him. In theory he did not believe in it: if morality were no more than a matter of convenience good and evil had no meaning. He did not like to be illogical, but here was simple goodness, natural and without effort, and he thought it beautiful. Meditating, he slowly tore the letter into little pieces; he did not see how he could go without Mildred, and he did not want to go with her.

It was very hot, the sky was cloudless, and they had been driven to a shady corner. The baby was gravely playing with stones on the beach, and now and then she crawled up to Philip and gave him one to hold, then took it away again and placed it carefully down. She was playing a mysterious and complicated game known only to herself. Mildred was asleep. She lay with her head thrown back and her mouth slightly open; her legs were stretched out, and her boots protruded from her petticoats in a grotesque fashion. His eyes had been resting on her vaguely, but now he looked at her with peculiar attention. He remembered how passionately he had loved her, and he wondered why now he was entirely indifferent to her. The change in him filled him with dull pain. It seemed to him that all he had suffered had been sheer waste. The touch of her hand had filled him with ecstasy; he had desired to enter into her soul so that he could share every thought with her and every feeling; he had suffered acutely because, when silence had fallen between them, a remark of hers showed how far their thoughts had travelled apart, and he had rebelled against the unsurmountable wall which seemed to divide every personality from every other. He found it strangely tragic that he had loved her so madly and now loved her not at all. Sometimes he hated her. She was incapable of learning, and the experience of life had taught her nothing. She was as unmannerly as she had always been. It revolted Philip to hear the insolence with which she treated the hard-worked servant at the boarding-house.

Presently he considered his own plans. At the end of his fourth year he would be able to take his examination in midwifery, and a year more would see him qualified. Then he might manage a journey to Spain. He wanted to see the pictures which he knew only from photographs; he felt deeply that El Greco held a secret of peculiar moment to him; and he fancied that in Toledo he would surely find it out. He did not wish to do things grandly, and on a hundred pounds he might live for six months in Spain: if Macalister put him on to another good thing he could make that easily. His heart warmed at the thought of those old beautiful cities, and the tawny plains of Castile. He was convinced that more might be got out of life than offered itself at present, and he thought that in Spain he could live with greater intensity: it might be possible to practise in one of those old cities, there were a good many foreigners, passing or resident, and he should be able to pick up a living. But that would be much later; first he must get one or two hospital appointments; they gave experience and made it easy to get jobs afterwards. He wished to get a berth as ship's doctor on one of the large tramps that took things leisurely enough for a man to see something of the places at which they stopped. He wanted to go to the East; and his fancy was rich with pictures of Bangkok and Shanghai, and the ports of Japan: he pictured to himself palm-trees and skies blue and hot, dark-skinned people, pagodas; the scents of the Orient intoxicated his nostrils. His heart beat with passionate desire for the beauty and the strangeness of the world.

Mildred awoke.

"I do believe I've been asleep," she said. "Now then, you naughty girl, what have you been doing to yourself? Her dress was clean yesterday and just look at it now, Philip."

Chapter 95

When they returned to London Philip began his dressing in the surgical wards. He was not so much interested in surgery as in medicine, which, a more empirical science, offered greater scope to the imagination. The work was a little harder than the corresponding work on the medical side. There was a lecture from nine till ten, when he went into the wards; there wounds had to be dressed, stitches taken out, bandages renewed: Philip prided himself a little on his skill in bandaging, and it amused him to wring a word of approval from a nurse. On certain afternoons in the week there were operations; and he stood in the well of the theatre, in a white jacket, ready to hand the operating surgeon any instrument he wanted or to sponge the blood away so that he could see what he was about. When some rare operation was to be performed the theatre would fill up, but generally there were not more than half a dozen students present, and then the proceedings had a cosiness which Philip enjoyed. At that time the world at large seemed to have a passion for appendicitis, and a good many cases came to the operating theatre for this complaint:

the surgeon for whom Philip dressed was in friendly rivalry with a colleague as to which could remove an appendix in the shortest time and with the smallest incision.

In due course Philip was put on accident duty. The dressers took this in turn; it lasted three days, during which they lived in hospital and ate their meals in the common room; they had a room on the ground floor near the casualty ward, with a bed that shut up during the day into a cupboard. The dresser on duty had to be at hand day and night to see to any casualty that came in. You were on the move all the time, and not more than an hour or two passed during the night without the clanging of the bell just above your head, which made you leap out of bed instinctively. Saturday night was of course the busiest time and the closing of the public houses the busiest hour. Men would be brought in by the police dead drunk and it would be necessary to administer a stomach-pump; women, rather the worse for liquor themselves, would come in with a wound on the head or a bleeding nose which their husbands had given them: some would vow to have the law on him, and others, ashamed, would declare that it had been an accident. What the dresser could manage himself he did, but if there was anything important he sent for the house-surgeon: he did this with care, since the house-surgeon was not vastly pleased to be dragged down five flights of stairs for nothing. The cases ranged from a cut finger to a cut throat. Boys came in with hands mangled by some machine, men were brought who had been knocked down by a cab, and children who had broken a limb while playing: now and then attempted suicides were carried in by the police: Philip saw a ghastly, wild-eyed man with a great gash from ear to ear, and he was in the ward for weeks afterwards in charge of a constable, silent, angry, because he was alive, and sullen; he made no secret of the fact that he would try again to kill himself as soon as he was released. The wards were crowded, and the house-surgeon was faced with a dilemma when patients were brought in by the police: if they were sent on to the station and died there disagreeable things were said in the papers; and it was very difficult sometimes to tell if a man was dying or drunk. Philip did not go to bed till he was tired out, so that he should not have the bother of getting up again in an hour; and he sat in the casualty ward talking in the intervals of work with the night-nurse. She was a grey-haired woman of masculine appearance, who had been night-nurse in the casualty department for twenty years. She liked the work because she was her own mistress and had no sister to bother her. Her movements were slow, but she was immensely capable and she never failed in an emergency. The dressers, often inexperienced or nervous, found her a tower of strength. She had seen thousands of them, and they made no impression upon her: she always called them Mr. Brown; and when they expostulated and told her their real names, she merely nodded and went on calling them Mr. Brown. It interested Philip to sit with her in the bare room, with its two horse-hair couches and the flaring gas, and listen to her. She had long ceased to look upon the people who came in as human beings; they were drunks, or broken arms, or cut throats. She took the vice and misery and cruelty of the world as a matter of course; she found nothing to praise or blame in human actions: she accepted. She had a certain grim humour.

"I remember one suicide," she said to Philip, "who threw

himself into the Thames. They fished him out and brought him here, and ten days later he developed typhoid fever from swallowing Thames water."

"Did he die?"

"Yes, he did all right. I could never make up my mind if it was suicide or not…. They're a funny lot, suicides. I remember one man who couldn't get any work to do and his wife died, so he pawned his clothes and bought a revolver; but he made a mess of it, he only shot out an eye and he got all right. And then, if you please, with an eye gone and a piece of his face blow away, he came to the conclusion that the world wasn't such a bad place after all, and he lived happily ever afterwards. Thing I've always noticed, people don't commit suicide for love, as you'd expect, that's just a fancy of novelists; they commit suicide because they haven't got any money. I wonder why that is."

"I suppose money's more important than love," suggested Philip.

Money was in any case occupying Philip's thoughts a good deal just then. He discovered the little truth there was in the airy saying, which himself had repeated, that two could live as cheaply as one, and his expenses were beginning to worry him. Mildred was not a good manager, and it cost them as much to live as if they had eaten in restaurants; the child needed clothes, and Mildred boots, an umbrella, and other small things which it was impossible for her to do without. When they returned from Brighton she had announced her intention of getting a job, but she took no definite steps, and presently a bad cold laid her up for a fortnight. When she was well she answered one or two advertisements, but nothing came of it: either she arrived too late and the vacant place was filled, or the work was more than she felt strong enough to do. Once she got an offer, but the wages were only fourteen shillings a week, and she thought she was worth more than that.

"It's no good letting oneself be put upon," she remarked. "People don't respect you if you let yourself go too cheap."

"I don't think fourteen shillings is so bad," answered Philip drily.

He could not help thinking how useful it would be towards the expenses of the household, and Mildred was already beginning to hint that she did not get a place because she had not got a decent dress to interview employers in. He gave her the dress, and she made one or two more attempts, but Philip came to the conclusion that they were not serious. She did not want to work. The only way he knew to make money was on the Stock Exchange, and he was very anxious to repeat the lucky experiment of the summer; but war had broken out with the Transvaal and nothing was doing in South Africa. Macalister told him that Redvers Buller would march into Pretoria in a month and then everything would boom. The only thing was to wait patiently. What they wanted was a British reverse to knock things down a bit, and then it might be worth while buying. Philip began reading assiduously the "city chat" of his favourite newspaper. He was worried and irritable. Once or twice he spoke sharply to Mildred, and since she was neither tactful nor patient she answered with temper, and they quarrelled. Philip always expressed his regret for what he had said, but Mildred had not a forgiving nature, and she would sulk for a couple of days. She got on his nerves in all sorts of ways; by the manner in which she ate, and by the untidiness which made her leave articles of clothing about their sitting-room: Philip was excited by the war and devoured the papers, morning and evening; but she took no interest in anything that happened. She had made the acquaintance of two or three people who lived in the street, and one of them had asked if she would like the curate to call on her. She wore a wedding-ring and called herself Mrs. Carey. On Philip's walls were two or three of the drawings which he had made in Paris, nudes, two of women and one of Miguel Ajuria, standing very square on his feet, with clenched fists. Philip kept them because they were the best things he had done, and they reminded him of happy days. Mildred had long looked at them with disfavour.

"I wish you'd take those drawings down, Philip," she said to him at last. "Mrs. Foreman, of number thirteen, came in yesterday afternoon, and I didn't know which way to look. I saw her staring at them."

"What's the matter with them?"

"They're indecent. Disgusting, that's what I call it, to have drawings of naked people about. And it isn't nice for baby either. She's beginning to notice things now."

"How can you be so vulgar?"

"Vulgar? Modest, I call it. I've never said anything, but d'you think I like having to look at those naked people all day long."

"Have you no sense of humour at all, Mildred?" he asked frigidly.

"I don't know what sense of humour's got to do with it. I've got a good mind to take them down myself. If you want to know what I think about them, I think they're disgusting."

"I don't want to know what you think about them, and I forbid you to touch them."

When Mildred was cross with him she punished him through the baby. The little girl was as fond of Philip as he was of her, and it was her great pleasure every morning to crawl into his room (she was getting on for two now and could walk pretty well), and be taken up into his bed. When Mildred stopped this the poor child would cry bitterly. To Philip's remonstrances she replied:

"I don't want her to get into habits."

And if then he said anything more she said:

"It's nothing to do with you what I do with my child. To hear you talk one would think you was her father. I'm her mother, and I ought to know what's good for her, oughtn't I?"

Philip was exasperated by Mildred's stupidity; but he was so indifferent to her now that it was only at times she made him angry. He grew used to having her about. Christmas came, and with it a couple of days' holiday for Philip. He brought some holly in and decorated the flat, and on Christmas Day he gave small presents to Mildred and the baby. There were only two of them, so they could not have a turkey, but Mildred roasted a chicken and boiled a Christmas pudding which she had bought at a local grocer's. They stood themselves a bottle of wine. When they had dined Philip sat in his armchair by the fire, smoking his pipe; and the unaccustomed wine had made him forget for a while the anxiety about money which was so constantly with him. He felt happy and comfortable. Presently Mildred came in to tell him that the baby wanted him to kiss her good night, and with a smile he went into Mildred's bedroom. Then, telling the child to go to sleep, he turned down the gas and, leaving the door open in case she cried, went back into the sitting-room.

"Where are you going to sit?" he asked Mildred.

"You sit in your chair. I'm going to sit on the floor."

When he sat down she settled herself in front of the fire and leaned against his knees. He could not help remembering that this was how they had sat together in her rooms in the Vauxhall Bridge Road, but the positions had been reversed; it was he who had sat on the floor and leaned his head against her knee. How passionately he had loved her then! Now he felt for her a tenderness he had not known for a long time. He seemed still to feel twined round his neck the baby's soft little arms.

"Are you comfy?" he asked.

She looked up at him, gave a slight smile, and nodded. They gazed into the fire dreamily, without speaking to one another. At last she turned round and stared at him curiously.

"D'you know that you haven't kissed me once since I came here?" she said suddenly.

"D'you want me to?" he smiled.

"I suppose you don't care for me in that way any more?"

"I'm very fond of you."

"You're much fonder of baby."

He did not answer, and she laid her cheek against his hand.

"You're not angry with me any more?" she asked presently, with her eyes cast down.

"Why on earth should I be?"

"I've never cared for you as I do now. It's only since I passed through the fire that I've learnt to love you."

It chilled Philip to hear her make use of the sort of phrase she read in the penny novelettes which she devoured. Then he wondered whether what she said had any meaning for her: perhaps she knew no other way to express her genuine feelings than the stilted language of *The Family Herald*.

"It seems so funny our living together like this."

He did not reply for quite a long time, and silence fell upon them again; but at last he spoke and seemed conscious of no interval.

"You mustn't be angry with me. One can't help these things. I remember that I thought you wicked and cruel because you did this, that, and the other; but it was very silly of me. You didn't love me, and it was absurd to blame you for that. I thought I could make you love me, but I know now that was impossible. I don't know what it is that makes someone love you, but whatever it is, it's the only thing that matters, and if it isn't there you won't create it by kindness, or generosity, or anything of that sort."

"I should have thought if you'd loved me really you'd have loved me still."

"I should have thought so too. I remember how I used to think that it would last for ever; I felt I would rather die than be without you, and I used to long for the time when you would be faded and wrinkled so that nobody cared for you any more and I should have you all to myself."

She did not answer, and presently she got up and said she was going to bed. She gave a timid little smile.

"It's Christmas Day, Philip, won't you kiss me good night?"

He gave a laugh, blushed slightly, and kissed her. She went to her bedroom and he began to read.

Chapter 96

The climax came two or three weeks later. Mildred was driven by Philip's behaviour to a pitch of strange exasperation. There were many different emotions in her soul, and she passed from mood to mood with facility. She spent a great deal of time alone and brooded over her position. She did not put all her feelings into words, she did not even know what they were, but certain things stood out in her mind, and she thought of them over and over again. She had never understood Philip, nor had very much liked him; but she was pleased to have him about her because she thought he was a gentleman. She was impressed because his father had been a doctor and his uncle was a clergyman. She despised him a little because she had made such a fool of him, and at the same time was never quite comfortable in his presence; she could not let herself go, and she felt that he was criticizing her manners.

When she first came to live in the little rooms in Kennington she was tired out and ashamed. She was glad to be left alone. It was a comfort to think that there was no rent to pay; she need not go out in all weathers, and she could lie quietly in bed if she did not feel well. She had hated the life she led. It was horrible to have to be affable and subservient; and even now when it crossed her mind she cried with pity for herself as she thought of the roughness of men and their brutal language. But it crossed her mind very seldom. She was grateful to Philip for coming to her rescue, and when she remembered how honestly he had loved her and how badly she had treated him, she felt a pang of remorse. It was easy to make it up to him. It meant very little to her. She was surprised when he refused her suggestion, but she shrugged her shoulders: let him put on airs if he liked, she did not care, he would be anxious enough in a little while, and then it would be her turn to refuse; if he thought it was any deprivation to her he was very much mistaken. She had no doubt of her power over him. He was peculiar, but she knew him through and through. He had so often quarrelled with her and sworn he would never see her again, and then in a little while he had come on his knees begging to be forgiven. It gave her a thrill to think how he had cringed before her. He would have been glad to lie down on the ground for her to walk on him. She had seen him cry. She knew exactly how to treat him, pay no attention to him, just pretend you didn't notice his tempers, leave him severely alone, and in a little while he was sure to grovel. She laughed a little to herself, good-humouredly, when she thought how he had come and eaten dirt before her. She had had her fling now. She knew what men were and did not want to have anything more to do with them. She was quite ready to settle down with Philip. When all was said, he was a gentleman in every sense of the word, and that was something not to be sneezed at, wasn't it? Anyhow, she was in no hurry, and she was not going to take the first step. She was glad to see how fond he was growing of the baby, though it tickled her a good deal; it was comic that he should set so much store on another man's child. He *was* peculiar and no mistake.

But one or two things surprised her. She had been used to his subservience: he was only too glad to do anything for her in the old days, she was accustomed to see him cast down by a cross word and in ecstasy at a kind one; he was different now, and she said to herself that he had not improved in the last year. It never struck her for a moment that there could be any change in his feelings, and she thought it was only acting when he paid no heed to her bad temper. He wanted to read sometimes and told her to stop talking: she did not know whether to flare up or to sulk, and was so puzzled that she did neither. Then came the conversation in which he told her that he intended their relations to be platonic, and, remembering an incident of their common past, it occurred to her that he dreaded the possibility of her being pregnant. She took pains to reassure him. It made no difference. She was the sort of woman who was unable to realize that a man might not have her own obsession with sex; her relations with men had been purely on those lines; and she could not understand that they ever had other interests. The thought struck her that Philip was in love with somebody else, and she watched him, suspecting nurses at the hospital or people he met out; but artful questions led her to the conclusion that there was no one dangerous in the Athelny household; and it forced itself upon her also that Philip, like most medical students, was unconscious of the sex of the nurses with whom his work threw him in contact. They were associated in his mind with a faint odour of iodoform. Philip received no letters, and there was no girl's photograph among his belongings. If he was in love with someone, he was very clever at hiding it; and he answered all Mildred's questions with frankness and apparently without suspicion that there was any motive in them.

"I don't believe he's in love with anybody else," she said to herself at last.

It was a relief, for in that case he was certainly still in love with her; but it made his behaviour very puzzling. If he was going to treat her like that, why did he ask her to come and live at the flat? It was unnatural. Mildred was not a woman who conceived the possibility of compassion, generosity, or kindness. Her only conclusion was that Philip was queer. She took it into her head that the reasons for his conduct were chivalrous; and, her imagination filled with the extravagances of cheap fiction, she pictured to herself all sorts of romantic explanations for his delicacy. Her fancy ran riot with bitter misunderstandings, purifications by fire, snow-white souls, and death in the cruel cold of a Christmas night. She made up her mind that when they went to Brighton she would put an end to all his nonsense; they would be alone there, everyone would think them husband and wife, and there would be the pier and the band. When she found that nothing would induce Philip to share the same room with her, when he spoke to her about it with a tone in his voice she had never heard before, she suddenly realized that he did not want her. She was astounded. She remembered all he had said in the past and how desperately he had loved her. She felt humiliated and angry, but she had a sort of native insolence which carried her through. He needn't think she was in love with him, because she wasn't. She hated him sometimes, and she longed to humble him; but she found herself singularly powerless; she did not know which way to handle him. She began to be a little nervous with him. Once or twice she cried. Once or twice she set herself to be particularly nice to him; but when she took his arm while they walked along the front at night he made some excuse in a while to release himself, as though it were unpleasant for him to be touched by her. She could not make it out. The only hold she had over him was through the baby, of whom he seemed to grow fonder and fonder: she could make him white with anger by giving the child a slap or a push; and the only time the old, tender smile came back into his eyes was when she stood with the baby in her arms. She noticed it when she was being photographed like that by a man on the beach, and afterwards she often stood in the same way for Philip to look at her.

When they got back to London Mildred began looking for the work she had asserted was so easy to find; she wanted now to be independent of Philip; and she thought of the satisfaction with which she would announce to him that she was going into rooms and would take the child with her. But her heart failed her when she came into closer contact with the possibility. She had grown unused to the long hours, she did not want to be at the beck and call of a manageress, and her dignity revolted at the thought of wearing once more a uniform. She had made out to such of the neighbours as she knew that they were comfortably off: it would be a come-down if they heard that she had to go out and work. Her natural indolence asserted itself. She did not want to leave

Philip, and so long as he was willing to provide for her, she did not see why she should. There was no money to throw away, but she got her board and lodging, and he might get better off. His uncle was an old man and might die any day, he would come into a little then, and even as things were, it was better than slaving from morning till night for a few shillings a week. Her efforts relaxed; she kept on reading the advertisement columns of the daily paper merely to show that she wanted to do something if anything that was worth her while presented itself. But panic seized her, and she was afraid that Philip would grow tired of supporting her. She had no hold over him at all now, and she fancied that he only allowed her to stay there because he was fond of the baby. She brooded over it all, and she thought to herself angrily that she would make him pay for all this some day. She could not reconcile herself to the fact that he no longer cared for her. She would make him. She suffered from pique, and sometimes in a curious fashion she desired Philip. He was so cold now that it exasperated her. She thought of him in that way incessantly. She thought that he was treating her very badly, and she did not know what she had done to deserve it. She kept on saying to herself that it was unnatural they should live like that. Then she thought that if things were different and she were going to have a baby, he would be sure to marry her. He was funny, but he was a gentleman in every sense of the word, no one could deny that. At last it became an obsession with her, and she made up her mind to force a change in their relations. He never even kissed her now, and she wanted him to: she remembered how ardently he had been used to press her lips. It gave her a curious feeling to think of it. She often looked at his mouth.

One evening, at the beginning of February, Philip told her that he was dining with Lawson, who was giving a party in his studio to celebrate his birthday; and he would not be in till late; Lawson had bought a couple of bottles of the punch they favoured from the tavern in Beak Street, and they proposed to have a merry evening. Mildred asked if there were going to be women there, but Philip told her there were not; only men had been invited; and they were just going to sit and talk and smoke: Mildred did not think it sounded very amusing; if she were a painter she would have half a dozen models about. She went to bed, but could not sleep, and presently an idea struck her; she got up and fixed the catch on the wicket at the landing, so that Philip could not get in. He came back about one, and she heard him curse when he found that the wicket was closed. She got out of bed and opened.

"Why on earth did you shut yourself in? I'm sorry I've dragged you out of bed."

"I left it open on purpose, I can't think how it came to be shut."

"Hurry up and get back to bed, or you'll catch cold."

He walked into the sitting-room and turned up the gas. She followed him in. She went up to the fire.

"I want to warm my feet a bit. They're like ice."

He sat down and began to take off his boots. His eyes were shining and his cheeks were flushed. She thought he had been drinking.

"Have you been enjoying yourself?" she asked, with a smile.

"Yes, I've had a ripping time."

Philip was quite sober, but he had been talking and laughing, and he was excited still. An evening of that sort reminded him of the old days in Paris. He was in high spirits. He took his pipe out of his pocket and filled it.

"Aren't you going to bed?" she asked.

"Not yet, I'm not a bit sleepy. Lawson was in great form. He talked sixteen to the dozen from the moment I got there till the moment I left."

"What did you talk about?"

"Heaven knows! Of every subject under the sun. You should have seen us all shouting at the tops of our voices and nobody listening."

Philip laughed with pleasure at the recollection, and Mildred laughed too. She was pretty sure he had drunk more than was good for him. That was exactly what she had expected. She knew men.

"Can I sit down?" she said.

Before he could answer she settled herself on his knees.

"If you're not going to bed you'd better go and put on a dressing-gown."

"Oh, I'm all right as I am." Then putting her arms round his neck, she placed her face against his and said: "Why are you so horrid to me, Phil?"

He tried to get up, but she would not let him.

"I do love you, Philip," she said.

"Don't talk damned rot."

"It isn't, it's true. I can't live without you. I want you."

He released himself from her arms.

"Please get up. You're making a fool of yourself and you're making me feel a perfect idiot."

"I love you, Philip. I want to make up for all the harm I did you. I can't go on like this, it's not in human nature."

He slipped out of the chair and left her in it.

"I'm very sorry, but it's too late."

She gave a heart-rending sob.

"But why? How can you be so cruel?"

"I suppose it's because I loved you too much. I wore the passion out. The thought of anything of that sort horrifies me. I can't look at you now without thinking of Emil and Griffiths. One can't help those things. I suppose it's just nerves."

She seized his hand and covered it with kisses.

"Don't," he cried.

She sank back into the chair.

"I can't go on like this. If you won't love me, I'd rather go away."

"Don't be foolish, you haven't anywhere to go. You can stay here as long as you like, but it must be on the definite understanding that we're friends and nothing more."

Then she dropped suddenly the vehemence of passion and gave a soft, insinuating laugh. She sidled up to Philip and put her arms round him. She made her voice low and wheedling.

"Don't be such an old silly. I believe you're nervous. You don't know how nice I can be."

She put her face against his and rubbed his cheek with hers. To Philip her smile was an abominable leer, and the suggestive glitter of her eyes filled him with horror. He drew back instinctively.

"I won't," he said.

But she would not let him go. She sought his mouth with her lips. He took her hands and tore them roughly apart and pushed her away.

"You disgust me," he said.

"Me?"

She steadied herself with one hand on the chimney-piece. She looked at him for an instant, and two red spots suddenly appeared on her cheeks. She gave a shrill, angry laugh.

"I disgust *you*."

She paused and drew in her breath sharply. Then she burst into a furious torrent of abuse. She shouted at the top of her voice. She called him every foul name she could think of. She used language so obscene that Philip was astounded; she was always so anxious to be refined, so shocked by coarseness, that it had never occurred to him that she knew the words she used now. She came up to him and thrust her face in his. It was distorted with passion, and in her tumultuous speech the spittle dribbled over her lips.

"I never cared for you, not once, I was making a fool of you always, you bored me, you bored me stiff, and I hated you, I would never have let you touch me only for the money, and it used to make me sick when I had to let you kiss me. We laughed at you, Griffiths and me, we laughed because you was such a mug. A mug! A mug!"

Then she burst again into abominable invective. She accused him of every mean fault; she said he was stingy, she said he was dull, she said he was vain, selfish; she cast virulent ridicule on everything upon which he was most sensitive. And at last she turned to go. She kept on, with hysterical violence, shouting at him an opprobrious, filthy epithet. She seized the handle of the door and flung it open. Then she turned round and hurled at him the injury which she knew was the only one that really touched him. She threw into the word all the malice and all the venom of which she was capable. She flung it at him as though it were a blow.

"Cripple!"

Chapter 97

Philip awoke with a start next morning, conscious that it was late, and looking at his watch found it was nine o'clock. He jumped out of bed and went into the kitchen to get himself some hot water to shave with. There was no sign of Mildred, and the things which she had used for her supper the night before still lay in the sink unwashed. He knocked at her door.

"Wake up, Mildred. It's awfully late."

She did not answer, even after a second louder knocking, and he concluded that she was sulking. He was in too great a hurry to bother about that. He put some water on to boil and jumped into his bath, which was always poured out the night before in order to take the chill off. He presumed that Mildred would cook his breakfast while he was dressing and leave it in the sitting-room. She had done that two or three times when she was out of temper. But he heard no sound of her moving, and realized that if he wanted anything to eat he would have to get it himself. He was irritated that she should play him such a trick on a morning when he had overslept himself. There was still no sign of her when he was ready, but he heard her moving about her room. She was evidently getting up. He made himself some tea and cut himself a couple of pieces of bread and butter, which he ate while he was putting on his boots, then bolted downstairs and along the street into the main road to catch his tram. While his eyes sought out the newspaper shops to see the war news on the placards, he thought of the scene of the night before: now that it was over and he had slept on it, he could not help thinking it grotesque; he supposed he had been ridiculous, but he was not master of his feelings; at the time they had been overwhelming. He was angry with Mildred because she had forced him into that absurd position, and then with renewed astonishment he thought of her outburst and the filthy language she had used. He could not help flushing when he remembered her final jibe; but he shrugged his shoulders contemptuously. He had long known that when his fellows were angry with him they never failed to taunt him with his deformity. He had seen men at the hospital imitate his walk, not before him as they used at school, but when they thought he was not looking. He knew now that they did it from no wilful unkindness, but because man is naturally an imitative animal, and because it was an easy way to make people laugh: he knew it, but he could never resign himself to it.

He was glad to throw himself into his work. The ward seemed pleasant and friendly when he entered it. The sister greeted him with a quick, businesslike smile.

"You're very late, Mr. Carey."

"I was out on the loose last night."

"You look it."

"Thank you."

Laughing, he went to the first of his cases, a boy with tuberculous ulcers, and removed his bandages. The boy was pleased to see him, and Philip chaffed him as he put a clean dressing on the wound. Philip was a favourite with the patients; he treated them good-humouredly; and he had gentle, sensitive hands which did not hurt them: some of the dressers were a little rough and happy-go-lucky in their methods. He lunched with his friends in the club-room, a frugal meal consisting of a scone and butter, with a cup of cocoa, and they talked of the war. Several men were going out, but the authorities were particular and refused everyone who had not had a hospital appointment. Someone suggested that, if the war went on, in a while they would be glad to take anyone who was qualified; but the general opinion was that it would be over in a month. Now that Roberts was there things would get all right in no time. This was Macalister's opinion too, and he had told Philip that they must watch their chance and buy just before peace was declared. There would be a boom then, and they might all make a bit of money. Philip had left with Macalister instructions to buy him stock whenever the opportunity presented itself. His appetite had been whetted by the thirty pounds he had made in the summer, and he wanted now to make a couple of hundred.

He finished his day's work and got on a tram to go back to Kennington. He wondered how Mildred would behave that evening. It was a nuisance to think that she would probably be surly and refuse to answer his questions. It was a warm evening for the time of year, and even in those grey streets of South London there was the languor of February; nature is restless then after the long winter months, growing things awake from their sleep, and there is a rustle in the earth, a forerunner of spring, as it resumes its eternal activities. Philip would have liked to drive on further, it was distasteful to him to go back to his rooms, and he wanted the air; but the desire to see the child clutched suddenly at his heart strings, and he smiled to himself as he thought of her toddling towards him with a crow of delight. He was surprised, when he reached the house and looked up mechanically at the windows, to see that there was no light. He went upstairs and knocked, but got no answer. When Mildred went out she left the key under the mat and he found it there now. He let himself in and going into the sitting-room struck a match. Something had happened, he did not at once know what; he turned the gas on full and lit it; the room was suddenly filled with the glare and he looked round. He gasped. The whole place was wrecked. Everything in it had been wilfully destroyed. Anger seized him, and he rushed into Mildred's room. It was dark and empty. When he had got a light he saw that she had taken away all her things and the baby's (he had noticed on entering that the go-cart was not in its usual place on the landing, but thought Mildred had taken the baby out); and all the things on the washing-stand had been broken, a knife had been drawn cross-ways through the seats of the two chairs, the pillow had been slit open, there were large gashes in the sheets and the counterpane, the looking-glass appeared to have been broken with a hammer. Philip was bewildered. He went into his own room, and here too everything was in confusion. The basin and the ewer had been smashed, the looking-glass was in fragments, and the sheets were in ribands. Mildred had made a slit large enough to put her hand into the pillow and had scattered the feathers about the room. She had jabbed a knife into the blankets. On the dressing-table were photographs of Philip's mother, the frames had been smashed and the glass shivered. Philip went into the tiny kitchen. Everything that was breakable was broken, glasses, pudding-basins, plates, dishes.

It took Philip's breath away. Mildred had left no letter, nothing but this ruin to mark her anger, and he could imagine the set face with which she had gone about her work. He went back into the sitting-room and looked about him. He was so astonished that he no longer felt angry. He looked curiously at the kitchen-knife and the coal-hammer, which were lying on the table where she had left them. Then his eye caught a large carving-knife in the fireplace which had been broken. It must have taken her a long time to do so much damage. Lawson's portrait of him had been cut cross-ways and gaped hideously. His own drawings had been ripped in pieces; and the photographs, Manet's *Olympia* and the *Odalisque* of Ingres, the portrait of Philip IV, had been smashed with great blows of the coal-hammer. There were gashes in the table-cloth and in the curtains and in the two armchairs. They were quite ruined. On one wall over the table which Philip used as his desk was the little bit of Persian rug which Cronshaw had given him. Mildred had always hated it.

"If it's a rug it ought to go on the floor," she said, "and it's a dirty stinking bit of stuff, that's all it is."

It made her furious because Philip told her it contained the answer to a great riddle. She thought he was making fun of her. She had drawn the knife right through it three times, it must have required some strength, and it hung now in tatters. Philip had two or three blue and white plates, of no value, but he had bought them one by one for very small sums and liked them for their associations. They littered the floor in fragments. There were long gashes on the backs of his books, and she had taken the trouble to tear pages out of the unbound French ones. The little ornaments on the chimney-piece lay on the hearth in bits. Everything that it had been possible to destroy with a knife or a hammer was destroyed.

The whole of Philip's belongings would not have sold for thirty pounds, but most of them were old friends, and he was a domestic creature, attached to all those odds and ends because they were his; he had been proud of his little home, and on so little money had made it pretty and characteristic. He sank down now in despair. He asked himself how she could have been so cruel. A sudden fear got him on his feet again and into the passage, where stood a cupboard in which he kept his clothes. He opened it and gave a sigh of relief. She had apparently forgotten it and none of his things was touched.

He went back into the sitting-room and, surveying the scene, wondered what to do; he had not the heart to begin trying to set things straight; besides there was no food in the house, and he was hungry. He went out and got himself something to eat. When he came in he was cooler. A little pang seized him as he thought of the child, and he wondered whether she would miss him, at first perhaps, but in a week she would have forgotten him; and he was thankful to be rid of Mildred. He did not think of her with wrath, but with an overwhelming sense of boredom.

"I hope to God I never see her again," he said aloud.

The only thing now was to leave the rooms, and he made up his mind to give notice the next morning. He could not afford to make good the damage done, and he had so little money left that he must find cheaper lodgings still. He would be glad to get out of them. The expense had worried him, and now the recollection of Mildred would be in them always. Philip was impatient and could never rest till he had put in action the plan which he had in mind; so on the following afternoon he got in a dealer in second-hand furniture who offered him three pounds for all his goods damaged and undamaged; and two days later he moved into the house opposite the hospital in which he had had rooms when first he became a medical student. The landlady was a very decent woman. He took a bedroom at the top, which she let him have for six shillings a week; it was small and shabby and looked on the yard of the house that backed on to it, but he had nothing now except his clothes and a box of books, and he was glad to lodge so cheaply.

Chapter 98

And now it happened that the fortunes of Philip Carey, of no consequence to any but himself, were affected by the events through which his country was passing. History was being made, and the process was so significant that it seemed absurd it should touch the life of an obscure medical student. Battle after battle, Magersfontein, Colenso, Spion Kop, lost on the playing fields of Eton, had humiliated the nation and dealt the death-blow to the prestige of the aristocracy and gentry who till then had found no one seriously to oppose their assertion that they possessed a natural instinct of government. The old order was being swept away: history was being made indeed. Then the colossus put forth his strength, and, blundering again, at last blundered into the semblance of victory. Cronje surrendered at Paardeberg, Ladysmith was relieved, and at the beginning of March Lord Roberts marched into Bloemfontein.

It was two or three days after the news of this reached London that Macalister came into the tavern in Beak Street and announced joyfully that things were looking brighter on the Stock

Exchange. Peace was in sight, Roberts would march into Pretoria within a few weeks, and shares were going up already. There was bound to be a boom.

"Now's the time to come in," he told Philip. "It's no good waiting till the public gets on to it. It's now or never."

He had inside information. The manager of a mine in South Africa had cabled to the senior partner of his firm that the plant was uninjured. They would start working again as soon as possible. It wasn't a speculation, it was an investment. To show how good a thing the senior partner thought it Macalister told Philip that he had bought five hundred shares for both his sisters; he never put them into anything that wasn't as safe as the Bank of England.

"I'm going to put my shirt on it myself," he said.

The shares were two and an eighth to a quarter. He advised Philip not to be greedy, but to be satisfied with a ten-shilling rise. He was buying three hundred for himself and suggested that Philip should do the same. He would hold them and sell when he thought fit. Philip had great faith in him, partly because he was a Scotsman and therefore by nature cautious, and partly because he had been right before. He jumped at the suggestion.

"I daresay we shall be able to sell before the account," said Macalister, "but if not, I'll arrange to carry them over for you."

It seemed a capital system to Philip. You held on till you got your profit, and you never even had to put your hand in your pocket. He began to watch the Stock Exchange columns of the paper with new interest. Next day everything was up a little, and Macalister wrote to say that he had had to pay two and a quarter for the shares. He said that the market was firm. But in a day or two there was a set-back. The news that came from South Africa was less reassuring, and Philip with anxiety saw that his shares had fallen to two; but Macalister was optimistic, the Boers couldn't hold out much longer, and he was willing to bet a top-hat that Roberts would march into Johannesburg before the middle of April. At the account Philip had to pay out nearly forty pounds. It worried him considerably, but he felt that the only course was to hold on: in his circumstances the loss was too great for him to pocket. For two or three weeks nothing happened; the Boers would not understand that they were beaten and nothing remained for them but to surrender: in fact they had one or two small successes, and Philip's shares fell half a crown more. It became evident that the war was not finished. There was a lot of selling. When Macalister saw Philip he was pessimistic.

"I'm not sure if the best thing wouldn't be to cut the loss. I've been paying out about as much as I want to in differences."

Philip was sick with anxiety. He could not sleep at night; he bolted his breakfast, reduced now to tea and bread and butter, in order to get over to the club reading-room and see the paper; sometimes the news was bad, and sometimes there was no news at all, but when the shares moved it was to go down. He did not know what to do. If he sold now he would lose altogether hard on three hundred and fifty pounds; and that would leave him only eighty pounds to go on with. He wished with all his heart that he had never been such a fool as to dabble on the Stock Exchange, but the only thing was to hold on; something decisive might happen any day and the shares would go up; he did not hope now for a profit, but he wanted to make good his loss. It was his only chance of finishing his course at the hospital. The Summer session was beginning in May, and at the end of it he meant to take the examination in midwifery. Then he would only have a year more; he reckoned it out carefully and came to the conclusion that he could manage it, fees and all, on a hundred and fifty pounds; but that was the least it could possibly be done on.

Early in April he went to the tavern in Beak Street anxious to see Macalister. It eased him a little to discuss the situation with him; and to realize that numerous people beside himself were suffering from loss of money made his own trouble a little less intolerable. But when Philip arrived no one was there but Hayward, and no sooner had Philip seated himself than he said:

"I'm sailing for the Cape on Sunday."

"Are you!" exclaimed Philip.

Hayward was the last person he would have expected to do anything of the kind. At the hospital men were going out now in numbers; the Government was glad to get anyone who was qualified; and others, going out as troopers, wrote home that they had been put on hospital work as soon as it was learned that they were medical students. A wave of patriotic feeling had swept over the country, and volunteers were coming from all ranks of society.

"What are you going as?" asked Philip.

"Oh, in the Dorset Yeomanry. I'm going as a trooper."

Philip had known Hayward for eight years. The youthful intimacy which had come from Philip's enthusiastic admiration for the man who could tell him of art and literature had long since vanished; but habit had taken its place; and when Hayward was in London they saw one another once or twice a week. He still talked about books with a delicate appreciation. Philip was not yet tolerant, and sometimes Hayward's conversation irritated him. He no longer believed implicitly that nothing in the world was of consequence but art. He resented Hayward's contempt for action and success. Philip, stirring his punch, thought of his early friendship and his ardent expectation that Hayward would do great things; it was long since he had lost all such illusions, and he knew now that Hayward would never do anything but talk. He found his three hundred a year more difficult to live on now that he was thirty-five than he had when he was a young man; and his clothes, though still made by a good tailor, were worn a good deal longer than at one time he would have thought possible. He was too stout, and no artful arrangement of his fair hair could conceal the fact that he was bald. His blue eyes were dull and pale. It was not hard to guess that he drank too much.

"What on earth made you think of going out to the Cape?" asked Philip.

"Oh, I don't know, I thought I ought to."

Philip was silent. He felt rather silly. He understood that Hayward was being driven by an uneasiness in his soul which he could not account for. Some power within him made it seem necessary to go and fight for his country. It was strange, since he considered patriotism no more than a prejudice, and, flattering himself on his cosmopolitanism, he had looked upon England as a place of exile. His countrymen in the mass wounded his susceptibilities. Philip wondered what it was that made people do things which were so contrary to all their theories of life. It would have been reasonable for Hayward to stand aside and watch with a smile while the barbarians slaughtered one another. It looked as though men were puppets in the hands of an unknown force, which drove them to do this and that; and sometimes they used their reason to justify their actions; and when this was impossible they did the actions in despite of reason.

"People are very extraordinary," said Philip. "I should never have expected you to go out as a trooper."

Hayward smiled, slightly embarrassed, and said nothing.

"I was examined yesterday," he remarked at last. "It was worth while undergoing the *gêne* of it to know that one was perfectly fit."

Philip noticed that he still used a French word in an affected way when an English one would have served. But just then Macalister came in.

"I wanted to see you, Carey," he said. "My people don't feel inclined to hold those shares any more, the market's in such an awful state, and they want you to take them up."

Philip's heart sank. He knew that was impossible. It meant that he must accept the loss. His pride made him answer calmly.

"I don't know that I think that's worth while. You'd better sell them."

"It's all very fine to say that, I'm not sure if I can. The market's stagnant, there are no buyers."

"But they're marked down at one and an eighth."

"Oh yes, but that doesn't mean anything. You can't get that for them."

Philip did not say anything for a moment. He was trying to

collect himself.

"D'you mean to say they're worth nothing at all?"

"Oh, I don't say that. Of course they're worth something, but you see, nobody's buying them now."

"Then you must just sell them for what you can get."

Macalister looked at Philip narrowly. He wondered whether he was very hard hit.

"I'm awfully sorry, old man, but we're all in the same boat. No one thought the war was going to hang on this way. I put you into them, but I was in myself, too."

"It doesn't matter at all," said Philip. "One has to take one's chance."

He moved back to the table from which he had got up to talk to Macalister. He was dumbfounded; his head suddenly began to ache furiously; but he did not want them to think him unmanly. He sat on for an hour. He laughed feverishly at everything they said. At last he got up to go.

"You take it pretty coolly," said Macalister, shaking hands with him. "I don't suppose anyone likes losing between three and four hundred pounds."

When Philip got back to his shabby little room he flung himself on his bed, and gave himself over to his despair. He kept on regretting his folly bitterly; and though he told himself that it was absurd to regret, for what had happened was inevitable just because it had happened, he could not help himself. He was utterly miserable. He could not sleep. He remembered all the ways he had wasted money during the last few years. His head ached dreadfully.

The following evening there came by the last post the statement of his account. He examined his passbook. He found that when he had paid everything he would have seven pounds left. Seven pounds! He was thankful he had been able to pay. It would have been horrible to be obliged to confess to Macalister that he had not the money. He was dressing in the eye-department during the summer session, and he had bought an ophthalmoscope off a student who had one to sell. He had not paid for this, but he lacked the courage to tell the student that he wanted to go back on his bargain. Also he had to buy certain books. He had about five pounds to go on with. It lasted him six weeks; then he wrote to his uncle a letter which he thought very businesslike; he said that owing to the war he had had grave losses and could not go on with his studies unless his uncle came to his help. He suggested that the Vicar should lend him a hundred and fifty pounds paid over the next eighteen months in monthly instalments; he would pay interest on this and promised to refund the capital by degrees when he began to earn money. He would be qualified in a year and a half at the latest, and he could be pretty sure then of getting an assistantship at three pounds a week. His uncle wrote back that he could do nothing. It was not fair to ask him to sell out when everything was at its worst, and the little he had he felt that his duty to himself made it necessary for him to keep in case of illness. He ended the letter with a little homily. He had warned Philip time after time, and Philip had never paid any attention to him; he could not honestly say he was surprised; he had long expected that this would be the end of Philip's extravagance and want of balance. Philip grew hot and cold when he read this. It had never occurred to him that his uncle would refuse, and he burst into furious anger; but this was succeeded by utter blankness: if his uncle would not help him he could not go on at the hospital. Panic seized him and, putting aside his pride, he wrote again to the Vicar of Blackstable, placing the case before him more urgently; but perhaps he did not explain himself properly and his uncle did not realize in what desperate straits he was, for he answered that he could not change his mind; Philip was twenty-five and really ought to be earning his living. When he died Philip would come into a little, but till then he refused to give him a penny. Philip felt in the letter the satisfaction of a man who for many years had disapproved of his courses and now saw himself justified.

Chapter 99

Philip began to pawn his clothes. He reduced his expenses by eating only one meal a day beside his breakfast; and he ate it, bread and butter and cocoa, at four so that it should last him till next morning. He was so hungry by nine o'clock that he had to go to bed. He thought of borrowing money from Lawson, but the fear of a refusal held him back; at last he asked him for five pounds. Lawson lent it with pleasure, but, as he did so, said:

"You'll let me have it back in a week or so, won't you? I've got to pay my framer, and I'm awfully broke just now."

Philip knew he would not be able to return it, and the thought of what Lawson would think made him so ashamed that in a couple of days he took the money back untouched. Lawson was just going out to luncheon and asked Philip to come too. Philip could hardly eat, he was so glad to get some solid food. On Sunday he was sure of a good dinner from Athelny. He hesitated to tell the Athelnys what had happened to him: they had always looked upon him as comparatively well-to-do, and he had a dread that they would think less well of him if they knew he was penniless.

Though he had always been poor, the possibility of not having enough to eat had never occurred to him; it was not the sort of thing that happened to the people among whom he lived; and he was as ashamed as if he had some disgraceful disease. The situation in which he found himself was quite outside the range of his experience. He was so taken aback that he did not know what else to do than to go on at the hospital; he had a vague hope that something would turn up; he could not quite believe that what was happening to him was true; and he remembered how during his first term at school he had often thought his life was a dream from which he would awake to find himself once more at home. But very soon he foresaw that in a week or so he would have no money at all. He must set about trying to earn something at once. If he had been qualified, even with a club-foot, he could have gone out to the Cape, since the demand for medical men was now great. Except for his deformity he might have enlisted in one of the Yeomanry regiments which were constantly being sent out. He went to the secretary of the Medical School and asked if he could give him the coaching of some backward student; but the secretary held out no hope of getting him anything of the sort. Philip read the advertisement columns of the medical papers, and he applied for the post of unqualified assistant to a man who had a dispensary in the Fulham Road. When he went to see him, he saw the doctor glance at his club-foot; and on hearing that Philip was only in his fourth year at the hospital he said at once that his experience was insufficient: Philip understood that this was only an excuse; the man would not have an assistant who might not be as active as he wanted. Philip turned his attention to other means of earning money. He knew French and German and thought there might be some chance of finding a job as correspondence clerk; it made his heart sink, but he set his teeth; there was nothing else to do. Though too shy to answer the advertisements which demanded a personal application, he replied to those which asked for letters; but he had no experience to state and no recommendations: he was conscious that neither his German nor his French was commercial; he was ignorant of the terms used in business; he knew neither shorthand nor typewriting. He could not help recognizing that his case was hopeless. He thought of writing to the solicitor who had been his father's executor, but he could not bring himself to, for it was contrary to his express advice that he had sold the mortgages in which his money had been invested. He knew from his uncle that Mr. Nixon thoroughly disapproved of him. He had gathered from Philip's year in the accountant's office that he was idle and incompetent.

"I'd sooner starve," Philip muttered to himself.

Once or twice the possibility of suicide presented itself to him: it would be easy to get something from the hospital dispensary, and it was a comfort to think that if the worst came to the worst he had at hand means of making a painless end of himself; but it was not a course that he considered seriously. When Mildred had left him to go with Griffiths his anguish had been so great that he wanted to die in order to get rid of the pain. He did not feel like that now. He remembered that the Casualty Sister had told him how people oftener did away with themselves for want of money than for want of love; and he chuckled when he thought that he was an exception. He wished only that he could talk his worries over with somebody, but he could not bring himself to confess them. He was ashamed. He went on looking for work. He left his rent unpaid for three weeks, explaining to his landlady that he would get money at the end of the month; she did not say anything, but pursed her lips and looked grim. When the end of the month came and she asked if it would be convenient for him to pay something on account, it made him feel very sick to say that he could not; he told her he would write to his uncle and was sure to be able to settle his bill on the following Saturday.

"Well, I 'ope you will, Mr. Carey, because I 'ave my rent to pay, and I can't afford to let accounts run on." She did not speak with anger, but with a determination that was rather frightening. She paused for a moment and then said: "If you don't pay next Saturday, I shall 'ave to complain to the secretary of the 'ospital."

"Oh yes, that'll be all right."

She looked at him for a little and glanced round the bare room. When she spoke it was without any emphasis, as though it were quite a natural thing to say.

"I've got a nice 'ot joint downstairs, and if you like to come down to the kitchen you're welcome to a bit of dinner."

Philip felt himself redden to the soles of his feet, and a sob caught at his throat.

"Thank you very much, Mrs. Higgins, but I'm not at all hungry."

"Very good, sir."

When she left the room Philip threw himself on his bed. He had to clench his fists in order to prevent himself from crying.

Chapter 100

Saturday. It was the day on which he had promised to pay his landlady. He had been expecting something to turn up all through the week. He had found no work. He had never been driven to extremities before, and he was so dazed that he did not know what to do. He had at the back of his mind a feeling that the whole thing was a preposterous joke. He had no more than a few coppers left, he had sold all the clothes he could do without; he had some books and one or two odds and ends upon which he might have got a shilling or two, but the landlady was keeping an eye on his comings and goings: he was afraid she would stop him if he took anything more from his room. The only thing was to tell her that he could not pay his bill. He had not the courage. It was the middle of June. The night was fine and warm. He made up his mind to stay out. He walked slowly along the Chelsea Embankment, because the river was restful and quiet, till he was tired, and then sat on a bench and dozed. He did not know how long he slept; he awoke with a start, dreaming that he was being shaken by a policeman and told to move on; but when he opened his eyes he found himself alone. He walked on, he did not know why, and at last came to Chiswick, where he slept again. Presently the hardness of the bench roused him. The night seemed very long. He shivered. He was seized with a sense of his misery; and he did not know what on earth to do: he was ashamed at having slept on the Embankment; it seemed peculiarly humiliating, and he felt his cheeks flush in the darkness. He remembered stories he had heard of those who did and how among them were officers, clergymen, and men who had been to universities: he wondered if he would become one of them, standing in a line to get soup from a charitable institution. It would be much better to commit suicide. He could not go on like that: Lawson would help him when he knew what straits he was in; it was absurd to let his pride prevent him from asking for assistance. He wondered why he had come such a cropper. He had always tried to do what he thought best, and everything had gone wrong. He had helped people when he could, he did not think he had been more selfish than anyone else, it seemed horribly unjust that he should be reduced to such a pass.

But it was no good thinking about it. He walked on. It was now light: the river was beautiful in the silence, and there was something mysterious in the early day; it was going to be very fine, and the sky, pale in the dawn, was cloudless. He felt very tired, and hunger was gnawing at his entrails, but he could not sit still; he was constantly afraid of being spoken to by a policeman. He dreaded the mortification of that. He felt dirty and wished he could have a wash. At last he found himself at Hampton Court. He felt that if he did not have something to eat he would cry. He chose a cheap eating-house and went in; there was a smell of hot things, and it made him feel slightly sick: he meant to eat something nourishing enough to keep him up for the rest of the day, but his stomach revolted at the sight of food. He had a cup of tea and some bread and butter. He remembered then that it was Sunday and he could go to the Athelnys; he thought of the roast beef and the Yorkshire pudding they would eat; but he was fearfully tired and could not face the happy, noisy family. He was feeling morose and wretched. He wanted to be left alone. He made up his mind that he would go into the gardens of the palace and lie down. His bones ached. Perhaps he would find a pump so that he could wash his hands and face and drink something; he was very thirsty; and now that he was no longer hungry he thought with pleasure of the flowers and the lawns and the great leafy trees. He felt that there he could think out better what he must do. He lay on the grass, in the shade, and lit his pipe. For economy's sake he had for a long time confined himself to two pipes a day; he was thankful now that his pouch was full. He did not know what people did when they had no money. Presently he fell asleep. When he awoke it was nearly midday, and he thought that soon he must be setting out for London so as to be there in the early morning and answer any advertisements which seemed to promise. He thought of his uncle, who had told him that he would leave him at his death the little he had; Philip did not in the least know how much this was: it could not be more than a few hundred pounds. He wondered whether he could raise money on the reversion. Not without the old man's consent, and that he would never give.

"The only thing I can do is to hang on somehow till he dies."

Philip reckoned his age. The Vicar of Blackstable was well over seventy. He had chronic bronchitis, but many old men had that and lived on indefinitely. Meanwhile something must turn up; Philip could not get away from the feeling that his position was altogether abnormal; people in his particular station did not starve. It was because he could not bring himself to believe in the reality of his experience that he did not give way to utter despair. He made up his mind to borrow half a sovereign from Lawson. He stayed in the garden all day and smoked when he felt very hungry; he did not mean to eat anything until he was setting out again for London: it was a long way and he must keep up his strength for that. He started when the day began to grow cooler, and slept on benches when he was tired. No one disturbed him. He had a wash and brush up, and a shave at Victoria, some tea and bread and butter, and while he was eating this read the advertisement columns of the morning paper. As he looked down them his eye fell upon an announcement asking for a salesman in the "furnishing drapery" department of some well-known stores. He had a curious little sinking of the heart, for with his middle-class prejudices it seemed dreadful to go into a shop; but he shrugged his shoulders—after all what did it matter? —and he made up his mind to have a shot at it. He had a queer feeling that by accepting every humiliation, by going out to meet it even, he was forcing the hand of fate. When he presented himself, feeling horribly shy, in the department at nine o'clock he found that many others were there before him. They were of all ages, from boys of sixteen to men of forty; some were talking to one another in undertones, but most were silent; and when he took up his place those around him gave him a look of hostility. He heard one man say:

"The only thing I look forward to is getting my refusal soon enough to give me time to look elsewhere."

The man, standing next him, glanced at Philip and asked:

"Had any experience?"

"No," said Philip.

He paused a moment and then made a remark: "Even the smaller houses won't see you without appointment after lunch."

Philip looked at the assistants. Some were draping chintzes and cretonnes, and others, his neighbour told him, were preparing country orders that had come in by post. At about a quarter past nine the buyer arrived. He heard one of the men who were waiting say to another that it was Mr. Gibbons. He was middle-aged, short and corpulent, with a black beard and dark, greasy hair. He had brisk movements and a clever face. He wore a silk hat and a frock coat, the lapel of which was adorned with a white geranium surrounded by leaves. He went into his office, leaving the door open; it was very small and contained only an American roll-desk in the corner, a bookcase, and a cupboard. The men standing outside watched him mechanically take the geranium out of his coat and put it in an ink-pot filled with water. It was against the rules to wear flowers in business.

(During the day the department men who wanted to keep in with the governor admired the flower.

"I've never seen better," they said, "you didn't grow it yourself?"

"Yes I did," he smiled, and a gleam of pride filled his intelligent eyes.)

He took off his hat and changed his coat, glanced at the letters and then at the men who were waiting to see him. He made a slight sign with one finger, and the first in the queue stepped into the office. They filed past him one by one and answered his questions. He put them very briefly, keeping his eyes fixed on the applicant's face.

"Age? Experience? Why did you leave your job?"

He listened to the replies without expression. When it came to Philip's turn he fancied that Mr. Gibbons stared at him curiously. Philip's clothes were neat and tolerably cut. He looked a little different from the others.

"Experience?"

"I'm afraid I haven't any," said Philip.

"No good."

Philip walked out of the office. The ordeal had been so much less painful than he expected that he felt no particular disappointment. He could hardly hope to succeed in getting a place the first time he tried. He had kept the newspaper and now looked at the advertisements again: a shop in Holborn needed a salesman too, and he went there; but when he arrived he found that someone had already been engaged. If he wanted to get anything to eat that day he must go to Lawson's studio before he went out to luncheon, so he made his way along the Brompton Road to Yeoman's Row.

"I say, I'm rather broke till the end of the month," he said, as soon as he found an opportunity. "I wish you'd lend me half a sovereign, will you?"

It was incredible the difficulty he found in asking for money;

and he remembered the casual way, as though almost they were conferring a favour, men at the hospital had extracted small sums out of him which they had no intention of repaying.

"Like a shot," said Lawson.

But when he put his hand in his pocket he found that he had only eight shillings. Philip's heart sank.

"Oh well, lend me five bob, will you?" he said lightly.

"Here you are."

Philip went to the public baths in Westminster and spent sixpence on a bath. Then he got himself something to eat. He did not know what to do with himself in the afternoon. He would not go back to the hospital in case anyone should ask him questions, and besides, he had nothing to do there now; they would wonder in the two or three departments he had worked in why he did not come, but they must think what they chose, it did not matter: he would not be the first student who had dropped out without warning. He went to the free library, and looked at the papers till they wearied him, then he took out Stevenson's *New Arabian Nights*; but he found he could not read: the words meant nothing to him, and he continued to brood over his helplessness. He kept on thinking the same things all the time, and the fixity of his thoughts made his head ache. At last, craving for fresh air, he went into the Green Park and lay down on the grass. He thought miserably of his deformity, which made it impossible for him to go to the war. He went to sleep and dreamed that he was suddenly sound of foot and out at the Cape in a regiment of Yeomanry; the pictures he had looked at in the illustrated papers gave materials for his fancy; and he saw himself on the veldt, in khaki, sitting with other men round a fire at night. When he awoke he found that it was still quite light, and presently he heard Big Ben strike seven. He had twelve hours to get through with nothing to do. He dreaded the interminable night. The sky was overcast and he feared it would rain; he would have to go to a lodging-house where he could get a bed; he had seen them advertised on lamps outside houses in Lambeth: Good Beds, sixpence; he had never been inside one, and dreaded the foul smell and the vermin. He made up his mind to stay in the open air if he possibly could. He remained in the Park till it was closed and then began to walk about. He was very tired. The thought came to him that an accident would be a piece of luck, so that he could be taken to a hospital and lie there, in a clean bed, for weeks. At midnight he was so hungry that he could not go without food any more, so he went to a coffee stall at Hyde Park Corner and ate a couple of potatoes and had a cup of coffee. Then he walked again. He felt too restless to sleep, and he had a horrible dread of being moved on by the police. He noted that he was beginning to look upon the constable from quite a new angle. This was the third night he had spent out. Now and then he sat on the benches in Piccadilly and towards morning he strolled down to The Embankment. He listened to the striking of Big Ben, marking every quarter of an hour, and reckoned out how long it left till the City woke again. In the morning he spent a few coppers on making himself neat and clean, bought a paper to read the advertisements, and set out once more on the search for work.

He went on in this way for several days. He had very little food and began to feel weak and ill, so that he had hardly enough energy to go on looking for the work which seemed so desperately hard to find. He was growing used now to the long waiting at the back of a shop on the chance that he would be taken on, and the curt dismissal. He walked to all parts of London in answer to the advertisements, and he came to know by sight men who applied as fruitlessly as himself. One or two tried to make friends with him, but he was too tired and too wretched to accept their advances. He did not go any more to Lawson, because he owed him five shillings. He began to be too dazed to think clearly and ceased very much to care what would happen to him. He cried a good deal. At first he was very angry with himself for this and ashamed, but he found it relieved him and somehow made him feel less hungry. In the very early morning he suffered a good deal from cold. One night he went into his room to change his linen; he slipped in about three, when he was quite sure everyone would be asleep, and out again at five; he lay on the bed and its softness was enchanting; all his bones ached, and as he lay he revelled in the pleasure of it; it was so delicious that he did not want to go to sleep. He was growing used to want of food and did not feel very hungry, but only weak. Constantly now at the back of his mind was the thought of doing away with himself, but he used all the strength he had not to dwell on it, because he was afraid the temptation would get hold of him so that he would not be able to help himself. He kept on saying to himself that it would be absurd to commit suicide, since something must happen soon; he could not get over the impression that his situation was too preposterous to be taken quite seriously; it was like an illness which must be endured but from which he was bound to recover.

Every night he swore that nothing would induce him to put up with such another and determined next morning to write to his uncle, or to Mr. Nixon, the solicitor, or to Lawson; but when the time came he could not bring himself to make the humiliating confession of his utter failure. He did not know how Lawson would take it. In their friendship Lawson had been scatter-brained and he had prided himself on his common sense. He would have to tell the whole history of his folly. He had an uneasy feeling that Lawson, after helping him, would turn the cold shoulder on him. His uncle and the solicitor would of course do something for him, but he dreaded their reproaches. He did not want anyone to reproach him: he clenched his teeth and repeated that what had happened was inevitable just because it had happened. Regret was absurd.

The days were unending, and the five shillings Lawson had lent him would not last much longer. Philip longed for Sunday to come so that he could go to Athelny's. He did not know what prevented him from going there sooner, except perhaps that he wanted so badly to get through on his own; for Athelny, who had been in straits as desperate, was the only person who could do anything for him. Perhaps after dinner he could bring himself to tell Athelny that he was in difficulties. Philip repeated to himself over and over again what he should say to him. He was dreadfully afraid that Athelny would put him off with airy phrases: that would be so horrible that he wanted to delay as long as possible the putting of him to the test. Philip had lost all confidence in his fellows.

Saturday night was cold and raw. Philip suffered horribly.

From midday on Saturday till he dragged himself wearily to Athelny's house he ate nothing. He spent his last twopence on Sunday morning on a wash and a brush up in the lavatory at Charing Cross.

Chapter 101

When Philip rang a head was put out of the window, and in a minute he heard a noisy clatter on the stairs as the children ran down to let him in. It was a pale, anxious, thin face that he bent down for them to kiss. He was so moved by their exuberant affection that, to give himself time to recover, he made excuses to linger on the stairs. He was in a hysterical state and almost anything was enough to make him cry. They asked him why he had not come on the previous Sunday, and he told them he had been ill; they wanted to know what was the matter with him; and Philip, to amuse them, suggested a mysterious ailment, the name of which, double-barrelled and barbarous with its mixture of Greek and Latin (medical nomenclature bristled with such), made them shriek with delight. They dragged Philip into the parlour and made him repeat it for their father's edification. Athelny got up and shook hands with him. He stared at Philip, but with his round, bulging eyes he always seemed to stare. Philip did not know why on this occasion it made him self-conscious.

"We missed you last Sunday," he said.

Philip could never tell lies without embarrassment, and he was scarlet when he finished his explanation for not coming. Then Mrs. Athelny entered and shook hands with him.

"I hope you're better, Mr. Carey," she said.

He did not know why she imagined that anything had been the matter with him, for the kitchen door was closed when he came up with the children, and they had not left him.

"Dinner won't be ready for another ten minutes," she said, in her slow drawl. "Won't you have an egg beaten up in a glass of milk while you're waiting?"

There was a look of concern on her face which made Philip uncomfortable. He forced a laugh and answered that he was not at all hungry. Sally came in to lay the table, and Philip began to chaff her. It was the family joke that she would be as fat as an aunt of Mrs. Athelny, called Aunt Elizabeth, whom the children had never seen but regarded as the type of obscene corpulence.

"I say, what *has* happened since I saw you last, Sally?" Philip began.

"Nothing that I know of."

"I believe you've been putting on weight."

"I'm sure you haven't," she retorted. "You're a perfect skeleton."

Philip reddened.

"That's a *tu quoque*, Sally," cried her father. "You will be fined one golden hair of your head. Jane, fetch the shears."

"Well, he is thin, father," remonstrated Sally. "He's just skin and bone."

"That's not the question, child. He is at perfect liberty to be thin, but your obesity is contrary to decorum."

As he spoke he put his arm proudly round her waist and looked at her with admiring eyes.

"Let me get on with the table, father. If I am comfortable there are some who don't seem to mind it."

"The hussy!" cried Athelny, with a dramatic wave of the hand. "She taunts me with the notorious fact that Joseph, a son of Levi who sells jewels in Holborn, has made her an offer of marriage."

"Have you accepted him, Sally?" asked Philip.

"Don't you know father better than that by this time? There's not a word of truth in it."

"Well, if he hasn't made you an offer of marriage," cried Athelny, "by Saint George and Merry England, I will seize him by the nose and demand of him immediately what are his intentions."

"Sit down, father, dinner's ready. Now then, you children, get along with you and wash your hands all of you, and don't shirk it, because I mean to look at them before you have a scrap of dinner, so there."

Philip thought he was ravenous till he began to eat, but then discovered that his stomach turned against food, and he could eat hardly at all. His brain was weary; and he did not notice that Athelny, contrary to his habit, spoke very little. Philip was relieved to be sitting in a comfortable house, but every now and then he could not prevent himself from glancing out of the window. The day was tempestuous. The fine weather had broken; and it was cold, and there was a bitter wind; now and again gusts of rain drove against the window. Philip wondered what he should do that night. The Athelnys went to bed early, and he could not stay where he was after ten o'clock. His heart sank at the thought of going out into the bleak darkness. It seemed more terrible now that he was with his friends than when he was outside and alone. He kept on saying to himself that there were plenty more who would be spending the night out of doors. He strove to distract his mind by talking, but in the middle of his words a spatter of rain against the window would make him start.

"It's like March weather," said Athelny. "Not the sort of day one would like to be crossing the Channel."

Presently they finished, and Sally came in and cleared away.

"Would you like a twopenny stinker?" said Athelny, handing him a cigar.

Philip took it and inhaled the smoke with delight. It soothed him extraordinarily. When Sally had finished Athelny told her to shut the door after her.

"Now we shan't be disturbed," he said, turning to Philip. "I've arranged with Betty not to let the children come in till I call them."

Philip gave him a startled look, but before he could take in the meaning of his words, Athelny, fixing his glasses on his nose with the gesture habitual to him, went on.

"I wrote to you last Sunday to ask if anything was the matter with you, and as you didn't answer I went to your rooms on Wednesday."

Philip turned his head away and did not answer. His heart began to beat violently. Athelny did not speak, and presently the silence seemed intolerable to Philip. He could not think of a single word to say.

"Your landlady told me you hadn't been in since Saturday night, and she said you owed her for the last month. Where have you been sleeping all this week?"

It made Philip sick to answer. He stared out of the window.

"Nowhere."

"I tried to find you."

"Why?" asked Philip.

"Betty and I have been just as broke in our day, only we had babies to look after. Why didn't you come here?"

"I couldn't."

Philip was afraid he was going to cry. He felt very weak. He shut his eyes and frowned, trying to control himself. He felt a sudden flash of anger with Athelny because he would not leave him alone; but he was broken; and presently, his eyes still closed, slowly in order to keep his voice steady, he told him the story of his adventures during the last few weeks. As he spoke it seemed to him that he had behaved inanely, and it made it still harder to tell. He felt that Athelny would think him an utter fool.

"Now you're coming to live with us till you find something to do," said Athelny, when he had finished.

Philip flushed, he knew not why.

"Oh, it's awfully kind of you, but I don't think I'll do that."

"Why not?"

Philip did not answer. He had refused instinctively from fear that he would be a bother, and he had a natural bashfulness of accepting favours. He knew besides that the Athelnys lived from hand to mouth, and with their large family had neither space nor money to entertain a stranger.

"Of course you must come here," said Athelny. "Thorpe will tuck in with one of his brothers and you can sleep in his bed. You don't suppose your food's going to make any difference to us."

Philip was afraid to speak, and Athelny, going to the door, called to his wife.

"Betty," he said, when she came in, "Mr. Carey's coming to live with us."

"Oh, that is nice," she said. "I'll go and get the bed ready."

She spoke in such a hearty, friendly tone, taking everything for granted, that Philip was deeply touched. He never expected people to be kind to him, and when they were it surprised and moved him. Now he could not prevent two large tears from rolling down his cheeks. The Athelnys discussed the arrangements and pretended not to notice to what a state his weakness had brought him. When Mrs. Athelny left them Philip leaned back in his chair, and looking out of the window laughed a little.

"It's not a very nice night to be out, is it?"

Chapter 102

Athelny told Philip that he could easily get him something to do in the large firm of linen-drapers in which himself worked. Several of the assistants had gone to the war, and Lynn and Sedley with patriotic zeal had promised to keep their places open for them. They put the work of the heroes on those who remained, and since they did not increase the wages of these were able at once to exhibit public spirit and effect an economy; but the war continued and trade was less depressed; the holidays were coming, when numbers of the staff went away for a fortnight at a time: they were bound to engage more assistants. Philip's experience had made him doubtful whether even then they would engage him; but Athelny, representing himself as a person of consequence in the firm, insisted that the manager could refuse him nothing. Philip, with his training in Paris, would be very useful; it was only a matter of waiting a little and he was bound to get a well-paid job to design costumes and draw posters. Philip made a poster for the summer sale and Athelny took it away. Two days later he brought it back, saying that the manager admired it very much and regretted with all his heart that there was no vacancy just then in that department. Philip asked whether there was nothing else he could do.

"I'm afraid not."

"Are you quite sure?"

"Well, the fact is they're advertising for a shop-walker tomorrow," said Athelny, looking at him doubtfully through his glasses.

"D'you think I stand any chance of getting it?"

Athelny was a little confused; he had led Philip to expect something much more splendid; on the other hand he was too poor to go on providing him indefinitely with board and lodging.

"You might take it while you wait for something better. You always stand a better chance if you're engaged by the firm already."

"I'm not proud, you know," smiled Philip.

"If you decide on that you must be there at a quarter to nine tomorrow morning."

Notwithstanding the war there was evidently much difficulty in finding work, for when Philip went to the shop many men were waiting already. He recognized some whom he had seen in his own searching, and there was one whom he had noticed lying about the Park in the afternoon. To Philip now that suggested that he was as homeless as himself and passed the night out of doors. The men were of all sorts, old and young, tall and short; but every one had tried to make himself smart for the interview with the manager: they had carefully brushed hair and scrupulously clean hands. They waited in a passage which Philip learnt afterwards led up to the dining-hall and the work rooms; it was broken every few yards by five or six steps. Though there was electric light in the shop here was only gas, with wire cages over it for protection, and it flared noisily. Philip arrived punctually, but it was nearly ten o'clock when he was admitted into the office. It was three-cornered, like a cut of cheese lying on its side: on the walls were pictures of women in corsets, and two poster-proofs, one of a man in pyjamas, green and white in large stripes, and the other of a ship in full sail ploughing an azure sea: on the sail was printed in large letters "great white sale." The widest side of the office was the back of one of the shop-windows, which was being dressed at the time, and an assistant went to and fro during the interview. The manager was reading a letter. He was a florid man, with sandy hair and a large sandy moustache; from the middle of his watch-chain hung a bunch of football medals. He sat in his shirt sleeves at a large desk with a telephone by his side; before him were the day's advertisements, Athelny's work, and cuttings from newspapers pasted on a card. He gave Philip a glance but did not speak to him: he dictated a letter to the typist, a girl who sat at a small table in one corner; then he asked Philip his name, age, and what experience he had had. He spoke with a cockney twang in a high, metallic voice which he seemed not able always to control; Philip noticed that his upper teeth were large and protruding; they gave you the impression that they were loose and would come out if you gave them a sharp tug.

"I think Mr. Athelny has spoken to you about me," said Philip.

"Oh, you are the young feller who did that poster?"

"Yes, sir."

"No good to us, you know, not a bit of good."

He looked Philip up and down. He seemed to notice that Philip was in some way different from the men who had preceded him.

"You'd 'ave to get a frock coat, you know. I suppose you 'aven't got one. You seem a respectable young feller. I suppose you found art didn't pay."

Philip could not tell whether he meant to engage him or not. He threw remarks at him in a hostile way.

"Where's your home?"

"My father and mother died when I was a child."

"I like to give young fellers a chance. Many's the one I've given their chance to and they're managers of departments now. And they're grateful to me, I'll say that for them. They know what I done for them. Start at the bottom of the ladder, that's the only way to learn the business, and then if you stick to it there's no knowing what it can lead to. If you suit, one of these days you may find yourself in a position like what mine is. Bear that in mind, young feller."

"I'm very anxious to do my best, sir," said Philip.

He knew that he must put in the "sir" whenever he could, but it sounded odd to him, and he was afraid of overdoing it. The manager liked talking. It gave him a happy consciousness of his own importance, and he did not give Philip his decision till he had used a great many words.

"Well, I daresay you'll do," he said at last, in a pompous way. "Anyhow, I don't mind giving you a trial."

"Thank you very much, sir."

"You can start at once. I'll give you six shillings a week and your keep. Everything found, you know; the six shillings is only pocket money, to do what you like with, paid monthly. Start on Monday. I suppose you've got no cause of complaint with that."

"No, sir."

"Harrington Street—d'you know where that is? —Shaftesbury Avenue. That's where you sleep. Number ten, it is. You can sleep there on Sunday night, if you like; that's just as you please, or you can send your box there on Monday." The manager nodded: "Good morning."

Chapter 103

Mrs. Athelny lent Philip money to pay his landlady enough of her bill to let him take his things away. For five shillings and the pawn-ticket on a suit he was able to get from a pawnbroker a frockcoat which fitted him fairly well. He redeemed the rest of his clothes. He sent his box to Harrington Street by Carter Patterson and on Monday morning went with Athelny to the shop. Athelny introduced him to the buyer of the costumes and left him. The buyer was a pleasant, fussy little man of thirty, named Sampson; he shook hands with Philip, and, in order to show his own accomplishment of which he was very proud, asked him if he spoke French. He was surprised when Philip told him he did.

"Any other language?"

"I speak German."

"Oh! I go over to Paris myself occasionally. *Parlez-vous français?* Ever been to Maxim's?"

Philip was stationed at the top of the stairs in the "costumes." His work consisted in directing people to the various departments. There seemed a great many of them as Mr. Sampson tripped them off his tongue. Suddenly he noticed that Philip limped.

"What's the matter with your leg?" he asked.

"I've got a club-foot," said Philip. "But it doesn't prevent my walking or anything like that."

The buyer looked at it for a moment doubtfully, and Philip surmised that he was wondering why the manager had engaged him. Philip knew that he had not noticed there was anything the matter with him.

"I don't expect you to get them all correct the first day. If you're in any doubt all you've got to do is to ask one of the young ladies."

Mr. Sampson turned away; and Philip, trying to remember where this or the other department was, watched anxiously for the customer in search of information. At one o'clock he went up to dinner. The dining-room, on the top floor of the vast building, was large, long, and well lit; but all the windows were shut to keep out the dust, and there was a horrid smell of cooking. There were long tables covered with cloths, with big glass bottles of water at intervals, and down the centre salt cellars and bottles of vinegar. The assistants crowded in noisily, and sat down on forms still warm from those who had dined at twelve-thirty.

"No pickles," remarked the man next to Philip.

He was a tall thin young man, with a hooked nose and a pasty face; he had a long head, unevenly shaped as though the skull had been pushed in here and there oddly, and on his forehead and neck were large acne spots red and inflamed. His name was Harris. Philip discovered that on some days there were large soup-plates down the table full of mixed pickles. They were very popular. There were no knives and forks, but in a minute a large fat boy in a white coat came in with a couple of handfuls of them and threw them loudly on the middle of the table. Each man took what he wanted; they were warm and greasy from recent washing in dirty water. Plates of meat swimming in gravy were handed round by boys in white jackets, and as they flung each plate down with the quick gesture of a prestidigitator the gravy slopped over on to the tablecloth. Then they brought large dishes of cabbages and potatoes; the sight of them turned Philip's stomach; he noticed that everyone poured quantities of vinegar over them. The noise was awful. They talked and laughed and shouted, and there was the clatter of knives and forks, and strange sounds of eating. Philip was glad to get back into the department. He was beginning to remember where each one was, and had less often to ask one of the assistants, when somebody wanted to know the way.

"First to the right. Second on the left, madam."

One or two of the girls spoke to him, just a word when things were slack, and he felt they were taking his measure. At five he was sent up again to the dining-room for tea. He was glad to sit down. There were large slices of bread heavily spread with butter; and many had pots of jam, which were kept in the "store" and had their names written on.

Philip was exhausted when work stopped at half past six. Harris, the man he had sat next to at dinner, offered to take him over to Harrington Street to show him where he was to sleep. He told Philip there was a spare bed in his room, and, as the other rooms were full, he expected Philip would be put there. The house in Harrington Street had been a bootmaker's; and the shop was used as a bedroom; but it was very dark, since the window had been boarded three parts up, and as this did not open the only ventilation came from a small skylight at the far end. There was a musty smell, and Philip was thankful that he would not have to sleep there. Harris took him up to the sitting-room, which was on the first floor; it had an old piano in it with a keyboard that looked like a row of decayed teeth; and on the table in a cigar-box without a lid was a set of dominoes; old numbers of *The Strand Magazine* and of *The Graphic* were lying about. The other rooms were used as bedrooms. That in which Philip was to sleep was at the top of the house. There were six beds in it, and a trunk or a box stood by the side of each. The only furniture was a chest of drawers: it had four large drawers and two small ones, and Philip as the newcomer had one of these; there were keys to them, but as they were all alike they were not of much use, and Harris advised him to keep his valuables in his trunk. There was a looking-glass on the chimney-piece. Harris showed Philip the lavatory, which was a fairly large room with eight basins in a row, and here all the inmates did their washing. It led into another room in which were two baths, discoloured, the woodwork stained with soap; and in them were dark rings at various intervals which indicated the water marks of different baths.

When Harris and Philip went back to their bedroom they found a tall man changing his clothes and a boy of sixteen whistling as loud as he could while he brushed his hair. In a minute or two without saying a word to anybody the tall man went out. Harris winked at the boy, and the boy, whistling still, winked back. Harris told Philip that the man was called Prior; he had been in the army and now served in the silks; he kept pretty much to himself, and he went off every night, just like that, without so much as a good evening, to see his girl. Harris went out too, and only the boy remained to watch Philip curiously while he unpacked his things. His name was Bell and he was serving his time for nothing in the haberdashery. He was much interested in Philip's evening clothes. He told him about the other men in the room and asked him every sort of question about himself. He was a cheerful youth, and in the intervals of conversation sang in a half-broken voice snatches of music hall songs. When Philip had finished he went out to walk about the streets and look at the crowd; occasionally he stopped outside the doors of restaurants and watched the people going in; he felt hungry, so he bought a bath bun and ate it while he strolled along. He had been given a latchkey by the prefect, the man who turned out the gas at a quarter past eleven, but afraid of being locked out he returned in good time; he had learned already the system of fines: you had to pay a shilling if you came in after eleven, and half a crown after a quarter past, and you were reported besides: if it happened three times you were dismissed.

All but the soldier were in when Philip arrived and two were already in bed. Philip was greeted with cries.

"Oh, Clarence!Naughty boy!"

He discovered that Bell had dressed up the bolster in his evening clothes. The boy was delighted with his joke.

"You must wear them at the social evening, Clarence."

"He'll catch the belle of Lynn's, if he's not careful."

Philip had already heard of the social evenings, for the money stopped from the wages to pay for them was one of the grievances of the staff. It was only two shillings a month, and it covered medical attendance and the use of a library of worn novels; but as four shillings a month besides was stopped for washing, Philip discovered that a quarter of his six shillings a week would never be paid to him.

Most of the men were eating thick slices of fat bacon between a roll of bread cut in two. These sandwiches, the assistants' usual supper, were supplied by a small shop a few doors off at twopence each. The soldier rolled in; silently, rapidly, took off his clothes and threw himself into bed. At ten minutes past eleven the gas gave a big jump and five minutes later went out. The soldier went to sleep, but the others crowded round the big window in their pyjamas and nightshirts and, throwing remains of their sandwiches at the women who passed in the street below, shouted to them facetious remarks. The house opposite, six storeys high, was a workshop for Jewish tailors who left off work at eleven; the rooms were brightly lit and there were no blinds to the windows. The sweater's daughter—the family consisted of father, mother, two small boys, and a girl of twenty—went round the house to put out the lights when work was over, and sometimes she allowed herself to be made love to by one of the tailors. The shop assistants in Philip's room got a lot of amusement out of watching the manoeuvres of one man or another to stay behind, and they made small bets on which would succeed. At midnight the people were turned out of the "Harrington Arms" at the end of the street, and soon after they all went to bed: Bell, who slept nearest the door, made his way across the room by jumping from bed to bed, and even when he got to his own would not stop talking. At last everything was silent but for the steady snoring of the soldier, and Philip went to sleep.

He was awaked at seven by the loud ringing of a bell, and by a quarter to eight they were all dressed and hurrying downstairs in their stockinged feet to pick out their boots. They laced them as they ran along to the shop in Oxford Street for breakfast. If they were a minute later than eight they got none, nor, once in, were they allowed out to get themselves anything to eat. Sometimes, if they knew they could not get into the building in time, they stopped at the little shop near their quarters and bought a couple of buns; but this cost money, and most went without food till dinner. Philip ate some bread and butter, drank a cup of tea, and at half past eight began his day's work again.

"First to the right. Second on the left, madam."

Soon he began to answer the questions quite mechanically. The work was monotonous and very tiring. After a few days his feet hurt him so that he could hardly stand: the thick soft carpets made them burn, and at night his socks were painful to remove. It was a common complaint, and his fellow "floormen" told him that socks and boots just rotted away from the continual sweating. All the men in his room suffered in the same fashion, and they relieved the pain by sleeping with their feet outside the bed-clothes. At first Philip could not walk at all and was obliged to spend a good many of his evenings in the sitting-room at Harrington Street with his feet in a pail of cold water. His companion on these occasions was Bell, the lad in the haberdashery, who stayed in often to arrange the stamps he collected. As he fastened them with little pieces of stamp paper he whistled monotonously.

Chapter 104

The social evenings took place on alternate Mondays. There was one at the beginning of Philip's second week at Lynn's. He arranged to go with one of the women in his department.

"Meet 'em 'alf-way," she said, "same as I do."

This was Mrs. Hodges, a little woman of five-and-forty, with badly dyed hair; she had a yellow face with a network of small red veins all over it, and yellow whites to her pale blue eyes. She took a fancy to Philip and called him by his Christian name before he had been in the shop a week.

"We've both known what it is to come down," she said.

She told Philip that her real name was not Hodges, but she always referred to "me 'usband Misterodges"; he was a barrister and he treated her simply shocking, so she left him as she preferred to be independent like; but she had known what it was to drive in her own carriage, dear—she called everyone dear—and they always had late dinner at home. She used to pick her teeth with the pin of an enormous silver brooch. It was in the form of a whip and a hunting-crop crossed, with two spurs in the middle.

Philip was ill at ease in his new surroundings, and the girls in the shop called him "sidey." One addressed him as Phil, and he did not answer because he had not the least idea that she was speaking to him; so she tossed her head, saying he was a "stuck-up thing," and next time with ironical emphasis called him Mister Carey. She was a Miss Jewell, and she was going to marry a doctor. The other girls had never seen him, but they said he must be a gentleman as he gave her such lovely presents.

"Never you mind what they say, dear," said Mrs. Hodges. "I've 'ad to go through it same as you 'ave. They don't know any better, poor things. You take my word for it, they'll like you all right if you 'old your own same as I 'ave."

The social evening was held in the restaurant in the basement. The tables were put on one side so that there might be room for dancing, and smaller ones were set out for progressive whist.

"The 'eads 'ave to get there early," said Mrs. Hodges.

She introduced him to Miss Bennett, who was the belle of Lynn's. She was the buyer in the "Petticoats," and when Philip entered was engaged in conversation with the buyer in the "Gentlemen's Hosiery"; Miss Bennett was a woman of massive proportions, with a very large red face heavily powdered and a bust of imposing dimensions; her flaxen hair was arranged with elaboration. She was overdressed, but not badly dressed, in black with a high collar, and she wore black *glacé* gloves, in which she played cards; she had several heavy gold chains round her neck, bangles on her wrists, and circular photograph pendants, one being of Queen Alexandra; she carried a black satin bag and chewed Sen-sens.

"Please to meet you, Mr. Carey," she said. "This is your first visit to our social evenings, ain't it? I expect you feel a bit shy, but there's no cause to, I promise you that."

She did her best to make people feel at home. She slapped them on the shoulders and laughed a great deal.

"Ain't I a pickle?" she cried, turning to Philip. "What must you think of me? But I can't 'elp meself."

Those who were going to take part in the social evening came in, the younger members of the staff mostly, boys who had not girls of their own, and girls who had not yet found anyone to walk with. Several of the young gentlemen wore lounge suits with white evening ties and red silk handkerchiefs; they were going to perform, and they had a busy, abstracted air; some were self-confident, but others were nervous, and they watched their public with an anxious eye. Presently a girl with a great deal of hair sat at the piano and ran her hands noisily across the keyboard. When the audience had settled itself she looked round and gave the name of her piece.

"*A Drive in Russia.*"

There was a round of clapping, during which she deftly fixed bells to her wrists. She smiled a little and immediately burst into energetic melody. There was a great deal more clapping when she finished, and when this was over, as an encore, she gave a piece which imitated the sea; there were little trills to represent the lapping waves and thundering chords, with the loud pedal down, to suggest a storm. After this a gentleman sang a song called *Bid me Good-bye*, and as an encore obliged with *Sing me to Sleep*. The audience measured their enthusiasm with a nice discrimination. Everyone was applauded till he gave an encore, and so that there might be no jealousy no one was applauded more than anyone else. Miss Bennett sailed up to Philip.

"I'm sure you play or sing, Mr. Carey," she said archly. "I can see it in your face."

"I'm afraid I don't."

"Don't you even recite?"

"I have no parlour tricks."

The buyer in the "gentleman's Hosiery" was a well-known reciter, and he was called upon loudly to perform by all the assistants in his department. Needing no pressing, he gave a long poem of tragic character, in which he rolled his eyes, put his hand on his chest, and acted as though he were in great agony. The point, that he had eaten cucumber for supper, was divulged in the last line and was greeted with laughter, a little forced because everyone knew the poem well, but loud and long. Miss Bennett did not sing, play, or recite.

"Oh no, she 'as a little game of her own," said Mrs. Hodges.

"Now, don't you begin chaffing me. The fact is I know quite a lot about palmistry and second sight."

"Oh, do tell my 'and, Miss Bennett," cried the girls in her department, eager to please her.

"I don't like telling 'ands, I don't really. I've told people such terrible things and they've all come true, it makes one superstitious like."

"Oh, Miss Bennett, just for once."

A little crowd collected round her, and, amid screams

of embarrass-ment, giggles, blushings, and cries of dismay or admiration, she talked mysteriously of fair and dark men, of money in a letter, and of journeys, till the sweat stood in heavy beads on her painted face.

"Look at me," she said. "I'm all of a perspiration."

Supper was at nine. There were cakes, buns, sandwiches, tea, and coffee, all free; but if you wanted mineral water you had to pay for it. Gallantry often led young men to offer the ladies ginger beer, but common decency made them refuse. Miss Bennett was very fond of ginger beer, and she drank two and sometimes three bottles during the evening; but she insisted on paying for them herself. The men liked her for that.

"She's a rum old bird," they said, "but mind you, she's not a bad sort, she's not like what some are."

After supper progressive whist was played. This was very noisy, and there was a great deal of laughing and shouting as people moved from table to table. Miss Bennett grew hotter and hotter.

"Look at me," she said. "I'm all of a perspiration."

In due course one of the more dashing of the young men remarked that if they wanted to dance they'd better begin. The girl who had played the accompaniments sat at the piano and placed a decided foot on the loud pedal. She played a dreamy waltz, marking the time with the bass, while with the right hand she "tiddled" in alternate octaves. By way of a change she crossed her hands and played the air in the bass.

"She does play well, doesn't she?" Mrs. Hodges remarked to Philip. "And what's more she's never 'ad a lesson in 'er life; it's all ear."

Miss Bennett liked dancing and poetry better than anything in the world. She danced well, but very, very slowly, and an expression came into her eyes as though her thoughts were far, far away. She talked breathlessly of the floor and the heat and the supper. She said that the Portman Rooms had the best floor in London and she always liked the dances there; they were very select, and she couldn't bear dancing with all sorts of men you didn't know anything about; why, you might be exposing yourself to you didn't know what all. Nearly all the people danced very well, and they enjoyed themselves. Sweat poured down their faces, and the very high collars of the young men grew limp.

Philip looked on, and a greater depression seized him than he remembered to have felt for a long time. He felt intolerably alone. He did not go, because he was afraid to seem supercilious, and he talked with the girls and laughed, but in his heart was unhappiness. Miss Bennett asked him if he had a girl.

"No," he smiled.

"Oh, well, there's plenty to choose from here. And they're very nice respectable girls, some of them. I expect you'll have a girl before you've been here long."

She looked at him very archly.

"Meet 'em 'alfway," said Mrs. Hodges. "That's what I tell him."

It was nearly eleven o'clock, and the party broke up. Philip could not get to sleep. Like the others he kept his aching feet outside the bed-clothes. He tried with all his might not to think of the life he was leading. The soldier was snoring quietly.

Chapter 105

The wages were paid once a month by the secretary. On payday each batch of assistants, coming down from tea, went into the passage and joined the long line of people waiting orderly like the audience in a queue outside a gallery door. One by one they entered the office. The secretary sat at a desk with wooden bowls of money in front of him, and he asked the employe's name; he referred to a book, quickly, after a suspicious glance at the assistant, said aloud the sum due, and taking money out of the bowl counted it into his hand.

"Thank you," he said. "Next."

"Thank you," was the reply.

The assistant passed on to the second secretary and before leaving the room paid him four shillings for washing money, two shillings for the club, and any fines that he might have incurred. With what he had left he went back into his department and there waited till it was time to go. Most of the men in Philip's house were in debt with the woman who sold the sandwiches they generally ate for supper. She was a funny old thing, very fat, with a broad, red face, and black hair plastered neatly on each side of the forehead in the fashion shown in early pictures of Queen Victoria. She always wore a little black bonnet and a white apron; her sleeves were tucked up to the elbow; she cut the sandwiches with large, dirty, greasy hands; and there was grease on her bodice, grease on her apron, grease on her skirt. She was called Mrs. Fletcher, but everyone addressed her as "Ma"; she was really fond of the shop assistants, whom she called her boys; she never minded giving credit towards the end of the month, and it was known that now and then she had lent someone or other a few shillings when he was in straits. She was a good woman. When they were leaving or when they came back from the holidays, the boys kissed her fat red cheek; and more than one, dismissed and unable to find another job, had got for nothing food to keep body and soul together. The boys were sensible of her large heart and repaid her with genuine affection. There was a story they liked to tell of a man who had done well for himself at Bradford, and had five shops of his own, and had come back after fifteen years and visited Ma Fletcher and given her a gold watch.

Philip found himself with eighteen shillings left out of his month's pay. It was the first money he had ever earned in his life. It gave him none of the pride which might have been expected, but merely a feeling of dismay. The smallness of the sum emphasized the hopelessness of his position. He took fifteen shillings to Mrs. Athelny to pay back part of what he owed her, but she would not take more than half a sovereign.

"D'you know, at that rate it'll take me eight months to settle up with you."

"As long as Athelny's in work I can afford to wait, and who knows, p'raps they'll give you a rise."

Athelny kept on saying that he would speak to the manager about Philip, it was absurd that no use should be made of his talents; but he did nothing, and Philip soon came to the conclusion that the press agent was not a person of so much importance in the manager's eyes as in his own. Occasionally he saw Athelny in the shop. His flamboyance was extinguished; and in neat, commonplace, shabby clothes he hurried, a subdued, unassuming little man, through the departments as though anxious to escape notice.

"When I think of how I'm wasted there," he said at home, "I'm almost tempted to give in my notice. There's no scope for a man like me. I'm stunted, I'm starved."

Mrs. Athelny, quietly sewing, took no notice of his complaints. Her mouth tightened a little.

"It's very hard to get jobs in these times. It's regular and it's safe; I expect you'll stay there as long as you give satisfaction."

It was evident that Athelny would. It was interesting to see the ascendency which the uneducated woman, bound to him by no legal tie, had acquired over the brilliant, unstable man. Mrs. Athelny treated Philip with motherly kindness now that he was in a different position, and he was touched by her anxiety that he should make a good meal. It was the solace of his life (and when he grew used to it, the monotony of it was what chiefly appalled him) that he could go every Sunday to that friendly house. It was a joy to sit in the stately Spanish chairs and discuss all manner of things with Athelny. Though his condition seemed so desperate he never left him to go back to Harrington Street without a feeling of exultation. At first Philip, in order not to forget what he had learned, tried to go on reading his medical books, but he found it useless; he could not fix his attention on them after the exhausting work of the day; and it seemed hopeless to continue working when he did not know in how long he would be able to go back to the hospital. He dreamed constantly that he was in the wards. The awakening was painful. The sensation of other people sleeping in the room was inexpressibly irksome to him; he had been used to solitude, and to be with others always, never to be by himself for an instant, was at these moments horrible to him. It was then that he found it most difficult to combat his despair. He saw himself going on with that life, "First to the right, second on the left, madam," indefinitely; and having to be thankful if he was not sent away: the men who had gone to the war would be coming home soon, the firm had guaranteed to take them back, and this must mean that others would be sacked; he would have to stir himself even to keep the wretched post he had.

There was only one thing to free him and that was the death of his uncle. He would get a few hundred pounds then, and on this he could finish his course at the hospital. Philip began to wish with all his might for the old man's death. He reckoned out how long he could possibly live; he was well over seventy. Philip did not know his exact age, but he must be at least seventy-five; he suffered from chronic bronchitis and every winter had a bad cough. Though he knew them by heart Philip read over and over again the details in his text-book of medicine of chronic bronchitis in the old. A severe winter might be too much for the old man. With all his heart Philip longed for cold and rain. He thought of it constantly, so that it became a monomania. Uncle William was affected by the great heat too, and in August they had three weeks of sweltering weather. Philip imagined to himself that one day perhaps a telegram would come saying that the Vicar had died suddenly, and he pictured to himself his unutterable relief. As he stood at the top of the stairs and directed people to the departments they wanted, he occupied his mind with thinking incessantly what he would do with the money. He did not know how much it would be, perhaps no more than five hundred pounds, but even that would be enough. He would leave the shop at once, he would not bother to give notice, he would pack his box and go without saying a word to anybody; and then he would return to the hospital. That was the first thing. Would he have forgotten much? In six months he could get it all back, and then he would take his three examinations as soon as he could, midwifery first, then medicine and surgery. The awful fear seized him that his uncle, notwithstanding his promises, might leave everything he had to the parish or the church. The thought made Philip sick. He could not be so cruel. But if that happened Philip was quite determined what to do, he would not go on in that way indefinitely; his life was only tolerable because he could look forward to something better. If he had no hope he would have no fear. The only brave thing to do then would be to commit suicide, and, thinking this over too, Philip decided minutely what painless drug he would take and how he would get hold of it. It encouraged him to think that if things became unendurable, he had at all events a way out.

"Second to the right, madam, and down the stairs. First on the left and straight through. Mr. Philips, forward please."

Once a month, for a week, Philip was "on duty." He had to go to the department at seven in the morning and keep an eye on the sweepers. When they finished he had to take the sheets off the cases and the models. Then, in the evening when the assistants left, he had to put back the sheets on the models and the cases and "gang" the sweepers again. It was a dusty, dirty job. He was not allowed to read or write or smoke, but just had to walk about, and the time hung heavily on his hands. When he went off at half past nine he had supper given him, and this was the only consolation; for tea at five o'clock had left him with a healthy appetite, and the bread and cheese, the abundant cocoa, which the firm provided, were welcome.

One day when Philip had been at Lynn's for three months, Mr. Sampson, the buyer, came into the department, fuming with anger. The manager, happening to notice the costume window as he came in, had sent for the buyer and made satirical remarks upon the colour scheme. Forced to submit in silence to his superior's sarcasm, Mr. Sampson took it out of the assistants; and he rated the wretched fellow whose duty it was to dress the window.

"If you want a thing well done you must do it yourself," Mr. Sampson stormed. "I've always said it and I always shall. One can't leave anything to you chaps. Intelligent you call yourselves, do you? Intelligent!"

He threw the word at the assistants as though it were the bitterest term of reproach.

"Don't you know that if you put an electric blue in the window it'll kill all the other blues?"

He looked round the department ferociously, and his eye fell upon Philip.

"You'll dress the window next Friday, Carey. Let's see what you can make of it."

He went into his office, muttering angrily. Philip's heart sank. When Friday morning came he went into the window with a sickening sense of shame. His cheeks were burning. It was horrible to display himself to the passers-by, and though he told himself it was foolish to give way to such a feeling he turned his back to the street. There was not much chance that any of the students at the hospital would pass along Oxford Street at that hour, and he knew hardly anyone else in London; but as Philip worked, with a huge lump in his throat, he fancied that on turning round he would catch the eye of some man he knew. He made all the haste he could. By the simple observation that all reds went together, and by spacing the costumes more than was usual, Philip got a very good effect; and when the buyer went into the street to look at the result he was obviously pleased.

"I knew I shouldn't go far wrong in putting you on the window. The fact is, you and me are gentlemen; mind you, I wouldn't say this in the department, but you and me are gentlemen; and that always tells. It's no good your telling me it doesn't tell, because I know it does tell."

Philip was put on the job regularly, but he could not accustom himself to the publicity; and he dreaded Friday morning, on which the window was dressed, with a terror that made him awake at five o'clock and lie sleepless with sickness in his heart. The girls in the department noticed his shame-faced way, and they very soon discovered his trick of standing with his back to the street. They laughed at him and called him "sidey."

"I suppose you're afraid your aunt'll come along and cut you out of her will."

On the whole he got on well enough with the girls. They thought him a little queer; but his club-foot seemed to excuse his not being like the rest, and they found in due course that he was good-natured. He never minded helping anyone, and he was polite and even-tempered.

"You can see he's a gentleman," they said.

"Very reserved, isn't he?" said one young woman to whose passionate enthusiasm for the theatre he had listened unmoved.

Most of them had "fellers," and those who hadn't said they had rather than have it supposed that no one had an inclination for them. One or two showed signs of being willing to start a flirtation with Philip, and he watched their manoeuvres with grave amusement. He had had enough of love-making for some time; and he was nearly always tired and often hungry.

Chapter 106

Philip avoided the places he had known in happier times. The little gatherings at the tavern in Beak Street were broken up: Macalister, having let down his friends, no longer went there, and Hayward was at the Cape. Only Lawson remained; and Philip, feeling that now the painter and he had nothing in common, did not wish to see him; but one Saturday afternoon, after dinner, having changed his clothes he walked down Regent Street to go to the free library in St. Martin's Lane, meaning to spend the afternoon there, and suddenly found himself face to face with him. His first instinct was to pass on without a word, but Lawson did not give him the opportunity.

"Where on earth have you been all this time?" he cried.

"I?" said Philip.

"I wrote you and asked you to come to the studio for a beano and you never even answered."

"I didn't get your letter."

"No, I know. I went to the hospital to ask for you, and I saw my letter in the rack. Have you chucked the Medical?"

Philip hesitated for a moment. He was ashamed to tell the truth, but the shame he felt angered him, and he forced himself to speak. He could not help reddening.

"Yes, I lost the little money I had. I couldn't afford to go on with it."

"I say, I'm awfully sorry. What are you doing?"

"I'm a shop-walker."

The words choked Philip, but he was determined not to shirk the truth. He kept his eyes on Lawson and saw his embarrassment. Philip smiled savagely.

"If you went into Lynn and Sedley's, and made your way into the 'made Robes' department, you would see me in a frock coat, walking about with a *dégagé* air and directing ladies who want to buy petticoats or stockings. 'First to the right, madam, and second on the left.' "

Lawson, seeing that Philip was making a jest of it, laughed awkwardly. He did not know what to say. The picture that Philip called up horrified him, but he was afraid to show his sympathy.

"That's a bit of a change for you," he said.

His words seemed absurd to him, and immediately he wished he had not said them. Philip flushed darkly.

"A bit," he said. "By the way, I owe you five bob."

He put his hand in his pocket and pulled out some silver.

"Oh, it doesn't matter. I'd forgotten all about it."

"Go on, take it."

Lawson received the money silently. They stood in the middle of the pavement, and people jostled them as they passed. There was a sardonic twinkle in Philip's eyes, which made the painter intensely uncomfortable, and he could not tell that Philip's heart was heavy with despair. Lawson wanted dreadfully to do something, but he did not know what to do.

"I say, won't you come to the studio and have a talk?"

"No," said Philip.

"Why not?"

"There's nothing to talk about."

He saw the pain come into Lawson's eyes, he could not help it, he was sorry, but he had to think of himself; he could not bear the thought of discussing his situation, he could endure it only by determining resolutely not to think about it. He was afraid of his weakness if once he began to open his heart. Moreover, he took irresistible dislikes to the places where he had been miserable; he remembered the humiliation he had endured when he had waited in that studio, ravenous with hunger, for Lawson to offer him a meal, and the last occasion when he had taken the five shillings off him. He hated the sight of Lawson because he recalled those days of utter abasement.

"Then look here, come and dine with me one night. Choose your own evening."

Philip was touched with the painter's kindness. All sorts of people were strangely kind to him, he thought.

"It's awfully good of you, old man, but I'd rather not." He held out his hand. "Good-bye."

Lawson, troubled by a behaviour which seemed inexplicable, took his hand, and Philip quickly limped away. His heart was heavy; and, as was usual with him, he began to reproach himself for what he had done: he did not know what madness of pride had made him refuse the offered friendship. But he heard someone running behind him and presently Lawson's voice calling him; he stopped and suddenly the feeling of hostility got the better of him; he presented to Lawson a cold, set face.

"What is it?"

"I suppose you heard about Hayward, didn't you?"

"I know he went to the Cape."

"He died, you know, soon after landing."

For a moment Philip did not answer. He could hardly believe his ears.

"How?" he asked.

"Oh, enteric. Hard luck, wasn't it? I thought you mightn't know. Gave me a bit of a turn when I heard it."

Lawson nodded quickly and walked away. Philip felt a shiver pass through his heart. He had never before lost a friend of his own age, for the death of Cronshaw, a man so much older than himself, had seemed to come in the normal course of things. The news gave him a peculiar shock. It reminded him of his own mortality, for like everyone else Philip, knowing perfectly that all men must die, had no intimate feeling that the same must apply to himself; and Hayward's death, though he had long ceased to have any warm feeling for him, affected him deeply. He remembered on a sudden all the good talks they had had, and it pained him to think that they would never talk with one another again; he remembered their first meeting, and the pleasant months they had spent together in Heidelberg. Philip's heart sank as he thought of the lost years. He walked on mechanically, not noticing where he went, and realized suddenly, with a movement of irritation, that instead of turning down the Haymarket he had sauntered along Shaftesbury Avenue. It bored him to retrace his steps; and besides, with that news, he did not want to read, he wanted to sit alone and think. He made up his mind to go to the British Museum. Solitude was now his only luxury. Since he had been at Lynn's he had often gone there and sat in front of the groups from the Parthenon; and, not deliberately thinking, had allowed their divine masses to rest his troubled soul. But this afternoon they had nothing to say to him, and after a few minutes, impatiently, he wandered out of the room. There were too many people, provincials with foolish faces, foreigners poring over guide-books; their hideousness besmirched the everlasting masterpieces, their restlessness troubled the god's immortal repose. He went into another room and here there was hardly anyone. Philip sat down wearily. His nerves were on edge. He could not get the people out of his mind. Sometimes at Lynn's they affected him in the same way, and he looked at them file past him with horror; they were so ugly and there was such meanness in their faces, it was terrifying; their features were distorted with paltry desires, and you felt they were strange to any ideas of beauty. They had furtive eyes and weak chins. There was no wickedness in them, but only pettiness and vulgarity. Their humour was a low facetiousness. Sometimes he found himself looking at them to see what animal they resembled (he tried not to, for it quickly became an obsession), and he saw in them all the sheep or the horse or the fox or the goat. Human beings filled him with disgust.

But presently the influence of the place descended upon him. He felt quieter. He began to look absently at the tombstones with which the room was lined. They were the work of Athenian stone masons of the fourth and fifth centuries before Christ, and they were very simple, work of no great talent but with the exquisite spirit of Athens upon them; time had mellowed the marble to the colour of honey, so that unconsciously one thought of the bees of Hymettus, and softened their outlines. Some represented a nude figure, seated on a bench, some the departure of the dead from those who loved him, and some the dead clasping hands with one who remained behind. On all was the tragic word farewell; that and nothing more. Their simplicity was infinitely touching. Friend parted from friend, the son from his mother, and the restraint made the survivor's grief more poignant. It was so long, long ago, and century upon century had passed over that unhappiness; for two thousand years those who wept had been dust as those they wept for. Yet the woe was alive still, and it filled Philip's heart so that he felt compassion spring up in it, and he said:

"Poor things, poor things."

And it came to him that the gaping sightseers and the fat strangers with their guide-books, and all those mean, common people who thronged the shop, with their trivial desires and vulgar cares, were mortal and must die. They too loved and must part from those they loved, the son from his mother, the wife from her husband; and perhaps it was more tragic because their lives were ugly and sordid, and they knew nothing that gave beauty to the world. There was one stone which was very beautiful, a bas-relief of two young men holding each other's hand; and the reticence of line, the simplicity, made one like to think that the sculptor here had been touched with a genuine emotion. It was an exquisite memorial to that than which the world offers but one thing more precious, to a friendship; and as Philip looked at it, he felt the tears come to his eyes. He thought of Hayward and his eager admiration for him when first they met, and how disillusion had come and then indifference, till nothing held them together but habit and old memories. It was one of the queer things of life that you saw a person every day for months and were so intimate with him that you could not imagine existence without him; then separation came and everything went on in the same way, and the companion who had seemed essential proved unnecessary. Your life proceeded and you did not even miss him. Philip thought of those early days in Heidelberg when Hayward, capable of great things, had been full of enthusiasm for the future, and how, little by little, achieving nothing, he had resigned himself to failure. Now he was dead. His death had been as futile as his life. He died ingloriously, of a stupid disease, failing once more, even at the end, to accomplish anything. It was just the same now as if he had never lived.

Philip asked himself desperately what was the use of living at all. It all seemed inane. It was the same with Cronshaw: it was quite unimportant that he had lived; he was dead and forgotten, his book of poems sold in remainder by second-hand booksellers; his life seemed to have served nothing except to give a pushing journalist occasion to write an article in a review. And Philip cried out in his soul:

"What is the use of it?"

The effort was so incommensurate with the result. The

bright hopes of youth had to be paid for at such a bitter price of disillusionment. Pain and disease and unhappiness weighed down the scale so heavily. What did it all mean? He thought of his own life, the high hopes with which he had entered upon it, the limitations which his body forced upon him, his friendlessness, and the lack of affection which had surrounded his youth. He did not know that he had ever done anything but what seemed best to do, and what a cropper he had come! Other men, with no more advantages than he, succeeded, and others again, with many more, failed. It seemed pure chance. The rain fell alike upon the just and upon the unjust, and for nothing was there a why and a wherefore.

Thinking of Cronshaw, Philip remembered the Persian rug which he had given him, telling him that it offered an answer to his question upon the meaning of life; and suddenly the answer occurred to him: he chuckled: now that he had it, it was like one of the puzzles which you worry over till you are shown the solution and then cannot imagine how it could ever have escaped you. The answer was obvious. Life had no meaning. On the earth, satellite of a star speeding through space, living things had arisen under the influence of conditions which were part of the planet's history; and as there had been a beginning of life upon it, so, under the influence of other conditions, there would be an end: man, no more significant than other forms of life, had come not as the climax of creation but as a physical reaction to the environment. Philip remembered the story of the Eastern King who, desiring to know the history of man, was brought by a sage five hundred volumes; busy with affairs of state, he bade him go and condense it; in twenty years the sage returned and his history now was in no more than fifty volumes, but the King, too old then to read so many ponderous tomes, bade him go and shorten it once more; twenty years passed again and the sage, old and grey, brought a single book in which was the knowledge the King had sought; but the King lay on his death-bed, and he had no time to read even that; and then the sage gave him the history of man in a single line; it was this: he was born, he suffered, and he died. There was no meaning in life, and man by living served no end. It was immaterial whether he was born or not born, whether he lived or ceased to live. Life was insignificant and death without consequence. Philip exulted, as he had exulted in his boyhood when the weight of a belief in God was lifted from his shoulders: it seemed to him that the last burden of responsibility was taken from him; and for the first time he was utterly free. His insignificance was turned to power, and he felt himself suddenly equal with the cruel fate which had seemed to persecute him; for, if life was meaningless, the world was robbed of its cruelty. What he did or left undone did not matter. Failure was unimportant and success amounted to nothing. He was the most inconsiderate creature in that swarming mass of mankind which for a brief space occupied the surface of the earth; and he was almighty because he had wrenched from chaos the secret of its nothingness. Thoughts came tumbling over one another in Philip's eager fancy, and he took long breaths of joyous satisfaction. He felt inclined to leap and sing. He had not been so happy for months.

"Oh life," he cried in his heart, "oh life, where is thy sting?"

For the same uprush of fancy which had shown him with all

the force of mathematical demonstration that life had no meaning, brought with it another idea; and that was why Cronshaw, he imagined, had given him the Persian rug. As the weaver elaborated his pattern for no end but the pleasure of his aesthetic sense, so might a man live his life, or if one was forced to believe that his actions were outside his choosing, so might a man look at his life, that it made a pattern. There was as little need to do this as there was use. It was merely something he did for his own pleasure. Out of the manifold events of his life, his deeds, his feelings, his thoughts, he might make a design, regular, elaborate, complicated, or beautiful; and though it might be no more than an illusion that he had the power of selection, though it might be no more than a fantastic legerdemain in which appearances were interwoven with moonbeams, that did not matter: it seemed, and so to him it was. In the vast warp of life (a river arising from no spring and flowing endlessly to no sea), with the background to his fancies that there was no meaning and that nothing was important, a man might get a personal satisfaction in selecting the various strands that worked out the pattern. There was one pattern, the most obvious, perfect, and beautiful, in which a man was born, grew to manhood, married, produced children, toiled for his bread, and died; but there were others, intricate and wonderful, in which happiness did not enter and in which success was not attempted; and in them might be discovered a more troubling grace. Some lives, and Hayward's was among them, the blind indifference of chance cut off while the design was still imperfect; and then the solace was comfortable that it did not matter; other lives, such as Cronshaw's, offered a pattern which was difficult to follow: the point of view had to be shifted and old standards had to be altered before one could understand that such a life was its own justification. Philip thought that in throwing over the desire for happiness he was casting aside the last of his illusions. His life had seemed horrible when it was measured by its happiness, but now he seemed to gather strength as he realized that it might be measured by something else. Happiness mattered as little as pain. They came in, both of them, as all the other details of his life came in, to the elaboration of the design. He seemed for an instant to stand above the accidents of his existence, and he felt that they could not affect him again as they had done before. Whatever happened to him now would be one more motive to add to the complexity of the pattern, and when the end approached he would rejoice in its completion. It would be a work of art, and it would be none the less beautiful because he alone knew of its existence, and with his death it would at once cease to be.

Philip was happy.

Chapter 107

Mr. Sampson, the buyer, took a fancy to Philip. Mr. Sampson was very dashing, and the girls in his department said they would not be surprised if he married one of the rich customers. He lived out of town and often impressed the assistants by putting on his evening clothes in the office. Sometimes he would be seen by those on sweeping duty coming in next morning still dressed, and they would wink gravely to one another while he went into his office and changed into a frockcoat. On these occasions, having slipped out for a hurried breakfast, he also would wink at Philip as he walked up the stairs on his way back and rub his hands.

"What a night! What a night!" he said. "My word!"

He told Philip that he was the only gentleman there, and he and Philip were the only fellows who knew what life was. Having said this, he changed his manner suddenly, called Philip Mr. Carey instead of old boy, assumed the importance due to his position as buyer, and put Philip back into his place of shop-walker.

Lynn and Sedley received fashion papers from Paris once a week and adapted the costumes illustrated in them to the needs of their customers. Their clientele was peculiar. The most substantial part consisted of women from the smaller manufacturing towns, who were too elegant to have their frocks made locally and not sufficiently acquainted with London to discover good dressmakers within their means. Beside these, incongruously, was a large number of music hall artistes. This was a connection that Mr. Sampson had worked up for himself and took great pride in. They had begun by getting their stage-costumes at Lynn's, and he had induced many of them to get their other clothes there as well.

"As good as Paquin and half the price," he said.

He had a persuasive, hail-fellow-well-met air with him which appealed to customers of this sort, and they said to one another:

"What's the good of throwing money away when you can get a coat and skirt at Lynn's that nobody knows don't come from Paris?"

Mr. Sampson was very proud of his friendship with the popular favourites whose frocks he made, and when he went out to dinner at two o'clock on Sunday with Miss Victoria Virgo— "she was wearing that powder blue we made her and I lay she didn't let on it come from us, I 'ad to tell her meself that if I 'adn't designed it with my own hands I'd have said it must come from Paquin" —at her beautiful house in Tulse Hill, he regaled the department next day with abundant details. Philip had never paid much attention to women's clothes, but in course of time he began, a little amused at himself, to take a technical interest in them. He had an eye for colour which was more highly trained than that of anyone in the department, and he had kept from his student days in Paris some knowledge of line. Mr.

Sampson, an ignorant man conscious of his incompetence, but with a shrewdness that enabled him to combine other people's suggestions, constantly asked the opinion of the assistants in his department in making up new designs; and he had the quickness to see that Philip's criticisms were valuable. But he was very jealous, and would never allow that he took anyone's advice. When he had altered some drawing in accordance with Philip's suggestion, he always finished up by saying:

"Well, it comes round to my own idea in the end."

One day, when Philip had been at the shop for five months, Miss Alice Antonia, the well-known serio-comic, came in and asked to see Mr. Sampson. She was a large woman, with flaxen hair, and a boldly painted face, a metallic voice, and the breezy manner of a *comédienne* accustomed to be on friendly terms with the gallery boys of provincial music halls. She had a new song and wished Mr. Sampson to design a costume for her.

"I want something striking," she said. "I don't want any old thing, you know. I want something different from what anybody else has."

Mr. Sampson, bland and familiar, said he was quite certain they could get her the very thing she required. He showed her sketches.

"I know there's nothing here that would do, but I just want to show you the kind of thing I would suggest."

"Oh no, that's not the sort of thing at all," she said, as she glanced at them impatiently. "What I want is something that'll just hit 'em in the jaw and make their front teeth rattle."

"Yes, I quite understand, Miss Antonia," said the buyer, with a bland smile, but his eyes grew blank and stupid.

"I expect I shall 'ave to pop over to Paris for it in the end."

"Oh, I think we can give you satisfaction, Miss Antonia. What you can get in Paris you can get here."

When she had swept out of the department Mr. Sampson, a little worried, discussed the matter with Mrs. Hodges.

"She's a caution and no mistake," said Mrs. Hodges.

"Alice, where art thou?" remarked the buyer, irritably, and thought he had scored a point against her.

His ideas of music hall costumes had never gone beyond short skirts, a swirl of lace, and glittering sequins; but Miss Antonia had expressed herself on that subject in no uncertain terms.

"Oh, my aunt!" she said.

And the invocation was uttered in such a tone as to indicate a rooted antipathy to anything so commonplace, even if she had not added that sequins gave her the sick. Mr. Sampson "got out" one or two ideas, but Mrs. Hodges told him frankly she did not think they would do. It was she who gave Philip the suggestion:

"Can you draw, Phil? Why don't you try your 'and and see what you can do?"

Philip bought a cheap box of water colours, and in the evening while Bell, the noisy lad of sixteen, whistling three notes, busied himself with his stamps, he made one or two sketches. He remembered some of the costumes he had seen in Paris, and he adapted one of them, getting his effect from a combination of violent, unusual colours. The result amused him and next morning he showed it to Mrs. Hodges. She was somewhat astonished, but took it at once to the buyer.

"It's unusual," he said, "there's no denying that."

It puzzled him, and at the same time his trained eye saw that it would make up admirably. To save his face he began making suggestions for altering it, but Mrs. Hodges, with more sense, advised him to show it to Miss Antonia as it was.

"It's neck or nothing with her, and she may take a fancy to it."

"It's a good deal more nothing than neck," said Mr. Sampson, looking at the *décolletage*. "He can draw, can't he? Fancy 'im keeping it dark all this time."

When Miss Antonia was announced, the buyer placed the design on the table in such a position that it must catch her eye the moment she was shown into his office. She pounced on it at once.

"What's that?" she said. "Why can't I 'ave that?"

"That's just an idea we got out for you," said Mr. Sampson casually. "D'you like it?"

"Do I like it!" she said. "Give me 'alf a pint with a little drop of gin in it."

"Ah, you see, you don't have to go to Paris. You've only got to say what you want and there you are."

The work was put in hand at once, and Philip felt quite a thrill of satisfaction when he saw the costume completed. The buyer and Mrs. Hodges took all the credit of it; but he did not care, and when he went with them to the Tivoli to see Miss Antonia wear it for the first time he was filled with elation. In answer to her questions he at last told Mrs. Hodges how he had learnt to draw—fearing that the people he lived with would think he wanted to put on airs, he had always taken the greatest care to say nothing about his past occupations—and she repeated the information to Mr. Sampson. The buyer said nothing to him on the subject, but began to treat him a little more deferentially and presently gave him designs to do for two of the country customers. They met with satisfaction. Then he began to speak to his clients of a "clever young feller, Paris art student, you know," who worked for him; and soon Philip, ensconced behind a screen, in his shirt-sleeves, was drawing from morning till night. Sometimes he was so busy that he had to dine at three with the "stragglers." He liked it, because there were few of them and they were all too tired to talk; the food also was better, for it consisted of what was left over from the buyers' table. Philip's rise from shop-walker to designer of costumes had a great effect on the department. He realized that he was an object of envy. Harris, the assistant with the queer-shaped head, who was the first person he had known at the shop and had attached himself to Philip, could not conceal his bitterness.

"Some people 'ave all the luck," he said. "You'll be a buyer yourself one of these days, and we shall all be calling you 'sir'."

He told Philip that he should demand higher wages, for notwith-standing the difficult work he was now engaged in, he received no more than the six shillings a week with which he started. But it was a ticklish matter to ask for a rise. The manager had a sardonic way of dealing with such applicants.

"Think you're worth more, do you? How much d'you think you're worth, eh?"

The assistant, with his heart in his mouth, would suggest that he thought he ought to have another two shillings a week.

"Oh, very well, if you think you're worth it. You can 'ave it." Then he paused and sometimes, with a steely eye, added: "And you can 'ave your notice too."

It was no use then to withdraw your request, you had to go. The manager's idea was that assistants who were dissatisfied did not work properly, and if they were not worth a rise it was better to sack them at once. The result was that they never asked for one unless they were prepared to leave. Philip hesitated. He was a little suspicious of the men in his room who told him that the buyer could not do without him. They were decent fellows, but their sense of humour was primitive, and it would have seemed funny to them if they had persuaded Philip to ask for more wages and he were sacked. He could not forget the mortification he had suffered in looking for work, he did not wish to expose himself to that again, and he knew there was small chance of his getting elsewhere a post as designer: there were hundreds of people about who could draw as well as he. But he wanted money very badly; his clothes were worn out, and the heavy carpets rotted his socks and boots; he had almost persuaded himself to take the venturesome step when one morning, passing up from breakfast in the basement through the passage that led to the manager's office, he saw a queue of men waiting in answer to an advertisement. There were about a hundred of them, and whichever was engaged would be offered his keep and the same six shillings a week that Philip had. He saw some of them cast envious glances at him because he had employment. It made him shudder. He dared not risk it.

Chapter 108

The winter passed. Now and then Philip went to the hospital, slinking in when it was late and there was little chance of meeting anyone he knew, to see whether there were letters for him. At Easter he received one from his uncle. He was surprised to hear from him, for the Vicar of Blackstable had never written him more than half a dozen letters in his whole life, and they were on business matters.

> *Dear Philip,*
>
> *If you are thinking of taking a holiday soon and care to come down here I shall be pleased to see you. I was very ill with my bronchitis in the winter and Doctor Wigram never expected me to pull through. I have a wonderful constitution and I made, thank God, a marvellous recovery.*
>
> *Yours affectionately,*
> *William Carey.*

The letter made Philip angry. How did his uncle think he was living? He did not even trouble to inquire. He might have starved for all the old man cared. But as he walked home something struck him; he stopped under a lamp post and read the letter again; the handwriting had no longer the businesslike firmness which had characterised it; it was larger and wavering: perhaps the illness had shaken him more than he was willing to confess, and he sought in that formal note to express a yearning to see the only relation he had in the world. Philip wrote back that he could come down to Blackstable for a fortnight in July. The invitation was convenient, for he had not known what to do with his brief holiday. The Athelnys went hopping in September, but he could not then be spared, since during that month the autumn models were prepared. The rule of Lynn's was that everyone must take a fortnight whether he wanted it or not; and during that time, if he had nowhere to go, the assistant might sleep in his room, but he was not allowed food. A number had no friends within reasonable distance of London, and to these the holiday was an awkward interval when they had to provide food out of their small wages and, with the whole day on their hands, had nothing to spend. Philip had not been out of London since his visit to Brighton with Mildred, now two years before, and he longed for fresh air and the silence of the sea. He thought of it with such a passionate desire, all through May and June, that, when at length the time came for him to go, he was listless.

On his last evening, when he talked with the buyer of one or two jobs he had to leave over, Mr. Sampson suddenly said to him:

"What wages have you been getting?"

"Six shillings."

"I don't think it's enough. I'll see that you're put up to twelve when you come back."

"Thank you very much," smiled Philip. "I'm beginning to want some new clothes badly."

"If you stick to your work and don't go larking about with the girls like what some of them do, I'll look after you, Carey. Mind you, you've got a lot to learn, but you're promising, I'll say that for you, you're promising, and I'll see that you get a pound a week as soon as you deserve it."

Philip wondered how long he would have to wait for that. Two years?

He was startled at the change in his uncle. When last he had seen him he was a stout man who held himself upright, clean-shaven, with a round, sensual face; but he had fallen in strangely, his skin was yellow; there were great bags under the eyes, and he was bent and old. He had grown a beard during his last illness, and he walked very slowly.

"I'm not at my best today," he said, when Philip, having just arrived, was sitting with him in the dining-room. "The heat upsets me."

Philip, asking after the affairs of the parish, looked at him and wondered how much longer he could last. A hot summer would finish him; Philip noticed how thin his hands were; they trembled. It meant so much to Philip. If he died that summer he could go back to the hospital at the beginning of the winter session; his heart leaped at the thought of returning no more to Lynn's. At dinner the Vicar sat humped up on his chair, and the housekeeper who had been with him since his wife's death said:

"Shall Mr. Philip carve, sir?"

The old man, who had been about to do so from disinclination to confess his weakness, seemed glad at the first suggestion to relinquish the attempt.

"You've got a very good appetite," said Philip.

"Oh yes, I always eat well. But I'm thinner than when you were here last. I'm glad to be thinner, I didn't like being so fat. Dr. Wigram thinks I'm all the better for being thinner than I was."

When dinner was over the housekeeper brought him some medicine.

"Show the prescription to Master Philip," he said. "He's a doctor too. I'd like him to see that he thinks it's all right. I told Dr. Wigram that now you're studying to be a doctor he ought to make a reduction in his charges. It's dreadful the bills I've had to pay. He came every day for two months, and he charges five shillings a visit. It's a lot of money, isn't it? He comes twice a week still. I'm going to tell him he needn't come any more. I'll send for him if I want him."

He looked at Philip eagerly while he read the prescriptions. They were narcotics. There were two of them, and one was a medicine which the Vicar explained he was to use only if his neuritis grew unendurable.

"I'm very careful," he said. "I don't want to get into the opium habit."

He did not mention his nephew's affairs. Philip fancied that it was by way of precaution, in case he asked for money, that his uncle kept dwelling on the financial calls upon him. He had spent so much on the doctor and so much more on the chemist; while he was ill they had had to have a fire every day in his bedroom, and now on Sunday he needed a carriage to go to church in the evening as well as in the morning. Philip felt angrily inclined to say he need not be afraid, he was not going to borrow from him, but he held his tongue. It seemed to him that everything had left the old man now but two things, pleasure in his food and a grasping desire for money. It was a hideous old age.

In the afternoon Dr. Wigram came, and after the visit Philip walked with him to the garden gate.

"How d'you think he is?" said Philip.

Dr. Wigram was more anxious not to do wrong than to do right, and he never hazarded a definite opinion if he could help it. He had practised at Blackstable for five-and-thirty years. He had the reputation of being very safe, and many of his patients thought it much better that a doctor should be safe than clever. There was a new man at Blackstable—he had been settled there for ten years, but they still looked upon him as an interloper—and he was said to be very clever; but he had not much practice among the better people, because no one really knew anything about him.

"Oh, he's as well as can be expected," said Dr. Wigram in answer to Philip's inquiry.

"Has he got anything seriously the matter with him?"

"Well, Philip, your uncle is no longer a young man," said the doctor with a cautious little smile, which suggested that after all the Vicar of Blackstable was not an old man either.

"He seems to think his heart's in a bad way."

"I'm not satisfied with his heart," hazarded the doctor, "I think he should be careful, very careful."

On the tip of Philip's tongue was the question: how much longer can he live? He was afraid it would shock. In these matters a periphrase was demanded by the decorum of life, but, as he asked another question instead, it flashed through him that the doctor must be accustomed to the impatience of a sick man's relatives. He must see through their sympathetic expressions. Philip, with a faint smile at his own hypocrisy, cast down his eyes.

"I suppose he's in no immediate danger?"

This was the kind of question the doctor hated. If you said a patient couldn't live another month the family prepared itself for a bereavement, and if then the patient lived on they visited the medical attendant with the resentment they felt at having tormented themselves before it was necessary. On the other hand, if you said the patient might live a year and he died in a week the family said you did not know your business. They thought of all the affection they would have lavished on the defunct if they had known the end was so near. Dr. Wigram made the gesture of washing his hands.

"I don't think there's any grave risk so long as he—remains as he is," he ventured at last. "But on the other hand, we mustn't forget that he's no longer a young man, and—well, the machine is wearing out. If he gets over the hot weather I don't see why he shouldn't get on very comfortably till the winter, and then if the winter does not bother him too much, well, I don't see why anything should happen."

Philip went back to the dining-room where his uncle was sitting. With his skull-cap and a crochet shawl over his shoulders he looked grotesque. His eyes had been fixed on the door, and they rested on Philip's face as he entered. Philip saw that his uncle had been waiting anxiously for his return.

"Well, what did he say about me?"

Philip understood suddenly that the old man was frightened of dying. It made Philip a little ashamed, so that he looked away involuntarily. He was always embarrassed by the weakness of human nature.

"He says he thinks you're much better," said Philip.

A gleam of delight came into his uncle's eyes.

"I've got a wonderful constitution," he said. "What else did he say?" he added suspiciously.

Philip smiled.

"He said that if you take care of yourself there's no reason why you shouldn't live to be a hundred."

"I don't know that I can expect to do that, but I don't see why I shouldn't see eighty. My mother lived till she was eighty-four."

There was a little table by the side of Mr. Carey's chair, and on it were a Bible and the large volume of the Common Prayer from which for so many years he had been accustomed to read to his household. He stretched out now his shaking hand and took his Bible.

"Those old patriarchs lived to a jolly good old age, didn't they?" he said, with a queer little laugh in which Philip read a sort of timid appeal.

The old man clung to life. Yet he believed implicitly all that his religion taught him. He had no doubt in the immortality of the soul, and he felt that he had conducted himself well enough, according to his capacities, to make it very likely that he would go to heaven. In his long career to how many dying persons must he have administered the consolations of religion! Perhaps he was like the doctor who could get no benefit from his own prescriptions. Philip was puzzled and shocked by that eager cleaving to the earth. He wondered what nameless horror was at the back of the old man's mind. He would have liked to probe into his soul so that he might see in its nakedness the dreadful dismay of the unknown which he suspected.

The fortnight passed quickly and Philip returned to London. He passed a sweltering August behind his screen in the costumes department, drawing in his shirt-sleeves. The assistants in relays went for their holidays. In the evening Philip generally went into Hyde Park and listened to the band. Growing more accustomed to his work it tired him less, and his mind recovering from its long stagnation, sought for fresh activity. His whole desire now was set on his uncle's death. He kept on dreaming the same dream: a telegram was handed to him one morning, early, which announced the Vicar's sudden demise, and freedom was in his grasp. When he awoke and found it was nothing but a dream he was filled with sombre rage. He occupied himself, now that the event seemed likely to happen at any time, with elaborate plans for the future. In these he passed rapidly over the year which he must spend before it was possible for him to be qualified and dwelt on the journey to Spain on which his heart was set. He read books about that country, which he borrowed from the free library, and already he knew from photographs exactly what each city looked like. He saw himself lingering in Cordova on the bridge that spanned the Gaudalquivir; he wandered through tortuous streets in Toledo and sat in churches where he wrung from El Greco the secret which he felt the mysterious painter held for him. Athelny entered into his humour, and on Sunday afternoons they made out elaborate itineraries so that Philip should miss nothing that was noteworthy. To cheat his impatience Philip began to teach himself Spanish, and in the deserted sitting-room in Harrington Street he spent an hour every evening doing Spanish exercises and puzzling out with an English translation by his side the magnificent phrases of *Don Quixote*. Athelny gave him a lesson once a week, and Philip learned a few sentences to help him on his journey. Mrs. Athelny laughed at them.

"You two and your Spanish!" she said. "Why don't you do something useful?"

But Sally, who was growing up and was to put up her hair at Christmas, stood by sometimes and listened in her grave way while her father and Philip exchanged remarks in a language she did not understand. She thought her father the most wonderful man who had ever existed, and she expressed her opinion of Philip only through her father's commendations.

"Father thinks a rare lot of your Uncle Philip," she remarked to her brothers and sisters.

Thorpe, the eldest boy, was old enough to go on the *Arethusa*, and Athelny regaled his family with magnificent descriptions of the appearance the lad would make when he came back in uniform for his holidays. As soon as Sally was seventeen she was to be apprenticed to a dressmaker. Athelny in his rhetorical way talked of the birds, strong enough to fly now, who were leaving the parental nest, and with tears in his eyes told them that the nest would be there still if ever they wished to return to it. A shakedown and a dinner would always be theirs, and the heart of a father would never be closed to the troubles of his children.

"You do talk, Athelny," said his wife. "I don't know what trouble they're likely to get into so long as they're steady. So long as you're honest and not afraid of work you'll never be out of a job, that's what I think, and I can tell you I shan't be sorry when I see the last of them earning their own living."

Child-bearing, hard work, and constant anxiety were beginning to tell on Mrs. Athelny; and sometimes her back ached in the evening so that she had to sit down and rest herself. Her ideal of happiness was to have a girl to do the rough work so that she need not herself get up before seven. Athelny waved his beautiful white hand.

"Ah, my Betty, we've deserved well of the state, you and I. We've reared nine healthy children, and the boys shall serve their king; the girls shall cook and sew and in their turn breed healthy children." He turned to Sally, and to comfort her for the anti-climax of the contrast added grandiloquently: "They also serve who only stand and wait."

Athelny had lately added socialism to the other contradictory theories he vehemently believed in, and he stated now:

"In a socialist state we should be richly pensioned, you and I, Betty."

"Oh, don't talk to me about your socialists, I've got no patience with them," she cried. "It only means that another lot of lazy loafers will make a good thing out of the working classes. My motto is, leave me alone; I don't want anyone interfering with me;

I'll make the best of a bad job, and the devil take the hindmost."

"D'you call life a bad job?" said Athelny. "Never! We've had our ups and downs, we've had our struggles, we've always been poor, but it's been worth it, ay, worth it a hundred times I say when I look round at my children."

"You do talk, Athelny," she said, looking at him, not with anger but with scornful calm. "You've had the pleasant part of the children, I've had the bearing of them, and the bearing with them. I don't say that I'm not fond of them, now they're there, but if I had my time over again I'd remain single. Why, if I'd remained single I might have a little shop by now, and four or five hundred pounds in the bank, and a girl to do the rough work. Oh, I wouldn't go over my life again, not for something."

Philip thought of the countless millions to whom life is no more than unending labour, neither beautiful nor ugly, but just to be accepted in the same spirit as one accepts the changes of the seasons. Fury seized him because it all seemed useless. He could not reconcile himself to the belief that life had no meaning and yet everything he saw, all his thoughts, added to the force of his conviction. But though fury seized him it was a joyful fury. Life was not so horrible if it was meaningless, and he faced it with a strange sense of power.

Chapter 109

The autumn passed into winter. Philip had left his address with Mrs. Foster, his uncle's housekeeper, so that she might communicate with him, but still went once a week to the hospital on the chance of there being a letter. One evening he saw his name on an envelope in a handwriting he had hoped never to see again. It gave him a queer feeling. For a little while he could not bring himself to take it. It brought back a host of hateful memories. But at length, impatient with himself, he ripped open the envelope.

7 William Street,

Fitzroy Square

Dear Phil,

Can I see you for a minute or two as soon as possible. I am in awful trouble and don't know what to do. It's not money.

Yours truly,

Mildred.

He tore the letter into little bits and going out into the street scattered them in the darkness.

"I'll see her damned," he muttered.

A feeling of disgust surged up in him at the thought of seeing her again. He did not care if she was in distress, it served her right whatever it was; he thought of her with hatred, and the love he had had for her aroused his loathing. His recollections filled him with nausea, and as he walked across the Thames he drew himself aside in an instinctive withdrawal from his thought of her. He went to bed, but he could not sleep; he wondered what was the matter with her, and he could not get out of his head the fear that she was ill and hungry; she would not have written to him unless she were desperate. He was angry with himself for his weakness, but he knew that he would have no peace unless he saw her. Next morning he wrote a letter-card and posted it on his way to the shop. He made it as stiff as he could and said merely that he was sorry she was in difficulties and would come to the address she had given at seven o'clock that evening.

It was that of a shabby lodging-house in a sordid street; and when, sick at the thought of seeing her, he asked whether she was in, a wild hope seized him that she had left. It looked the sort of place people moved in and out of frequently. He had not thought of looking at the postmark on her letter and did not know how many days it had lain in the rack. The woman who answered the bell did not reply to his inquiry, but silently preceded him along the passage and knocked on a door at the back.

"Mrs. Miller, a gentleman to see you," she called.

The door was slightly opened, and Mildred looked out suspiciously.

"Oh, it's you," she said. "Come in."

He walked in and she closed the door. It was a very small bedroom, untidy as was every place she lived in; there was a pair of shoes on the floor, lying apart from one another and uncleaned; a hat was on the chest of drawers, with false curls beside it; and there was a blouse on the table. Philip looked for somewhere to put his hat. The hooks behind the door were laden with skirts, and he noticed that they were muddy at the hem.

"Sit down, won't you?" she said. Then she gave a little awkward laugh. "I suppose you were surprised to hear from me again."

"You're awfully hoarse," he answered. "Have you got a sore throat?"

"Yes, I have had for some time."

He did not say anything. He waited for her to explain why she wanted to see him. The look of the room told him clearly enough that she had gone back to the life from which he had taken her. He wondered what had happened to the baby; there was a photograph of it on the chimney-piece, but no sign in the room that a child was ever there. Mildred was holding her handkerchief. She made it into a little ball, and passed it from hand to hand. He saw that she was very nervous. She was staring at the fire, and he could look at her without meeting her eyes. She was much thinner than when she had left him; and the skin, yellow and dryish, was drawn more tightly over her cheekbones. She had dyed her hair and it was now flaxen: it altered her a good deal, and made her look more vulgar.

"I was relieved to get your letter, I can tell you," she said at last. "I thought p'raps you weren't at the 'ospital any more."

Philip did not speak.

"I suppose you're qualified by now, aren't you?"

"No."

"How's that?"

"I'm no longer at the hospital. I had to give it up eighteen months ago."

"You are changeable. You don't seem as if you could stick to anything."

Philip was silent for another moment, and when he went on it was with coldness.

"I lost the little money I had in an unlucky speculation and I couldn't afford to go on with the Medical. I had to earn my living as best I could."

"What are you doing then?"

"I'm in a shop."

"Oh!"

She gave him a quick glance and turned her eyes away at once. He thought that she reddened. She dabbed her palms nervously with the handkerchief.

"You've not forgotten all your doctoring, have you?" She jerked the words out quite oddly.

"Not entirely."

"Because that's why I wanted to see you." Her voice sank to a hoarse whisper. "I don't know what's the matter with me."

"Why don't you go to a hospital?"

"I don't like to do that, and have all the stoodents staring at me, and I'm afraid they'd want to keep me."

"What are you complaining of?" asked Philip coldly, with the stereotyped phrase used in the out-patients' room.

"Well, I've come out in a rash, and I can't get rid of it."

Philip felt a twinge of horror in his heart. Sweat broke out on his forehead.

"Let me look at your throat?"

He took her over to the window and made such examination as he could. Suddenly he caught sight of her eyes. There was deadly fear in them. It was horrible to see. She was terrified. She wanted him to reassure her; she looked at him pleadingly, not daring to ask for words of comfort but with all her nerves astrung to receive them: he had none to offer her.

"I'm afraid you're very ill indeed," he said.

"What d'you think it is?"

When he told her she grew deathly pale, and her lips even turned yellow: she began to cry, hopelessly, quietly at first and then with choking sobs.

"I'm awfully sorry," he said at last. "But I had to tell you."

"I may just as well kill myself and have done with it."

He took no notice of the threat.

"Have you got any money?" he asked.

"Six or seven pounds."

"You must give up this life, you know. Don't you think you could find some work to do? I'm afraid I can't help you much. I only get twelve bob a week."

"What is there I can do now?" she cried impatiently.

"Damn it all, you *must* try to get something."

He spoke to her very gravely, telling her of her own danger and the danger to which she exposed others, and she listened sullenly. He tried to console her. At last he brought her to a sulky acquiescence in which she promised to do all he advised. He wrote a prescription, which he said he would leave at the nearest chemist's, and he impressed upon her the necessity of taking her medicine with the utmost regularity. Getting up to go, he held out his hand.

"Don't be downhearted, you'll soon get over your throat."

But as he went her face became suddenly distorted, and she caught hold of his coat.

"Oh, don't leave me," she cried hoarsely. "I'm so afraid, don't leave me alone yet. Phil, please. There's no one else I can go to, you're the only friend I've ever had."

He felt the terror of her soul, and it was strangely like that terror he had seen in his uncle's eyes when he feared that he might die. Philip looked down. Twice that woman had come into his life and made him wretched; she had no claim upon him; and yet, he knew not why, deep in his heart was a strange aching; it was that which, when he received her letter, had left him no peace till he obeyed her summons.

"I suppose I shall never really quite get over it," he said to himself.

What perplexed him was that he felt a curious physical distaste, which made it uncomfortable for him to be near her.

"What do you want me to do?" he asked.

"Let's go out and dine together. I'll pay."

He hesitated. He felt that she was creeping back again into his life when he thought she was gone out of it for ever. She watched him with sickening anxiety.

"Oh, I know I've treated you shocking, but don't leave me alone now. You've had your revenge. If you leave me by myself now I don't know what I shall do."

"All right, I don't mind," he said, "but we shall have to do it on the cheap, I haven't got money to throw away these days."

She sat down and put her shoes on, then changed her skirt and put on a hat; and they walked out together till they found a restaurant in the Tottenham Court Road. Philip had got out of the habit of eating at those hours, and Mildred's throat was so sore that she could not swallow. They had a little cold ham and Philip drank a glass of beer. They sat opposite one another, as they had so often sat before; he wondered if she remembered; they had nothing to say to one another and would have sat in silence if Philip had not forced himself to talk. In the bright light of the restaurant, with its vulgar looking-glasses that reflected in an endless series, she looked old and haggard. Philip was anxious to know about the child, but he had not the courage to ask. At last she said:

"You know baby died last summer."

"Oh!" he said.

"You might say you're sorry."

"I'm not," he answered, "I'm very glad."

She glanced at him and, understanding what he meant, looked away.

"You were rare stuck on it at one time, weren't you? I always thought it funny like how you could see so much in another man's child."

When they had finished eating they called at the chemist's for the medicine Philip had ordered, and going back to the shabby room he made her take a dose. Then they sat together till it was time for Philip to go back to Harrington Street. He was hideously bored.

Philip went to see her every day. She took the medicine he had prescribed and followed his directions, and soon the results were so apparent that she gained the greatest confidence in Philip's skill. As she grew better she grew less despondent. She talked more freely.

"As soon as I can get a job I shall be all right," she said. "I've had my lesson now and I mean to profit by it. No more racketing about for yours truly."

Each time he saw her, Philip asked whether she had found work. She told him not to worry, she would find something to do as soon as she wanted it; she had several strings to her bow; it was all the better not to do anything for a week or two. He could not deny this, but at the end of that time he became more insistent. She laughed at him, she was much more cheerful now, and said he was a fussy old thing. She told him long stories of the manageresses she interviewed, for her idea was to get work at some eating-house; what they said and what she answered. Nothing definite was fixed, but she was sure to settle something at the beginning of the following week: there was no use hurrying, and it would be a mistake to take something unsuitable.

"It's absurd to talk like that," he said impatiently. "You must take anything you can get. I can't help you, and your money won't last for ever."

"Oh, well, I've not come to the end of it yet and chance it."

He looked at her sharply. It was three weeks since his first visit, and she had then less than seven pounds. Suspicion seized him. He remembered some of the things she had said. He put two and two together. He wondered whether she had made any attempt to find work. Perhaps she had been lying to him all the time. It was very strange that her money should have lasted so long.

"What is your rent here?"

"Oh, the landlady's very nice, different from what some of them are; she's quite willing to wait till it's convenient for me to pay."

He was silent. What he suspected was so horrible that he hesitated. It was no use to ask her, she would deny everything; if he wanted to know he must find out for himself. He was in the habit of leaving her every evening at eight, and when the clock struck he got up; but instead of going back to Harrington Street he stationed himself at the corner of Fitzroy Square so that he could see anyone who came along William Street. It seemed to him that he waited an interminable time, and he was on the point of going away, thinking his surmise had been mistaken, when the door of No.7 opened and Mildred came out. He fell back into the darkness and watched her walk towards him. She had on the hat with a quantity of feathers on it which he had seen in her room, and she wore a dress he recognized, too showy for the street and unsuitable to the time of year. He followed her slowly till she came into the Tottenham Court Road, where she slackened her pace; at the corner of Oxford Street she stopped, looked round, and crossed over to a music hall. He went up to her and touched her on the arm. He saw that she had rouged her cheeks and painted her lips.

"Where are you going, Mildred?"

She started at the sound of his voice and reddened as she always did when she was caught in a lie; then the flash of anger which he knew so well came into her eyes as she instinctively sought to defend herself by abuse. But she did not say the words which were on the tip of her tongue.

"Oh, I was only going to see the show. It gives me the hump sitting every night by myself."

He did not pretend to believe her.

"You mustn't. Good heavens, I've told you fifty times how dangerous it is. You must stop this sort of thing at once."

"Oh, hold your jaw," she cried roughly. "How d'you suppose I'm going to live?"

He took hold of her arm and without thinking what he was doing tried to drag her away.

"For God's sake come along. Let me take you home. You don't know what you're doing. It's criminal."

"What do I care? Let them take their chance. Men haven't been so good to me that I need bother my head about them."

She pushed him away and walking up to the box-office put down her money. Philip had threepence in his pocket. He could not follow. He turned away and walked slowly down Oxford Street.

"I can't do anything more," he said to himself.

That was the end. He did not see her again.

Chapter 110

Christmas that year falling on Thursday, the shop was to close for four days: Philip wrote to his uncle asking whether it would be convenient for him to spend the holidays at the vicarage. He received an answer from Mrs. Foster, saying that Mr. Carey was not well enough to write himself, but wished to see his nephew and would be glad if he came down. She met Philip at the door, and when she shook hands with him, said:

"You'll find him changed since you was here last, sir; but you'll pretend you don't notice anything, won't you, sir? He's that nervous about himself."

Philip nodded, and she led him into the dining-room.

"Here's Mr. Philip, sir."

The Vicar of Blackstable was a dying man. There was no mistaking that when you looked at the hollow cheeks and the shrunken body. He sat huddled in the armchair, with his head strangely thrown back, and a shawl over his shoulders. He could not walk now without the help of sticks, and his hands trembled so that he could only feed himself with difficulty.

"He can't last long now," thought Philip, as he looked at him.

"How d'you think I'm looking?" asked the Vicar. "D'you think I've changed since you were here last?"

"I think you look stronger than you did last summer."

"It was the heat. That always upsets me."

Mr. Carey's history of the last few months consisted in the number of weeks he had spent in his bedroom and the number of weeks he had spent downstairs. He had a hand-bell by his side and while he talked he rang it for Mrs. Foster, who sat in the next room ready to attend to his wants, to ask on what day of the month he had first left his room.

"On the seventh of November, sir."

Mr. Carey looked at Philip to see how he took the information.

"But I eat well still, don't I, Mrs. Foster?"

"Yes, sir, you've got a wonderful appetite."

"I don't seem to put on flesh though."

Nothing interested him now but his health. He was set upon one thing indomitably and that was living, just living, notwithstanding the monotony of his life and the constant pain which allowed him to sleep only when he was under the influence of morphia.

"It's terrible, the amount of money I have to spend on doctor's bills." He tinkled his bell again. "Mrs. Foster, show Master Philip the chemist's bill."

Patiently she took it off the chimney-piece and handed it to Philip.

"That's only one month. I was wondering if as you're

873

doctoring yourself you couldn't get me the drugs cheaper. I thought of getting them down from the stores, but then there's the postage."

Though apparently taking so little interest in him that he did not trouble to inquire what Philip was doing, he seemed glad to have him there. He asked how long he could stay, and when Philip told him he must leave on Tuesday morning, expressed a wish that the visit might have been longer. He told him minutely all his symptoms and repeated what the doctor had said of him. He broke off to ring his bell, and when Mrs. Foster came in, said:

"Oh, I wasn't sure if you were there. I only rang to see if you were."

When she had gone he explained to Philip that it made him uneasy if he was not certain that Mrs. Foster was within earshot; she knew exactly what to do with him if anything happened. Philip, seeing that she was tired and that her eyes were heavy from want of sleep, suggested that he was working her too hard.

"Oh, nonsense," said the Vicar, "she's as strong as a horse." And when next she came in to give him his medicine he said to her:

"Master Philip says you've got too much to do, Mrs. Foster. You like looking after me, don't you?"

"Oh, I don't mind, sir. I want to do everything I can."

Presently the medicine took effect and Mr. Carey fell asleep. Philip went into the kitchen and asked Mrs. Foster whether she could stand the work. He saw that for some months she had had little peace.

"Well, sir, what can I do?" she answered. "The poor old

gentleman's so dependent on me, and, although he is troublesome sometimes, you can't help liking him, can you? I've been here so many years now, I don't know what I shall do when he comes to go."

Philip saw that she was really fond of the old man. She washed and dressed him, gave him his food, and was up half a dozen times in the night; for she slept in the next room to his and whenever he awoke he tinkled his little bell till she came in. He might die at any moment, but he might live for months. It was wonderful that she should look after a stranger with such patient tenderness, and it was tragic and pitiful that she should be alone in the world to care for him.

It seemed to Philip that the religion which his uncle had preached all his life was now of no more than formal importance to him: every Sunday the curate came and administered to him Holy Communion, and he often read his Bible; but it was clear that he looked upon death with horror. He believed that it was the gateway to life everlasting, but he did not want to enter upon that life. In constant pain, chained to his chair, and having given up the hope of ever getting out into the open again, like a child in the hands of a woman to whom he paid wages, he clung to the world he knew.

In Philip's head was a question he could not ask, because he was aware that his uncle would never give any but a conventional answer: he wondered whether at the very end, now that the machine was painfully wearing itself out, the clergyman still believed in immortality; perhaps at the bottom of his soul, not allowed to shape itself into words in case it became urgent, was the conviction that there was no God and after this life nothing.

On the evening of Boxing Day Philip sat in the dining-room with his uncle. He had to start very early next morning in order to get to the shop by nine, and he was to say good night to Mr. Carey then. The Vicar of Blackstable was dozing and Philip, lying on the sofa by the window, let his book fall on his knees and looked idly round the room. He asked himself how much the furniture would fetch. He had walked round the house and looked at the things he had known from his childhood; there were a few pieces of china which might go for a decent price and Philip wondered if it would be worth while to take them up to London; but the furniture was of the Victorian order, of mahogany, solid and ugly; it would go for nothing at an auction. There were three or four thousand books, but everyone knew how badly they sold, and it was not probable that they would fetch more than a hundred pounds. Philip did not know how much his uncle would leave, and he reckoned out for the hundredth time what was the least sum upon which he could finish the curriculum at the hospital, take his degree, and live during the time he wished to spend on hospital appointments. He looked at the old man, sleeping restlessly: there was no humanity left in that shrivelled face; it was the face of some queer animal. Philip thought how easy it would be to finish that useless life. He had thought it each evening when Mrs. Foster prepared for his uncle the medicine which was to give him an easy night. There were two bottles: one contained a drug which he took regularly, and the other an opiate if the pain grew unendurable. This was poured out for him and left by his bedside. He generally took it at three or four in the morning. It would be a simple thing to double the dose; he would die in the night, and no one would suspect anything; for that was how Doctor Wigram expected him to die. The end would be painless. Philip clenched his hands as he thought of the money he wanted so badly. A few more months of that wretched life could matter nothing to the old man, but the few more months meant everything to him: he was getting to the end of his endurance, and when he thought of going back to work in the morning he shuddered with horror. His heart beat quickly at the thought which obsessed him, and though he made an effort to put it out of his mind he could not. It would be so easy, so desperately easy. He had no feeling for the old man, he had never liked him; he had been selfish all his life, selfish to his wife who adored him, indifferent to the boy who had been put in his charge; he was not a cruel man, but a stupid, hard man, eaten up with a small sensuality. It would be easy, desperately easy. Philip did not dare. He was afraid of remorse; it would be no good having the money if he regretted all his life what he had done. Though he had told himself so often that regret was futile, there were certain things that came back to him occasionally and worried him. He wished they were not on his conscience.

His uncle opened his eyes; Philip was glad, for he looked a little more human then. He was frankly horrified at the idea that had come to him, it was murder that he was meditating; and he wondered if other people had such thoughts or whether he was abnormal and depraved. He supposed he could not have done it when it came to the point, but there the thought was, constantly recurring: if he held his hand it was from fear. His uncle spoke.

"You're not looking forward to my death, Philip?"

Philip felt his heart beat against his chest.

"Good heavens, no."

"That's a good boy. I shouldn't like you to do that. You'll get a little bit of money when I pass away, but you mustn't look forward to it. It wouldn't profit you if you did."

He spoke in a low voice, and there was a curious anxiety in his tone. It sent a pang into Philip's heart. He wondered what strange insight might have led the old man to surmise what strange desires were in Philip's mind.

"I hope you'll live for another twenty years," he said.

"Oh, well, I can't expect to do that, but if I take care of myself I don't see why I shouldn't last another three or four."

He was silent for a while, and Philip found nothing to say. Then, as if he had been thinking it all over, the old man spoke again.

"Everyone has the right to live as long as he can."

Philip wanted to distract his mind.

"By the way, I suppose you never hear from Miss Wilkinson now?"

"Yes, I had a letter some time this year. She's married, you know."

"Really?"

"Yes, she married a widower. I believe they're quite comfortable."

Chapter 111

Next day Philip began work again, but the end which he expected within a few weeks did not come. The weeks passed into months. The winter wore away, and in the parks the trees burst into bud and into leaf. A terrible lassitude settled upon Philip. Time was passing, though it went with such heavy feet, and he thought that his youth was going and soon he would have lost it and nothing would have been accomplished. His work seemed more aimless now that there was the certainty of his leaving it. He became skilful in the designing of costumes, and though he had no inventive faculty acquired quickness in the adaptation of French fashions to the English market. Sometimes he was not displeased with his drawings, but they always bungled them in the execution. He was amused to notice that he suffered from a lively irritation when his ideas were not adequately carried out. He had to walk warily. Whenever he suggested something original Mr. Sampson turned it down: their customers did not want anything *outré*, it was a very respectable class of business, and when you had a connection of that sort it wasn't worth while taking liberties with it. Once or twice he spoke sharply to Philip; he thought the young man was getting a bit above himself because Philip's ideas did not always coincide with his own.

"You jolly well take care, my fine young fellow, or one of these days you'll find yourself in the street."

Philip longed to give him a punch on the nose, but he restrained himself. After all it could not possibly last much longer, and then he would be done with all these people for ever. Sometimes in comic desperation he cried out that his uncle must be made of iron. What a constitution! The ills he suffered from would have killed any decent person twelve months before. When at last the news came that the Vicar was dying Philip, who had been thinking of other things, was taken by surprise. It was in July, and in another fortnight he was to have gone for his holiday. He received a letter from Mrs. Foster to say the doctor did not give Mr. Carey many days to live, and if Philip wished to see him again he must come at once. Philip went to the buyer and told him he wanted to leave. Mr. Sampson was a decent fellow, and when he knew the circumstances made no difficulties. Philip said good-bye to the people in his department; the reason of his leaving had spread among them in an exaggerated form, and they thought he had come into a fortune. Mrs. Hodges had tears in her eyes when she shook hands with him.

"I suppose we shan't often see you again," she said.

"I'm glad to get away from Lynn's," he answered.

It was strange, but he was actually sorry to leave these people whom he thought he had loathed, and when he drove away from the house in Harrington Street it was with no exultation. He had so anticipated the emotions he would experience on this occasion that now he felt nothing: he was as unconcerned as though he were going for a few days' holiday.

"I've got a rotten nature," he said to himself. "I look forward to things awfully, and then when they come I'm always disappointed."

He reached Blackstable early in the afternoon. Mrs. Foster met him at the door, and her face told him that his uncle was not yet dead.

"He's a little better today," she said. "He's got a wonderful constitution."

She led him into the bedroom where Mr. Carey lay on his back. He gave Philip a slight smile, in which was a trace of satisfied cunning at having circumvented his enemy once more.

"I thought it was all up with me yesterday," he said, in an exhausted voice. "They'd all given me up, hadn't you, Mrs. Foster?"

"You've got a wonderful constitution, there's no denying that."

"There's life in the old dog yet."

Mrs. Foster said that the Vicar must not talk, it would tire him; she treated him like a child, with kindly despotism; and there was something childish in the old man's satisfaction at having cheated all their expectations. It struck him at once that Philip had been sent for, and he was amused that he had been brought on a fool's errand. If he could only avoid another of his heart attacks he would get well enough in a week or two; and he had had the attacks several times before; he always felt as if he were going to die, but he never did. They all talked of his constitution, but they none of them knew how strong it was.

"Are you going to stay a day or two?" He asked Philip, pretending to believe he had come down for a holiday.

"I was thinking of it," Philip answered cheerfully.

"A breath of sea air will do you good."

Presently Dr. Wigram came, and after he had seen the Vicar talked with Philip. He adopted an appropriate manner.

"I'm afraid it is the end this time, Philip," he said. "It'll be a great loss to all of us. I've known him for five-and-thirty years."

"He seems well enough now," said Philip.

"I'm keeping him alive on drugs, but it can't last. It was dreadful these last two days, I thought he was dead half a dozen times."

The doctor was silent for a minute or two, but at the gate he said suddenly to Philip:

"Has Mrs. Foster said anything to you?"

"What d'you mean?"

"They're very superstitious, these people: she's got hold of an idea that he's got something on his mind, and he can't die till he gets rid of it; and he can't bring himself to confess it."

Philip did not answer, and the doctor went on.

"Of course it's nonsense. He's led a very good life, he's done his duty, he's been a good parish priest, and I'm sure we shall all miss him; he can't have anything to reproach himself with. I very much doubt whether the next vicar will suit us half so well."

For several days Mr. Carey continued without change. His appetite which had been excellent left him, and he could eat little.

Dr. Wigram did not hesitate now to still the pain of the neuritis which tormented him; and that, with the constant shaking of his palsied limbs, was gradually exhausting him. His mind remained clear. Philip and Mrs. Foster nursed him between them. She was so tired by the many months during which she had been attentive to all his wants that Philip insisted on sitting up with the patient so that she might have her night's rest. He passed the long hours in an armchair so that he should not sleep soundly, and read by the light of shaded candles *The Thousand and One Nights*. He had not read them since he was a little boy, and they brought back his childhood to him. Sometimes he sat and listened to the silence of the night. When the effects of the opiate wore off Mr. Carey grew restless and kept him constantly busy.

At last, early one morning, when the birds were chattering noisily in the trees, he heard his name called. He went up to the bed. Mr. Carey was lying on his back, with his eyes looking at the ceiling; he did not turn them on Philip. Philip saw that sweat was on his forehead, and he took a towel and wiped it.

"Is that you, Philip?" the old man asked.

Philip was startled because the voice was suddenly changed. It was hoarse and low. So would a man speak if he was cold with fear.

"Yes, d'you want anything?"

There was a pause, and still the unseeing eyes stared at the ceiling. Then a twitch passed over the face.

"I think I'm going to die," he said.

"Oh, what nonsense!" cried Philip. "You're not going to die for years."

Two tears were wrung from the old man's eyes. They moved Philip horribly. His uncle had never betrayed any particular emotion in the affairs of life; and it was dreadful to see them now, for they signified a terror that was unspeakable.

"Send for Mr. Simmonds," he said. "I want to take the Communion."

Mr. Simmonds was the curate.

"Now?" asked Philip.

"Soon, or else it'll be too late."

Philip went to awake Mrs. Foster, but it was later than he thought and she was up already. He told her to send the gardener with a message, and he went back to his uncle's room.

"Have you sent for Mr. Simmonds?"

"Yes."

There was a silence. Philip sat by the bedside, and occasionally wiped the sweating forehead.

"Let me hold your hand, Philip," the old man said at last.

Philip gave him his hand and he clung to it as to life, for comfort in his extremity. Perhaps he had never really loved anyone in all his days, but now he turned instinctively to a human being. His hand was wet and cold. It grasped Philip's with feeble, despairing energy. The old man was fighting with the fear of death. And Philip thought that all must go through that. Oh, how monstrous it was, and they could believe in a God that allowed His creatures to suffer such a cruel torture! He had never cared for his uncle, and for two years he had longed every day for his death; but now he could not overcome the compassion that filled his heart. What a price it was to pay for being other than the beasts!

They remained in silence broken only once by a low inquiry from Mr. Carey:

"Hasn't he come yet?"

At last the housekeeper came in softly to say that Mr. Simmonds was there. He carried a bag in which were his surplice and his hood. Mrs. Foster brought the Communion plate. Mr. Simmonds shook hands silently with Philip, and then with professional gravity went to the sick man's side. Philip and the maid went out of the room.

Philip walked round the garden all fresh and dewy in the morning. The birds were singing gaily. The sky was blue, but the air, salt-laden, was sweet and cool. The roses were in full bloom. The green of the trees, the green of the lawns, was eager and brilliant. Philip walked, and as he walked he thought of the mystery which was proceeding in that bedroom. It gave him a peculiar emotion. Presently Mrs. Foster came out to him and said that his uncle wished to see him. The curate was putting his things back into the black bag. The sick man turned his head a little and greeted him with a smile. Philip was astonished, for there was a change in him, an extraordinary change; his eyes had no longer the terror-stricken look, and the pinching of his face had gone: he looked happy and serene.

"I'm quite prepared now," he said, and his voice had a different tone in it. "When the Lord sees fit to call me I am ready to give my soul into His hands."

Philip did not speak. He could see that his uncle was sincere. It was almost a miracle. He had taken the body and blood of his

Saviour, and they had given him strength so that he no longer feared the inevitable passage into the night. He knew he was going to die: he was resigned. He only said one thing more:

"I shall rejoin my dear wife."

It startled Philip. He remembered with what a callous selfishness his uncle had treated her, how obtuse he had been to her humble, devoted love. The curate, deeply moved, went away and Mrs. Foster, weeping, accompanied him to the door. Mr. Carey, exhausted by his effort, fell into a light doze, and Philip sat down by the bed and waited for the end. The morning wore on, and the old man's breathing grew stertorous. The doctor came and said he was dying. He was unconscious and he pecked feebly at the sheets; he was restless and he cried out. Dr. Wigram gave him a hypodermic injection.

"It can't do any good now, he may die at any moment."

The doctor looked at his watch and then at the patient. Philip saw that it was one o'clock. Dr. Wigram was thinking of his dinner.

"It's no use your waiting," he said.

"There's nothing I can do," said the doctor.

When he was gone Mrs. Foster asked Philip if he would go to the carpenter, who was also the undertaker, and tell him to send up a woman to lay out the body.

"You want a little fresh air," she said, "it'll do you good."

The undertaker lived half a mile away. When Philip gave him his message, he said:

"When did the poor old gentleman die?"

Philip hesitated. It occurred to him that it would seem brutal to fetch a woman to wash the body while his uncle still lived, and he wondered why Mrs. Foster had asked him to come. They would think he was in a great hurry to kill the old man off. He thought the undertaker looked at him oddly. He repeated the question. It irritated Philip. It was no business of his.

"When did the Vicar pass away?"

Philip's first impulse was to say that it had just happened, but then it would seem inexplicable if the sick man lingered for several hours. He reddened and answered awkwardly:

"Oh, he isn't exactly dead yet."

The undertaker looked at him in perplexity, and he hurried to explain.

"Mrs. Foster is all alone and she wants a woman there. You understood, don't you? He may be dead by now."

The undertaker nodded.

"Oh, yes, I see. I'll send someone up at once."

When Philip got back to the vicarage he went up to the bedroom. Mrs. Foster rose from her chair by the bedside.

"He's just as he was when you left," she said.

She went down to get herself something to eat, and Philip watched curiously the process of death. There was nothing human now in the unconscious being that struggled feebly. Sometimes a muttered ejaculation issued from the loose mouth. The sun beat down hotly from a cloudless sky, but the trees in the garden were pleasant and cool. It was a lovely day. A bluebottle buzzed against the windowpane. Suddenly there was a loud rattle, it made Philip start, it was horribly frightening, a movement passed through the limbs and the old man was dead. The machine had run down. The bluebottle buzzed, buzzed noisily against the windowpane.

Chapter 112

Josiah Graves in his masterful way made arrangements, becoming but economical, for the funeral; and when it was over came back to the vicarage with Philip. The will was in his charge, and with a due sense of the fitness of things he read it to Philip over an early cup of tea. It was written on half a sheet of paper and left everything Mr. Carey had to his nephew. There was the furniture, about eighty pounds at the bank, twenty shares in the A. B. C. company, a few in Allsop's brewery, some in the Oxford music hall, and a few more in a London restaurant. They had been bought under Mr. Graves's direction, and he told Philip with satisfaction:

"You see, people must eat, they will drink, and they want amusement. You're always safe if you put your money in what the public thinks necessities."

His words showed a nice discrimination between the grossness of the vulgar, which he deplored but accepted, and the finer taste of the elect. Altogether in investments there was about five hundred pounds; and to that must be added the balance at the bank and what the furniture would fetch. It was riches to Philip. He was not happy but infinitely relieved.

Mr. Graves left him, after they had discussed the auction which must be held as soon as possible, and Philip sat himself down to go through the papers of the deceased. The Rev. William Carey had prided himself on never destroying anything and there were piles of correspondence dating back for fifty years and bundle upon bundle of neatly docketed bills. He had kept not only letters addressed to him, but letters which himself had written. There was a yellow packet of letters which he had written to his father in the forties, when as an Oxford undergraduate he had gone to Germany for the long vacation. Philip read them idly. It was a different William Carey from the William Carey he had known, and yet there were traces in the boy which might to an acute observer have suggested the man. The letters were formal and a little stilted. He showed himself strenuous to see all that was noteworthy, and he described with a fine enthusiasm the castles of the Rhine. The falls of Schaffhausen made him "offer reverent thanks to the all-powerful Creator of the universe, whose works were wondrous and beautiful," and he could not help thinking that they who lived in sight of "this handiwork of their blessed Maker must be moved by the contemplation to lead pure and holy lives." Among some bills Philip found a miniature which had been painted of William Carey soon after he was ordained. It represented a thin young curate, with long hair that fell over his head in natural curls, with dark eyes, large and dreamy, and a pale ascetic face. Philip remembered the chuckle with which his uncle used to tell of the dozens of slippers which were worked for him by adoring ladies.

The rest of the afternoon and all the evening Philip toiled through the innumerable correspondence. He glanced at the address and at the signature, then tore the letter in two and threw it into the washing-basket by his side. Suddenly he came upon one signed Helen. He did not know the writing. It was thin, angular, and old-fashioned. It began: my dear William, and ended: Your affectionate sister. Then it struck him that it was from his own mother? He had never seen a letter of hers before, and her handwriting was strange to him. It was about himself.

My dear William,

    Stephen wrote to you to thank you for your congratulations on the birth of our son and your kind wishes to myself. Thank God we are both well and I am deeply thankful for the great mercy which has been shown me. Now that I can hold a pen I want to tell you and dear Louisa myself how truly grateful I am to you both for all your kindness to me now and always since my marriage. I am going to ask you to do me a great favour. Both Stephen and I wish you to be the boy's godfather, and we hope that you will consent. I know I am not asking a small thing, for I am sure you will take the responsibilities of the position very seriously, but I am especially anxious that you should undertake this office because you are a clergyman as well as the boy's uncle. I am very anxious for the boy's welfare and I pray God night and day that he may grow into a good, honest, and Christian man. With you to guide him I hope that he will become a soldier in Christ's Faith and be all the days of his life God-fearing, humble, and pious.

Your affectionate sister,

Helen.

Philip pushed the letter away and, leaning forward, rested his face on his hands. It deeply touched and at the same time surprised him. He was astonished at its religious tone, which seemed to him neither mawkish nor sentimental. He knew nothing of his mother, dead now for nearly twenty years, but that she was beautiful and it was strange to learn that she was simple and pious. He had never thought of that side of her. He read again what she said about him, what she expected and thought about him; he had turned out very differently; he looked at himself for a moment; perhaps it was better that she was dead. Then a sudden impulse caused him to tear up the letter; its tenderness and simplicity made it seem peculiarly private; he had a queer feeling that there was something indecent in his reading what exposed his mother's gentle soul. He went on with the Vicar's dreary correspondence.

A few days later he went up to London, and for the first time for two years entered by day the hall of St. Luke's Hospital. He went to see the secretary of the Medical School; he was surprised to see him and asked Philip curiously what he had been doing. Philip's experiences had given him a certain confidence in himself and a different outlook upon many things: such a question would have embarrassed him before; but now he answered coolly, with a deliberate vagueness which prevented further inquiry, that private affairs had obliged him to make a break in the curriculum; he was now anxious to qualify as soon as possible. The first examination he could take was in Midwifery and the Diseases of Women, and he put his name down to be a clerk in the ward devoted to feminine ailments; since it was holiday time there happened to be no difficulty in getting a post as obstetric clerk; he arranged to undertake that duty during the last week of August and the first two of September. After this interview Philip walked through the Medical School, more or less deserted, for the examinations at the end of the summer session were all over; and he wandered along the terrace by the riverside. His heart was full. He thought that now he could begin a new life, and he would put behind him all the errors, follies, and miseries of the past. The flowing river suggested that everything passed, was passing always, and nothing mattered; the future was before him rich with possibilities.

He went back to Blackstable and busied himself with the settling up of his uncle's estate. The auction was fixed for the middle of August, when the presence of visitors for the summer holidays would make it possible to get better prices. Catalogues were made out and sent to the various dealers in second-hand books at Tercanbury, Maidstone, and Ashford.

One afternoon Philip took it into his head to go over to Tercanbury and see his old school. He had not been there since the day when, with relief in his heart, he had left it with the feeling that thenceforward he was his own master. It was strange to wander through the narrow streets of Tercanbury which he had known so well for so many years. He looked at the old shops, still there, still selling the same things; the booksellers with school-books, pious works, and the latest novels in one window and photographs of the Cathedral and of the city in the other; the games shop, with its cricket bats, fishing tackle, tennis rackets, and footballs; the tailor from whom he had got clothes all through his boyhood; and the fishmonger where his uncle whenever he came to Tercanbury bought fish. He wandered along the sordid street in which, behind a high wall, lay the red-brick house which was the preparatory school. Further on was the gateway that led into King's School, and he stood in the quadrangle round which were the various buildings. It was just four and the boys were hurrying out of school. He saw the masters in their gowns and mortar-boards, and they were strange to him. It was more than ten years since he had left and many changes had taken place. He saw the headmaster; he walked slowly down from the schoolhouse to his own, talking to a big boy who Philip supposed was in the sixth; he was little changed, tall, cadaverous, romantic as Philip remembered him, with the same wild eyes; but the black beard was streaked with grey now and the dark, sallow face was more deeply lined. Philip had an impulse to go up and speak to him, but he was afraid he would have forgotten him, and he hated the thought of explaining who he was.

Boys lingered talking to one another, and presently some who had hurried to change came out to play fives; others straggled out in twos and threes and went out of the gateway: Philip knew they were going up to the cricket ground; others again went into the precincts to bat at the nets. Philip stood among them a stranger; one or two gave him an indifferent glance; but visitors, attracted by the Norman staircase, were not rare and excited little attention. Philip looked at them curiously. He thought with melancholy of the distance that separated him from them, and he thought bitterly how much he had wanted to do and how little done. It seemed to him that all those years, vanished beyond recall, had been utterly wasted. The boys, fresh and buoyant, were doing the same things that he had done; it seemed that not a day had passed since he left the school, and yet in that place where at least by name he had known everybody, now he knew not a soul. In a few years these too, others taking their place, would stand alien as he stood; but the reflection brought him no solace; it merely impressed upon him the futility of human existence. Each generation repeated the trivial round. He wondered what had become of the boys who were his companions: they were nearly thirty now; some would be dead, but others were married and had children; they were soldiers and parsons, doctors, lawyers; they were staid men who were beginning to put youth behind them. Had any of them made such a hash of life as he? He thought of the boy he had been devoted to; it was funny, he could not recall his name; he remembered exactly what he looked like, he had been his greatest friend; but his name would not come back to him. He looked back with amusement on the jealous emotions he had suffered on his account. It was irritating not to recollect his name. He longed to be a boy again, like those he saw sauntering through the quadrangle, so that, avoiding his mistakes, he might start afresh and make something more out of life. He felt an intolerable loneliness. He almost regretted the penury which he had suffered during the last two years, since the desperate struggle merely to keep body and soul together had deadened the pain of living. In *the sweat of thy brow shalt thou earn thy daily bread*: it was not a curse upon mankind, but the balm which reconciled it to existence.

But Philip was impatient with himself; he called to mind his idea of the pattern of life: the unhappiness he had suffered was no more than part of a decoration which was elaborate and beautiful; he told himself strenuously that he must accept with gaiety everything, dreariness and excitement, pleasure and pain, because it added to the richness of the design. He sought for beauty consciously, and he remembered how even as a boy he had taken pleasure in the Gothic cathedral as one saw it from the precincts; he went there and looked at the massive pile, grey under the cloudy sky, with the central tower that rose like the praise of men to their God; but the boys were batting at the nets, and they were lissom and strong and active; he could not help hearing their shouts and laughter. The cry of youth was insistent, and he saw the beautiful thing before him only with his eyes.

Chapter 113

At the beginning of the last week in August Philip entered upon his duties in the "district." They were arduous, for he had to attend on an average three confinements a day. The patient had obtained a "card" from the hospital some time before; and when her time came it was taken to the porter by a messenger, generally a little girl, who was then sent across the road to the house in which Philip lodged. At night the porter, who had a latchkey, himself came over and awoke Philip. It was mysterious then to get up in the darkness and walk through the deserted streets of the South Side. At those hours it was generally the husband who brought the card. If there had been a number of babies before, he took it for the most part with surly indifference, but if newly married he was nervous and then sometimes strove to allay his anxiety by getting drunk. Often there was a mile or more to walk, during which Philip and the messenger discussed the conditions of labour and the cost of living; Philip learnt about the various trades which were practised on that side of the river. He inspired confidence in the people among whom he was thrown, and during the long hours that he waited in a stuffy room, the woman in labour lying on a large bed that took up half of it, her mother and the midwife talked to him as naturally as they talked to one another. The circumstances in which he had lived during the last two years had taught him several things about the life of the very poor, which it amused them to find he knew; and they were impressed because he was not deceived by their little subterfuges. He was kind, and he had gentle hands, and he did not lose his temper. They were pleased because he was not above drinking a cup of tea with them, and when the dawn came and they were still waiting they offered him a slice of bread and dripping; he was not squeamish and could eat most things now with a good appetite. Some of the houses he went to, in filthy courts off a dingy street, huddled against one another without light or air, were merely squalid; but others, unexpectedly, though dilapidated, with worm-eaten floors and leaking roofs, had the grand air: you found in them oak balusters exquisitely carved, and the walls had still their paneling. These were thickly inhabited. One family lived in each room, and in the daytime there was the incessant noise of children playing in the court. The old walls were the breeding-place of vermin; the air was so foul that often, feeling sick, Philip had to light his pipe. The people who dwelt here lived from hand to mouth. Babies were unwelcome, the man received them with surly anger, the mother with despair; it was one more mouth to feed, and there was little enough wherewith to feed those already there. Philip often discerned the wish that the child might be born dead or might die quickly. He delivered one woman of twins (a source of humour to the facetious) and when she was told she burst into a long, shrill wail of misery. Her mother said outright:

"I don't know how they're going to feed 'em."

"Maybe the Lord'll see fit to take 'em to 'imself," said the midwife.

Philip caught sight of the husband's face as he looked at the tiny pair lying side by side, and there was a ferocious sullenness in it which startled him. He felt in the family assembled there a hideous resentment against those poor atoms who had come into the world unwished for; and he had a suspicion that if he did not speak firmly an "accident" would occur. Accidents occurred often; mothers "overlaid" their babies, and perhaps errors of diet were not always the result of carelessness.

"I shall come every day," he said. "I warn you that if anything happens to them there'll have to be an inquest."

The father made no reply, but he gave Philip a scowl. There was murder in his soul.

"Bless their little 'earts," said the grandmother, "what should 'appen to them?"

The great difficulty was to keep the mothers in bed for ten days, which was the minimum upon which the hospital practice insisted. It was awkward to look after the family, no one would see to the children without payment, and the husband grumbled because his tea was not right when he came home tired from his work and hungry. Philip had heard that the poor helped one another, but woman after woman complained to him that she could not get anyone in to clean up and see to the children's dinner without paying for the service, and she could not afford to pay. By listening to the women as they talked and by chance remarks from which he could deduce much that was left unsaid, Philip learned how little there was in common between the poor and the classes above them. They did not envy their betters, for the life was too different, and they had an ideal of ease which made the existence of the middle-classes seem formal and stiff; moreover, they had a certain contempt for them because they were soft and did not work with their hands. The proud merely wished to be left alone, but the majority looked upon the well-to-do as people to be exploited; they knew what to say in order to get such advantages as the charitable put at their disposal, and they accepted benefits as a right which came to them from the folly of their superiors and their own astuteness. They bore the curate with contemptuous indifference, but the district visitor excited their bitter hatred. She came in and opened your windows without so much as a "by your leave" or "with your leave," "and me with my bronchitis, enough to give me my death of cold"; she poked her nose into corners, and if she didn't say the place was dirty you saw what she thought right enough, " an' it's all very well for them as 'as servants, but I'd like to see what she'd make of 'er room if she 'ad four children, and 'ad to do the cookin', and mend their clothes, and wash them."

Philip discovered that the greatest tragedy of life to these people was not separation or death, that was natural and the grief of it could be assuaged with tears, but loss of work. He saw a man come home one afternoon, three days after his wife's confinement, and tell her he had been dismissed; he was a builder and at that time work was slack; he stated the fact, and sat down to his tea.

"Oh, Jim," she said.

The man ate stolidly some mess which had been stewing in a sauce-pan against his coming; he stared at his plate; his wife looked at him two or three times, with little startled glances, and then quite silently began to cry. The builder was an uncouth little fellow with a rough, weather-beaten face and a long white scar on his forehead; he had large, stubbly hands. Presently he pushed aside his plate as if he must give up the effort to force himself to eat, and turned a fixed gaze out of the window. The room was at the top of the house, at the back, and one saw nothing but sullen clouds. The silence seemed heavy with despair. Philip felt that there was nothing to be said, he could only go; and as he walked away, wearily, for he had been up most of the night, his heart was filled with rage against the cruelty of the world. He knew the hopelessness of the search for work and the desolation which is harder to bear than hunger. He was thankful not to have to believe in God, for then such a condition of things would be intolerable; one could reconcile oneself to existence only because it was meaningless.

It seemed to Philip that the people who spent their time in helping the poorer classes erred, because they sought to remedy things which would harass them if themselves had to endure them without thinking that they did not in the least disturb those who were used to them. The poor did not want large airy rooms; they suffered from cold, for their food was not nourishing and their circulation bad; space gave them a feeling of chilliness, and they wanted to burn as little coal as need be; there was no hardship for several to sleep in one room, they preferred it; they were never alone for a moment, from the time they were born to the time they died, and loneliness oppressed them; they enjoyed the promiscuity in which they dwelt, and the constant noise of their surroundings pressed upon their ears unnoticed. They did not feel the need of taking a bath constantly, and Philip often heard them speak with indignation of the necessity to do so with which they were faced on entering the hospital: it was both an affront and a discomfort. They wanted chiefly to be left alone; then if the man was in regular work life went easily and was not without its pleasures: there was plenty of time for gossip, after the day's work a glass of beer was very good to drink, the streets were a constant source of entertainment, if you wanted to read there was *Reynolds's* or *The News of the World*; "but there, you couldn't make out 'ow the time did fly, the truth was and that's a fact, you was a rare one for reading when you was a girl, but what with one thing and another you didn't get no time now not even to read the paper."

The usual practice was to pay three visits after a confinement, and one Sunday Philip went to see a patient at the dinner hour. She was up for the first time.

"I couldn't stay in bed no longer, I really couldn't. I'm not one for idling, and it gives me the fidgets to be there and do nothing all day long, so I said to 'Erb, I'm just going to get up and cook your dinner for you."

'Erb was sitting at table with his knife and fork already in his hands. He was a young man, with an open face and blue eyes. He was earning good money, and as things went the couple were in easy circumstances. They had only been married a few months, and were both delighted with the rosy boy who lay in the cradle at the foot of the bed. There was a savoury smell of beefsteak in the room and Philip's eyes turned to the range.

"I was just going to dish up this minute," said the woman.

"Fire away," said Philip. "I'll just have a look at the son and heir and then I'll take myself off."

Husband and wife laughed at Philip's expression, and 'Erb getting up went over with Philip to the cradle. He looked at his baby proudly.

"There doesn't seem much wrong with him, does there?" said Philip.

He took up his hat, and by this time 'Erb's wife had dished up the beefsteak and put on the table a plate of green peas.

"You're going to have a nice dinner," smiled Philip.

"He's only in of a Sunday and I like to 'ave something special for him, so as he shall miss his 'ome when he's out at work."

"I suppose you'd be above sittin' down and 'avin' a bit of dinner with us?" said 'Erb.

"Oh, 'Erb," said his wife, in a shocked tone.

"Not if you ask me," answered Philip, with his attractive smile.

"Well, that's what I call friendly; I knew 'e wouldn't take offence, Polly. Just get another plate, my girl."

Polly was flustered, and she thought 'Erb a regular caution, you never knew what ideas 'e'd get in 'is 'ead next; but she got a plate and wiped it quickly with her apron, then took a new knife and fork from the chest of drawers, where her best cutlery rested among her best clothes. There was a jug of stout on the table, and 'Erb poured Philip out a glass. He wanted to give him the lion's share of the beefsteak, but Philip insisted that they should share alike. It was a sunny room with two windows that reached to the floor; it had been the parlour of a house which at one time was if not fashionable at least respectable: it might have been inhabited fifty years before by a well-to-do tradesman or an officer on half pay. 'Erb had been a football player before he married, and there were photographs on the wall of various teams in self-conscious attitudes, with neatly plastered hair, the captain seated proudly in the middle holding a cup. There were other signs of prosperity: photographs of the relations of 'Erb and his wife in Sunday clothes; on the chimney-piece an elaborate arrangement of shells stuck on a miniature rock; and on each side mugs, "A present from Southend" in Gothic letters, with pictures of a pier and a parade on them. 'Erb was something of a character; he was a non-union man and expressed himself with indignation at the efforts of the union to force him to join. The union wasn't no good to him, he never found no difficulty in getting work, and there was good wages for anyone as 'ad a head on his shoulders and wasn't above puttin' 'is 'and to anything as come 'is way. Polly was timorous. If she was 'im she'd join the union, the last time there was a strike she was expectin' 'im to be brought back in an ambulance every time he went out. She turned to Philip.

"He's that obstinate, there's no doing anything with 'im."

"Well, what I say is, it's a free country, and I won't be dictated to."

"It's no good saying it's a free country," said Polly, "that won't prevent 'em bashin' your 'ead in if they get the chanst."

When they had finished Philip passed his pouch over to

'Erb and they lit their pipes; then he got up, for a "call" might be waiting for him at his rooms, and shook hands. He saw that it had given them pleasure that he shared their meal, and they saw that he had thoroughly enjoyed it.

"Well, good-bye, sir," said 'Erb, "and I 'ope we shall 'ave as nice a doctor next time the missus disgraces 'erself."

"Go on with you, 'Erb," she retorted. " 'Ow d'you know there's going to be a next time?"

Chapter 114

The three weeks which the appointment lasted drew to an end. Philip had attended sixty-two cases, and he was tired out. When he came home about ten o'clock on his last night he hoped with all his heart that he would not be called out again. He had not had a whole night's rest for ten days. The case which he had just come from was horrible. He had been fetched by a huge, burly man, the worse for liquor, and taken to a room in an evil-smelling court, which was filthier than any he had seen: it was a tiny attic; most of the space was taken up by a wooden bed, with a canopy of dirty red hangings, and the ceiling was so low that Philip could touch it with the tips of his fingers; with the solitary candle that afforded what light there was he went over it, frizzling up the bugs that crawled upon it. The woman was a blowsy creature of middle age, who had had a long succession of still-born children. It was a story that Philip was not unaccustomed to: the husband had been a soldier in India; the legislation forced upon that country by the prudery of the English public had given a free run to the most distressing of all diseases; the innocent suffered. Yawning,

Philip undressed and took a bath, then shook his clothes over the water and watched the animals that fell out wriggling. He was just going to get into bed when there was a knock at the door, and the hospital porter brought him a card.

"Curse you," said Philip. "You're the last person I wanted to see tonight. Who's brought it?"

"I think it's the 'usband, sir. Shall I tell him to wait?"

Philip looked at the address, saw that the street was familiar to him, and told the porter that he would find his own way. He dressed himself and in five minutes, with his black bag in his hand, stepped into the street. A man, whom he could not see in the darkness, came up to him and said he was the husband.

"I thought I'd better wait, sir," he said. "It's a pretty rough neighbour'ood, and them not knowing who you was."

Philip laughed.

"Bless your heart, they all know the doctor. I've been in some damned sight rougher places than Waver Street."

It was quite true. The black bag was a passport through wretched alleys and down foul-smelling courts into which a policeman was not ready to venture by himself. Once or twice a little group of men had looked at Philip curiously as he passed; he heard a mutter of observations and then one say:

"It's the 'orspital doctor."

As he went by one or two of them said: "Good night, sir."

"We shall 'ave to step out if you don't mind, sir," said the man who accompanied him now. "They told me there was no time to lose."

"Why did you leave it so late?" asked Philip, as he quickened his pace.

He glanced at the fellow as they passed a lamp post.

"You look awfully young," he said.

"I'm turned eighteen, sir."

He was fair, and he had not a hair on his face, he looked no more than a boy; he was short, but thickset.

"You're young to be married," said Philip.

"We 'ad to."

"How much d'you earn?"

"Sixteen, sir."

Sixteen shillings a week was not much to keep a wife and child on. The room the couple lived in showed that their poverty was extreme. It was a fair size, but it looked quite large, since there was hardly any furniture in it; there was no carpet on the floor; there were no pictures on the walls; and most rooms had something, photographs or supplements in cheap frames from the Christmas numbers of the illustrated papers. The patient lay on a little iron bed of the cheapest sort. It startled Philip to see how young she was.

"By Jove, she can't be more than sixteen," he said to the woman who had come in to "see her through."

She had given her age as eighteen on the card, but when they were very young they often put on a year or two. Also she was pretty, which was rare in those classes in which the constitution has been undermined by bad food, bad air, and unhealthy occupations; she had delicate features and large blue eyes, and a mass of dark hair done in the elaborate fashion of the coster girl. She and her husband were very nervous.

"You'd better wait outside, so as to be at hand if I want you," Philip said to him.

Now that he saw him better Philip was surprised again at his boyish air: you felt that he should be larking in the street with the other lads instead of waiting anxiously for the birth of a child. The hours passed, and it was not till nearly two that the baby was born. Everything seemed to be going satisfactorily; the husband was called in, and it touched Philip to see the awkward, shy way in which he kissed his wife; Philip packed up his things. Before going he felt once more his patient's pulse.

"Hulloa!" he said.

He looked at her quickly: something had happened. In cases of emergency the S. O. C. —senior obstetric clerk—had to be sent for; he was a qualified man, and the "district" was in his charge. Philip scribbled a note, and giving it to the husband told him to run with it to the hospital; he bade him hurry, for his wife was in a dangerous state. The man set off. Philip waited anxiously; he knew the woman was bleeding to death; he was afraid she would die before his chief arrived; he took what steps he could. He hoped fervently that the S. O. C. would not have been called elsewhere. The minutes were interminable. He came at last, and, while he examined the patient, in a low voice asked Philip questions. Philip saw by his face that he thought the case very grave. His name was Chandler. He was a tall man of few words, with a long nose and a thin face much lined for his age. He shook his head.

"It was hopeless from the beginning. Where's the husband?"

"I told him to wait on the stairs," said Philip.

"You'd better bring him in."

Philip opened the door and called him. He was sitting in the dark on the first step of the flight that led to the next floor. He came up to the bed.

"What's the matter?" he asked.

"Why, there's internal bleeding. It's impossible to stop it." The S. O. C. hesitated a moment, and because it was a painful thing to say he forced his voice to become brusque. "She's dying."

The man did not say a word; he stopped quite still, looking at his wife, who lay, pale and unconscious, on the bed. It was the midwife who spoke.

"The gentlemen 'ave done all they could, 'Arry," she said. "I saw what was comin' from the first."

"Shut up," said Chandler.

There were no curtains on the windows, and gradually the night seemed to lighten; it was not yet the dawn, but the dawn was at hand. Chandler was keeping the woman alive by all the means in his power, but life was slipping away from her, and suddenly she died. The boy who was her husband stood at the end of the cheap iron bed with his hands resting on the rail; he did not speak; but he looked very pale and once or twice Chandler gave him an uneasy glance, thinking he was going to faint: his lips were grey. The midwife sobbed noisily, but he took no notice of her. His eyes were fixed upon his wife, and in them was an utter bewilderment. He reminded you of a dog whipped for something he did not know was wrong. When Chandler and Philip had gathered together their things Chandler turned to the husband.

"You'd better lie down for a bit. I expect you're about done up."

"There's nowhere for me to lie down, sir," he answered, and there was in his voice a humbleness which was very distressing.

"Don't you know anyone in the house who'll give you a shakedown?"

"No, sir."

"They only moved in last week," said the midwife. "They don't know nobody yet."

Chandler hesitated a moment awkwardly, then he went up to the man and said:

"I'm very sorry this has happened."

He held out his hand and the man, with an instinctive glance at his own to see if it was clean, shook it.

"Thank you, sir."

Philip shook hands with him too. Chandler told the midwife to come and fetch the certificate in the morning. They left the house and walked along together in silence.

"It upsets one a bit at first, doesn't it?" said Chandler at last.

"A bit," answered Philip.

"If you like I'll tell the porter not to bring you any more calls tonight."

"I'm off duty at eight in the morning in any case."

"How many cases have you had?"

"Sixty-three."

"Good. You'll get your certificate then."

They arrived at the hospital, and the S. O. C. went in to see if anyone wanted him. Philip walked on. It had been very hot all the day before, and even now in the early morning there was a balminess in the air. The street was very still. Philip did not feel inclined to go to bed. It was the end of his work and he need not hurry. He strolled along, glad of the fresh air and the silence; he thought that he would go on to the bridge and look at day-break on the river. A policeman at the corner bade him good morning. He knew who Philip was from his bag.

"Out late tonight, sir," he said.

Philip nodded and passed. He leaned against the parapet and looked towards the morning. At that hour the great city was like a city of the dead. The sky was cloudless, but the stars were dim at the approach of day; there was a light mist on the river, and the great buildings on the north side were like palaces in an enchanted island. A group of barges was moored in midstream. It was all of an unearthly violet, troubling somehow and awe-inspiring; but quickly everything grew pale, and cold, and grey. Then the sun rose, a ray of yellow gold stole across the sky, and the sky was iridescent. Philip could not get out of his eyes the dead girl lying on the bed, wan and white, and the boy who stood at the end of it like a stricken beast. The bareness of the squalid room made the pain of it more poignant. It was cruel that a stupid chance should have cut off her life when she was just entering upon it; but in the very moment of saying this to himself, Philip thought of the life which had been in store for her, the bearing of children, the dreary fight with poverty, the youth broken by toil and deprivation into a slatternly middle age—he saw the pretty face grow thin and white, the hair grow scanty, the pretty hands, worn down brutally by work, become like the claws of an old animal—then, when the man was past his prime, the difficulty of getting jobs, the small wages he had to take; and the inevitable, abject penury of the end: she might be energetic, thrifty, industrious, it would not have saved her; in the end was the workhouse or subsistence on the charity of her children. Who could pity her because she had died when life offered so little?

But pity was inane. Philip felt it was not that which these people needed. They did not pity themselves. They accepted their fate. It was the natural order of things. Otherwise, good heavens! otherwise they would swarm over the river in their multitude to the side where those great buildings were, secure and stately; and they would pillage, burn, and sack. But the day, tender and pale, had broken now, and the mist was tenuous; it bathed everything in a soft radiance; and the Thames was grey, rosy, and green; grey like mother-of-pearl and green like the heart of a yellow rose. The wharves and store-houses of the Surrey side were massed in disorderly loveliness. The scene was so exquisite that Philip's heart beat passionately. He was overwhelmed by the beauty of the world. Beside that nothing seemed to matter.

Chapter 115

Philip spent the few weeks that remained before the beginning of the winter session in the out-patients' department, and in October settled down to regular work. He had been away from the hospital for so long that he found himself very largely among new people; the men of different years had little to do with one another, and his contemporaries were now mostly qualified: some had left to take up assistantships or posts in country hospitals and infirmaries, and some held appointments at St. Luke's. The two years during which his mind had lain fallow had refreshed him, he fancied, and he was able now to work with energy.

The Athelnys were delighted with his change of fortune. He had kept aside a few things from the sale of his uncle's effects and gave them all presents. He gave Sally a gold chain that had belonged to his aunt. She was now grown up. She was apprenticed to a dressmaker and set out every morning at eight to work all day in a shop in Regent Street. Sally had frank blue eyes, a broad brow, and plentiful shining hair; she was buxom,

913

with broad hips and full breasts; and her father, who was fond of discussing her appearance, warned her constantly that she must not grow fat. She attracted because she was healthy, animal, and feminine. She had many admirers, but they left her unmoved; she gave one the impression that she looked upon lovemaking as nonsense; and it was easy to imagine that young men found her unapproachable. Sally was old for her years: she had been used to help her mother in the household work and in the care of the children, so that she had acquired a managing air, which made her mother say that Sally was a bit too fond of having things her own way. She did not speak very much, but as she grew older she seemed to be acquiring a quiet sense of humour, and sometimes uttered a remark which suggested that beneath her impassive exterior she was quietly bubbling with amusement at her fellow-creatures. Philip found that with her he never got on the terms of affectionate intimacy upon which he was with the rest of Athelny's huge family. Now and then her indifference slightly irritated him. There was something enigmatic in her.

When Philip gave her the necklace Athelny in his boisterous way insisted that she must kiss him; but Sally reddened and drew back.

"No, I'm not going to," she said.

"Ungrateful hussy!" cried Athelny. "Why not?"

"I don't like being kissed by men," she said.

Philip saw her embarrassment, and, amused, turned Athelny's attention to something else. That was never a very difficult thing to do. But evidently her mother spoke of the matter later, for next time Philip came she took the opportunity when they were alone for a couple of minutes to refer to it.

"You didn't think it disagreeable of me last week when I wouldn't kiss you?"

"Not a bit," he laughed.

"It's not because I wasn't grateful." She blushed a little as she uttered the formal phrase which she had prepared. "I shall always value the necklace, and it was very kind of you to give it me."

Philip found it always a little difficult to talk to her. She did all that she had to do very competently, but seemed to feel no need of conversation; yet there was nothing unsociable in her. One Sunday afternoon when Athelny and his wife had gone out together and Philip, treated as one of the family, sat reading in the parlour, Sally came in and sat by the window to sew. The girls' clothes were made at home and Sally could not afford to spend Sundays in idleness. Philip thought she wished to talk and put down his book.

"Go on reading," she said. "I only thought as you were alone I'd come and sit with you."

"You're the most silent person I've ever struck," said Philip.

"We don't want another one who's talkative in this house," she said.

There was no irony in her tone: she was merely stating a fact. But it suggested to Philip that she measured her father, alas, no longer the hero he was to her childhood, and in her mind joined together his entertaining conversation and the thriftlessness which often brought difficulties into their life; she compared his rhetoric with her mother's practical common sense; and though the liveliness of her father amused her she was perhaps sometimes a little impatient with it. Philip looked at her as she bent over her work; she was healthy, strong, and normal; it must be odd to see her among the other girls in the shop with their flat chests and anaemic faces. Mildred suffered from anaemia.

After a time it appeared that Sally had a suitor. She went out occasionally with friends she had made in the workroom, and had met a young man, an electrical engineer in a very good way of business, who was a most eligible person. One day she told her mother that he had asked her to marry him.

"What did you say?" said her mother.

"Oh, I told him I wasn't over-anxious to marry anyone just yet awhile." She paused a little as was her habit between observations. "He took on so that I said he might come to tea on Sunday."

It was an occasion that thoroughly appealed to Athelny. He rehearsed all the afternoon how he should play the heavy father for the young man's edification till he reduced his children to helpless giggling. Just before he was due Athelny routed out an Egyptian tarboosh and insisted on putting it on.

"Go on with you, Athelny," said his wife, who was in her best, which was of black velvet, and, since she was growing stouter every year, very tight for her. "You'll spoil the girl's chances."

She tried to pull it off, but the little man skipped nimbly out of her way.

"Unhand me, woman. Nothing will induce me to take it off. This young man must be shown at once that it is no ordinary family he is preparing to enter."

"Let him keep it on, mother," said Sally, in her even, indifferent fashion. "If Mr. Donaldson doesn't take it the way it's meant he can take himself off, and good riddance."

Philip thought it was a severe ordeal that the young man was being exposed to, since Athelny, in his brown velvet jacket, flowing black tie, and red tarboosh, was a startling spectacle for an innocent electrical engineer. When he came he was greeted by his host with the proud courtesy of a Spanish grandee and by Mrs. Athelny in an altogether homely and natural fashion. They sat down at the old ironing-table in the high-backed monkish chairs, and Mrs. Athelny poured tea out of a lustre teapot which gave a note of England and the countryside to the festivity. She had made little cakes with her own hand, and on the table was homemade jam. It was a farmhouse tea, and to Philip very quaint and charming in that Jacobean house. Athelny for some fantastic reason took it into his head to discourse upon Byzantine history; he had been reading the later volumes of the *Decline and Fall*; and, his forefinger dramatically extended, he poured into the astonished ears of the suitor scandalous stories about Theodora and Irene. He addressed himself directly to his guest with a torrent of rhodomontade; and the young man, reduced to helpless silence and shy, nodded his head at intervals to show that he took an intelligent interest. Mrs. Athelny paid no attention to Thorpe's conversation, but interrupted now and then to offer the young man more tea or to press upon him cake and jam. Philip watched Sally; she sat with downcast eyes, calm, silent, and observant; and her long eyelashes cast a pretty shadow on her cheek. You could not tell whether she was amused at the scene or if she cared for the young man. She was inscrutable. But one thing was certain: the electrical engineer was good-looking, fair and clean-shaven, with pleasant, regular features, and an honest face; he was tall and well made. Philip could not help thinking he would make an excellent mate for her, and he felt a pang of envy for the happiness which he fancied was in store for them.

Presently the suitor said he thought it was about time he was getting along. Sally rose to her feet without a word and accompanied him to the door. When she came back her father burst out:

"Well, Sally, we think your young man very nice. We are prepared to welcome him into our family. Let the banns be called and I will compose a nuptial song."

Sally set about clearing away the tea-things. She did not answer. Suddenly she shot a swift glance at Philip.

"What did you think of him, Mr. Philip?"

She had always refused to call him Uncle Phil as the other children did, and would not call him Philip.

"I think you'd make an awfully handsome pair."

She looked at him quickly once more, and then with a slight blush went on with her business.

"I thought him a very nice civil-spoken young fellow," said Mrs. Athelny, "and I think he's just the sort to make any girl happy."

Sally did not reply for a minute or two, and Philip looked at her curiously: it might be thought that she was meditating upon what her mother had said, and on the other hand she might be thinking of the man in the moon.

"Why don't you answer when you're spoken to, Sally?" remarked her mother, a little irritably.

"I thought he was a silly."

"Aren't you going to have him then?"

"No, I'm not."

"I don't know how much more you want," said Mrs. Athelny, and it was quite clear now that she was put out. "He's a very decent young fellow and he can afford to give you a thorough good home. We've got quite enough to feed here without you. If you get a chance like that it's wicked not to take it. And I daresay you'd be able to have a girl to do the rough work."

Philip had never before heard Mrs. Athelny refer so directly to the difficulties of her life. He saw how important it was that each child should be provided for.

"It's no good your carrying on, mother," said Sally in her quiet way. "I'm not going to marry him."

"I think you're a very hard-hearted, cruel, selfish girl."

"If you want me to earn my own living, mother, I can always go into service."

"Don't be so silly, you know your father would never let you do that."

Philip caught Sally's eye, and he thought there was in it a glimmer of amusement. He wondered what there had been in the conversation to touch her sense of humour. She was an odd girl.

Chapter 116

During his last year at St. Luke's Philip had to work hard.
He was contented with life. He found it very comfortable to
be heart-free and to have enough money for his needs. He had
heard people speak contemptuously of money: he wondered if
they had ever tried to do without it. He knew that the lack made
a man petty, mean, grasping; it distorted his character and caused
him to view the world from a vulgar angle; when you had to
consider every penny, money became of grotesque importance:
you needed a competency to rate it at its proper value. He lived
a solitary life, seeing no one except the Athelnys, but he was not
lonely; he busied himself with plans for the future, and sometimes
he thought of the past. His recollection dwelt now and then on
old friends, but he made no effort to see them. He would have
liked to know what was become of Norah Nesbit; she was Norah
something else now, but he could not remember the name of the
man she was going to marry; he was glad to have known her: she
was a good and a brave soul. One evening about half past eleven
he saw Lawson walking along Piccadilly; he was in evening clothes

and might be supposed to be coming back from a theatre. Philip gave way to a sudden impulse and quickly turned down a side street. He had not seen him for two years and felt that he could not now take up again the interrupted friendship. He and Lawson had nothing more to say to one another. Philip was no longer interested in art; it seemed to him that he was able to enjoy beauty with greater force than when he was a boy; but art appeared to him unimportant. He was occupied with the forming of a pattern out of the manifold chaos of life, and the materials with which he worked seemed to make preoccupation with pigments and words very trivial. Lawson had served his turn. Philip's friendship with him had been a motive in the design he was elaborating: it was merely sentimental to ignore the fact that the painter was of no further interest to him.

Sometimes Philip thought of Mildred. He avoided deliberately the streets in which there was a chance of seeing her; but occasionally some feeling, perhaps curiosity, perhaps something deeper which he would not acknowledge, made him wander about Piccadilly and Regent Street during the hours when she might be expected to be there. He did not know then whether he wished to see her or dreaded it. Once he saw a back which reminded him of hers, and for a moment he thought it was she; it gave him a curious sensation: it was a strange sharp pain in his heart, there was fear in it and a sickening dismay; and when he hurried on and found that he was mistaken he did not know whether it was relief that he experienced or disappointment.

At the beginning of August Philip passed his Surgery, his last examination, and received his diploma. It was seven years since he had entered St. Luke's Hospital. He was nearly thirty. He walked down the stairs of the Royal College of Surgeons with the roll in his hand which qualified him to practise, and his heart beat with satisfaction.

"Now I'm really going to begin life," he thought.

Next day he went to the secretary's office to put his name down for one of the hospital appointments. The secretary was a pleasant little man with a black beard, whom Philip had always found very affable. He congratulated him on his success, and then said:

"I suppose you wouldn't like to do a *locum* for a month on the South coast? Three guineas a week with board and lodging."

"I wouldn't mind," said Philip.

"It's at Farnley, in Dorsetshire. Doctor South. You'd have to go down at once; his assistant has developed mumps. I believe it's a very pleasant place."

There was something in the secretary's manner that puzzled Philip. It was a little doubtful.

"What's the crab in it?" he asked.

The secretary hesitated a moment and laughed in a conciliating fashion.

"Well, the fact is, I understand he's rather a crusty, funny old fellow. The agencies won't send him anyone any more. He speaks his mind very openly, and men don't like it."

"But d'you think he'll be satisfied with a man who's only just qualified? After all I have no experience."

"He ought to be glad to get you," said the secretary

diplomatically.

Philip thought for a moment. He had nothing to do for the next few weeks, and he was glad of the chance to earn a bit of money. He could put it aside for the holiday in Spain which he had promised himself when he had finished his appointment at St. Luke's or, if they would not give him anything there, at some other hospital.

"All right. I'll go."

"The only thing is, you must go this afternoon. Will that suit you? If so, I'll send a wire at once."

Philip would have liked a few days to himself; but he had seen the Athelnys the night before (he had gone at once to take them his good news) and there was really no reason why he should not start immediately. He had little luggage to pack. Soon after seven that evening he got out of the station at Farnley and took a cab to Doctor South's. It was a broad low stucco house, with a Virginia creeper growing over it. He was shown into the consulting-room. An old man was writing at a desk. He looked up as the maid ushered Philip in. He did not get up, and he did not speak; he merely stared at Philip. Philip was taken aback.

"I think you're expecting me," he said. "The secretary of St. Luke's wired to you this morning."

"I kept dinner back for half an hour. D'you want to wash?"

"I do," said Philip.

Doctor South amused him by his odd manner. He got up now, and Philip saw that he was a man of middle height, thin, with white hair cut very short and a long mouth closed so tightly that he seemed to have no lips at all; he was clean-shaven but for small white whiskers, and they increased the squareness of face which his firm jaw gave him. He wore a brown tweed suit and a white stock. His clothes hung loosely about him as though they had been made for a much larger man. He looked like a respectable farmer of the middle of the nineteenth century. He opened the door.

"There is the dining-room," he said, pointing to the door opposite. "Your bedroom is the first door you come to when you get on the landing. Come downstairs when you're ready."

During dinner Philip knew that Doctor South was examining him, but he spoke little, and Philip felt that he did not want to hear his assistant talk.

"When were you qualified?" he asked suddenly.

"Yesterday."

"Were you at a university?"

"No."

"Last year when my assistant took a holiday they sent me a 'Varsity man. I told 'em not to do it again. Too damned gentlemanly for me."

There was another pause. The dinner was very simple and very good. Philip preserved a sedate exterior, but in his heart he was bubbling over with excitement. He was immensely elated at being engaged as a *locum*; it made him feel extremely grown-up; he had an insane desire to laugh at nothing in particular; and the more he thought of his professional dignity the more he was inclined to chuckle.

But Doctor South broke suddenly into his thoughts.

"How old are you?"

"Getting on for thirty."

"How is it you're only just qualified?"

"I didn't go in for the Medical till I was nearly twenty-three, and I had to give it up for two years in the middle."

"Why?"

"Poverty."

Doctor South gave him an odd look and relapsed into silence. At the end of dinner he got up from the table.

"D'you know what sort of a practice this is?"

"No," answered Philip.

"Mostly fishermen and their families. I have the Union and the Seamen's Hospital. I used to be alone here, but since they tried to make this into a fashionable seaside resort a man has set up on the cliff, and the well-to-do people go to him. I only have those who can't afford to pay for a doctor at all."

Philip saw that the rivalry was a sore point with the old man.

"You know that I have no experience," said Philip.

"You none of you know anything."

He walked out of the room without another word and left Philip by himself. When the maid came in to clear away she told Philip that Doctor South saw patients from six till seven. Work for that night was over. Philip fetched a book from his room, lit his pipe, and settled himself down to read. It was a great comfort, since he had read nothing but medical books for the last few months. At ten o'clock Doctor South came in and looked at him. Philip hated not to have his feet up, and he had dragged up a chair for them.

"You seem able to make yourself pretty comfortable," said

Doctor South, with a grimness which would have disturbed Philip if he had not been in such high spirits.

Philip's eyes twinkled as he answered:

"Have you any objection?"

Doctor South gave him a look, but did not reply directly.

"What's that you're reading?"

"*Peregrine Pickle*. Smollett."

"I happen to know that Smollett wrote *Peregrine Pickle*."

"I beg your pardon. Medical men aren't much interested in literature, are they?"

Philip had put the book down on the table, and Doctor South took it up. It was a volume of an edition which had belonged to the Vicar of Blackstable. It was a thin book bound in faded morocco, with a copper-plate engraving as a frontispiece; the pages were musty with age and stained with mould. Philip, without meaning to, started forward a little as Doctor South took the volume in his hands, and a slight smile came into his eyes. Very little escaped the old doctor.

"Do I amuse you?" he asked icily.

"I see you're fond of books. You can always tell by the way people handle them."

Doctor South put down the novel immediately.

"Breakfast at eight-thirty," he said, and left the room.

"What a funny old fellow!" thought Philip.

He soon discovered why Doctor South's assistants found it difficult to get on with him. In the first place, he set his face firmly against all the discoveries of the last thirty years: he had no patience with the drugs which became modish, were thought to work marvellous cures, and in a few years were discarded; he had stock mixtures which he had brought from St. Luke's, where he had been a student, and had used all his life; he found them just as efficacious as anything that had come into fashion since. Philip was startled at Doctor South's suspicion of asepsis; he had accepted it in deference to universal opinion; but he used the precautions which Philip had known insisted upon so scrupulously at the hospital, with the disdainful tolerance of a man playing at soldiers with children.

"I've seen antiseptics come along and sweep everything before them, and then I've seen asepsis take their place. Bunkum!"

The young men who were sent down to him knew only hospital practice; and they came with the unconcealed scorn for the General Practitioner which they had absorbed in the air at the hospital; but they had seen only the complicated cases which appeared in the wards; they knew how to treat an obscure disease of the suprarenal bodies, but were helpless when consulted for a cold in the head. Their knowledge was theoretical and their self-assurance unbounded. Doctor South watched them with tightened lips; he took a savage pleasure in showing them how great was their ignorance and how unjustified their conceit. It was a poor practice, of fishing folk, and the doctor made up his own prescriptions. Doctor South asked his assistant how he expected to make both ends meet if he gave a fisherman with a stomachache a mixture consisting of half a dozen expensive drugs. He complained too that the young medical men were uneducated: their reading consisted of *The Sporting Times* and *The British Medical Journal;* they could neither write a legible hand nor spell correctly. For two or three days Doctor South watched Philip closely, ready to fall on him with acid sarcasm if he gave him the opportunity; and Philip, aware of this, went about his work with a quiet sense of amusement. He was pleased with the change of occupation. He liked the feeling of independence and of responsibility. All sorts of people came to the consulting-room. He was gratified because he seemed able to inspire his patients with confidence; and it was entertaining to watch the process of cure which at a hospital necessarily could be watched only at distant intervals. His rounds took him into low-roofed cottages in which were fishing tackle and sails and here and there mementoes of deep-sea travelling, a lacquer box from Japan, spears and oars from Melanesia, or daggers from the bazaars of Stamboul; there was an air of romance in the stuffy little rooms, and the salt of the sea gave them a bitter freshness. Philip liked to talk to the sailormen, and when they found that he was not supercilious they told him long yarns of the distant journeys of their youth.

Once or twice he made a mistake in diagnosis (he had never seen a case of measles before, and when he was confronted with the rash took it for an obscure disease of the skin), and once or twice his ideas of treatment differed from Doctor South's. The first time this happened Doctor South attacked him with savage irony; but Philip took it with good humour; he had some gift for repartee, and he made one or two answers which caused Doctor South to stop and look at him curiously. Philip's face was grave, but his eyes were twinkling. The old gentleman could not avoid the impression that Philip was chaffing him. He was used to being disliked and feared by his assistants, and this was a new experience.

He had half a mind to fly into a passion and pack Philip off by the next train, he had done that before with his assistants; but he had an uneasy feeling that Philip then would simply laugh at him outright; and suddenly he felt amused. His mouth formed itself into a smile against his will, and he turned away. In a little while he grew conscious that Philip was amusing himself systematically at his expense. He was taken aback at first and then diverted.

"Damn his impudence," he chuckled to himself. "Damn his impudence."

Chapter 117

Philip had written to Athelny to tell him that he was doing a *locum* in Dorsetshire and in due course received an answer from him. It was written in the formal manner he affected, studded with pompous epithets as a Persian diadem was studded with precious stones; and in the beautiful hand, like black letter and as difficult to read, upon which he prided himself. He suggested that Philip should join him and his family in the Kentish hop-field to which he went every year; and to persuade him said various beautiful and complicated things about Philip's soul and the winding tendrils of the hops. Philip replied at once that he would come on the first day he was free. Though not born there, he had a peculiar affection for the Isle of Thanet, and he was fired with enthusiasm at the thought of spending a fortnight so close to the earth and amid conditions which needed only a blue sky to be as idyllic as the olive groves of Arcady.

The four weeks of his engagement at Farnley passed quickly. On the cliff a new town was springing up, with red-brick villas round golf links, and a large hotel had recently been opened to cater for the summer visitors; but Philip went there seldom. Down below, by the harbour, the little stone houses of a past century were clustered in a delightful confusion, and the narrow streets, climbing down steeply, had an air of antiquity which appealed to the imagination. By the water's edge were neat cottages with trim, tiny gardens in front of them; they were inhabited by retired captains in the merchant service, and by mothers or widows of men who had gained their living by the sea; and they had an appearance which was quaint and peaceful. In the little harbour came tramps from Spain and the Levant, ships of small tonnage; and now and then a windjammer was borne in by the winds of romance. It reminded Philip of the dirty little harbour with its colliers at Blackstable, and he thought that there he had first acquired the desire, which was now an obsession, for Eastern lands and sunlit islands in a tropic sea. But here you felt yourself closer to the wide, deep ocean than on the shore of that North Sea which seemed always circumscribed; here you could draw a long breath as you looked out upon the even vastness; and the west wind, the dear soft salt wind of England, uplifted the heart and at the same time melted it to tenderness.

One evening, when Philip had reached his last week with Doctor South, a child came to the surgery door while the old doctor and Philip were making up prescriptions. It was a little ragged girl with a dirty face and bare feet. Philip opened the door.

"Please, sir, will you come to Mrs. Fletcher's in Ivy Lane at once?"

"What's the matter with Mrs. Fletcher?" called out Doctor South in his rasping voice.

The child took no notice of him, but addressed herself again to Philip.

"Please, sir, her little boy's had an accident and will you come at once?"

"Tell Mrs. Fletcher I'm coming," called out Doctor South.

The little girl hesitated for a moment, and putting a dirty finger in a dirty mouth stood still and looked at Philip.

"What's the matter, Kid?" said Philip, smiling.

"Please, sir, Mrs. Fletcher says, will the new doctor come?"

There was a sound in the dispensary and Doctor South came out into the passage.

"Isn't Mrs. Fletcher satisfied with me?" he barked. "I've attended Mrs. Fletcher since she was born. Why aren't I good enough to attend her filthy brat?"

The little girl looked for a moment as though she were going to cry, then she thought better of it; she put out her tongue deliberately at Doctor South, and, before he could recover from his astonishment, bolted off as fast as she could run. Philip saw that the old gentleman was annoyed.

"You look rather fagged, and it's a goodish way to Ivy Lane," he said, by way of giving him an excuse not to go himself.

Doctor South gave a low snarl.

"It's a damned sight nearer for a man who's got the use of both legs than for a man who's only got one and a half."

Philip reddened and stood silent for a while.

"Do you wish me to go or will you go yourself?" he said at last frigidly.

"What's the good of my going? They want you."

Philip took up his hat and went to see the patient. It was hard upon eight o'clock when he came back. Doctor South was standing in the dining-room with his back to the fireplace.

"You've been a long time," he said.

"I'm sorry. Why didn't you start dinner?"

"Because I chose to wait. Have you been all this while at Mrs. Fletcher's?"

"No, I'm afraid I haven't. I stopped to look at the sunset on my way back, and I didn't think of the time."

Doctor South did not reply, and the servant brought in some grilled sprats. Philip ate them with an excellent appetite. Suddenly Doctor South shot a question at him.

"Why did you look at the sunset?"

Philip answered with his mouth full:

"Because I was happy."

Doctor South gave him an odd look, and the shadow of a smile flickered across his old, tired face. They ate the rest of the dinner in silence; but when the maid had given them the port and left the room, the old man leaned back and fixed his sharp eyes on Philip.

"It stung you up a bit when I spoke of your game leg, young fellow?" he said.

"People always do, directly or indirectly, when they get angry with me."

"I suppose they know it's your weak point."

Philip faced him and looked at him steadily.

"Are you very glad to have discovered it?"

The doctor did not answer, but he gave a chuckle of bitter

mirth. They sat for a while staring at one another. Then Doctor South surprised Philip extremely.

"Why don't you stay here and I'll get rid of that damned fool with his mumps?"

"It's very kind of you, but I hope to get an appointment at the hospital in the autumn. It'll help me so much in getting other work later."

"I'm offering you a partnership," said Doctor South grumpily.

"Why?" asked Philip, with surprise.

"They seem to like you down here."

"I didn't think that was a fact which altogether met with your approval," Philip said drily.

"D'you suppose that after forty years' practice I care a twopenny damn whether people prefer my assistant to me? No, my friend. There's no sentiment between my patients and me. I don't expect gratitude from them. I expect them to pay my fees. Well, what d'you say to it?"

Philip made no reply, not because he was thinking over the proposal, but because he was astonished. It was evidently very unusual for someone to offer a partnership to a newly qualified man; and he realized with wonder that, although nothing would induce him to say so, Doctor South had taken a fancy to him. He thought how amused the secretary at St. Luke's would be when he told him.

"The practice brings in about seven hundred a year. We can reckon out how much your share would be worth, and you can pay me off by degrees. And when I die you can succeed me. I think that's better than knocking about hospitals for two or three years, and then taking assistantships until you can afford to set up for yourself."

Philip knew it was a chance that most people in his profession would jump at; the profession was overcrowded, and half the men he knew would be thankful to accept the certainty of even so modest a competence as that.

"I'm awfully sorry, but I can't," he said. "It means giving up everything I've aimed at for years. In one way and another I've had a roughish time, but I always had that one hope before me, to get qualified so that I might travel; and now, when I wake in the morning, my bones simply ache to get off, I don't mind where particularly, but just away, to places I've never been to."

Now the goal seemed very near. He would have finished his appointment at St. Luke's by the middle of the following year, and then he would go to Spain; he could afford to spend several months there, rambling up and down the land which stood to him for romance; after that he would get a ship and go to the East. Life was before him and time of no account. He could wander, for years if he chose, in unfrequented places, amid strange peoples, where life was led in strange ways. He did not know what he sought or what his journeys would bring him; but he had a feeling that he would learn something new about life and gain some clue to the mystery that he had solved only to find more mysterious. And even if he found nothing he would allay the unrest which gnawed at his heart. But Doctor South was showing him a great kindness, and it seemed ungrateful to refuse his offer for no adequate reason; so in his shy way, trying to appear as matter-of-fact as possible, he made some attempt to explain why it was so important to him to carry out the plans he had cherished so passionately.

Doctor South listened quietly, and a gentle look came into his shrewd old eyes. It seemed to Philip an added kindness that he did not press him to accept his offer. Benevolence is often very peremptory. He appeared to look upon Philip's reasons as sound. Dropping the subject, he began to talk of his own youth; he had been in the Royal Navy, and it was his long connection with the sea that, when he retired, had made him settle at Farnley. He told Philip of old days in the Pacific and of wild adventures in China. He had taken part in an expedition against the head-hunters of Borneo and had known Samoa when it was still an independent state. He had touched at coral islands. Philip listened to him entranced. Little by little he told Philip about himself. Doctor South was a widower, his wife had died thirty years before, and his daughter had married a farmer in Rhodesia; he had quarrelled with him, and she had not come to England for ten years. It was just as if he had never had wife or child. He was very lonely. His gruffness was little more than a protection which he wore to hide a complete disillusionment; and to Philip it seemed tragic to see him just waiting for death, not impatiently, but rather with loathing for it, hating old age and unable to resign himself to its limitations, and yet with the feeling that death was the only solution of the bitterness of his life. Philip crossed his path, and the natural affection which long separation from his daughter had killed—she had taken her husband's part in the quarrel and her children he had never seen—settled itself upon Philip. At first it made him angry, he told himself it was a sign of dotage; but there was something in Philip that attracted him, and he found himself smiling at him he knew not why. Philip did not bore him. Once or twice he put his hand on his shoulder: it was as near a caress as he had got since his daughter left England so many years before. When the time came for Philip to go Doctor South accompanied him to the station: he found himself unaccountably depressed.

"I've had a ripping time here," said Philip. "You've been awfully kind to me."

"I suppose you're very glad to go?"

"I've enjoyed myself here."

"But you want to get out into the world? Ah, you have youth." He hesitated a moment. "I want you to remember that if you change your mind my offer still stands."

"That's awfully kind of you."

Philip shook hands with him out of the carriage window, and the train steamed out of the station. Philip thought of the fortnight he was going to spend in the hop-field: he was happy at the idea of seeing his friends again, and he rejoiced because the day was fine. But Doctor South walked slowly back to his empty house. He felt very old and very lonely.

Chapter 118

It was late in the evening when Philip arrived at Ferne. It was Mrs. Athelny's native village, and she had been accustomed from her childhood to pick in the hop-field to which with her husband and her children she still went every year. Like many Kentish folk her family had gone out regularly, glad to earn a little money, but especially regarding the annual outing, looked forward to for months, as the best of holidays. The work was not hard, it was done in common, in the open air, and for the children it was a long, delightful picnic; here the young men met the maidens; in the long evenings when work was over they wandered about the lanes, making love; and the hopping season was generally followed by weddings. They went out in carts with bedding, pots and pans, chairs and tables; and Ferne while the hopping lasted was deserted. They were very exclusive and would have resented the intrusion of foreigners, as they called the people who came from London; they looked down upon them and feared them too; they were a rough lot, and the respectable country folk did not want to mix with them. In the old days the hoppers slept in barns, but ten years ago a row of huts had been erected at the side of a meadow; and the Athelnys, like many others, had the same hut every year.

Athelny met Philip at the station in a cart he had borrowed from the public-house at which he had got a room for Philip. It was a quarter of a mile from the hop-field. They left his bag there and walked over to the meadow in which were the huts. They were nothing more than a long, low shed, divided into little rooms about twelve feet square. In front of each was a fire of sticks, round which a family was grouped, eagerly watching the cooking of supper. The sea air and the sun had browned already the faces of Athelny's children. Mrs. Athelny seemed a different woman in her sunbonnet: you felt that the long years in the city had made no real difference to her; she was the country woman born and bred, and you could see how much at home she found herself in the country. She was frying bacon and at the same time keeping an eye on the younger children, but she had a hearty handshake and a jolly smile for Philip. Athelny was enthusiastic over the delights of a rural existence.

"We're starved for sun and light in the cities we live in. It isn't life, it's a long imprisonment. Let us sell all we have, Betty, and take a farm in the country."

"I can see you in the country," she answered with good-humoured scorn. "Why, the first rainy day we had in the winter you'd be crying for London." She turned to Philip. "Athelny's always like this when we come down here. Country, I like that! Why, he don't know a swede from a mangel-wurzel."

"Daddy was lazy today," remarked Jane, with the frankness which characterized her, "he didn't fill one bin."

"I'm getting into practice, child, and tomorrow I shall fill more bins than all of you put together."

"Come and eat your supper, children," said Mrs. Athelny. "Where's Sally?"

"Here I am, mother."

She stepped out of their little hut, and the flames of the wood fire leaped up and cast sharp colour upon her face. Of late Philip had only seen her in the trim frocks she had taken to since she was at the dressmaker's, and there was something very charming in the print dress she wore now, loose and easy to work in; the sleeves were tucked up and showed her strong, round arms. She too had a sunbonnet.

"You look like a milkmaid in a fairy story," said Philip, as he shook hands with her.

"She's the belle of the hop-fields," said Athelny. "My word, if the Squire's son sees you he'll make you an offer of marriage before you can say Jack Robinson."

"The Squire hasn't got a son, father," said Sally.

She looked about for a place to sit down in, and Philip made room for her beside him. She looked wonderful in the night lit by wood fires. She was like some rural goddess, and you thought of those fresh, strong girls whom old Herrick had praised in exquisite numbers. The supper was simple—bread and butter, crisp bacon, tea for the children, and beer for Mr. and Mrs. Athelny and Philip. Athelny, eating hungrily, praised loudly all he ate. He flung words of scorn at Lucullus and piled invectives upon Brillat-Savarin.

"There's one thing one can say for you, Athelny," said his wife, "you do enjoy your food and no mistake!"

"Cooked by your hand, my Betty," he said, stretching out an eloquent forefinger.

Philip felt himself very comfortable. He looked happily at the line of fires, with people grouped about them, and the colour of the flames against the night; at the end of the meadow was a line of great elms, and above the starry sky. The children talked and laughed, and Athelny, a child among them, made them roar by his tricks and fancies.

"They think a rare lot of Athelny down here," said his wife. "Why, Mrs. Bridges said to me, I don't know what we should do without Mr. Athelny now, she said. He's always up to something, he's more like a schoolboy than the father of a family."

Sally sat in silence, but she attended to Philip's wants in a thoughtful fashion that charmed him. It was pleasant to have her beside him, and now and then he glanced at her sunburned, healthy face. Once he caught her eyes, and she smiled quietly. When supper was over Jane and a small brother were sent down to a brook that ran at the bottom of the meadow to fetch a pail of water for washing up.

"You children, show your Uncle Philip where we sleep, and then you must be thinking of going to bed."

Small hands seized Philip, and he was dragged towards the hut. He went in and struck a match. There was no furniture in it; and beside a tin box, in which clothes were kept, there was nothing but the beds; there were three of them, one against each wall. Athelny followed Philip in and showed them proudly.

"That's the stuff to sleep on," he cried. "None of your spring-mattresses and swansdown. I never sleep so soundly anywhere as here. *You* will sleep between sheets. My dear fellow, I pity you from the bottom of my soul."

The beds consisted of a thick layer of hopvine, on the top of which was a coating of straw, and this was covered with a blanket. After a day in the open air, with the aromatic scent of the hops all round them, the happy pickers slept like tops. By nine o'clock all was quiet in the meadow and everyone in bed but one or two men who still lingered in the public-house and would not come back till it was closed at ten. Athelny walked there with Philip. But before he went Mrs. Athelny said to him:

"We breakfast about a quarter to six, but I daresay you won't want to get up as early as that. You see, we have to set to work at six."

"Of course he must get up early," cried Athelny, "and he must work like the rest of us. He's got to earn his board. No work, no dinner, my lad."

"The children go down to bathe before breakfast, and they can give you a call on their way back. They pass 'The Jolly Sailor'."

"If they'll wake me I'll come and bathe with them," said Philip.

Jane and Harold and Edward shouted with delight at the prospect, and next morning Philip was awakened out of a sound sleep by their bursting into his room. The boys jumped on his bed, and he had to chase them out with his slippers. He put on a coat and a pair of trousers and went down. The day had only just broken, and there was a nip in the air; but the sky was cloudless, and the sun was shining yellow. Sally, holding Connie's hand, was standing in the middle of the road, with a towel and a bathing-dress over her arm. He saw now that her sunbonnet was of the colour of lavender, and against it her face, red and brown, was like an apple. She greeted him with her slow, sweet smile, and he noticed suddenly that her teeth were small and regular and very white. He wondered why they had never caught his attention before.

"I was for letting you sleep on," she said, "but they would go up and wake you. I said you didn't really want to come."

"Oh, yes, I did."

They walked down the road and then cut across the marshes. That way it was under a mile to the sea. The water looked cold and grey, and Philip shivered at the sight of it; but the others tore off their clothes and ran in shouting. Sally did everything a little slowly, and she did not come into the water till all the rest were splashing round Philip. Swimming was his only accomplishment; he felt at home in the water; and soon he had them all imitating him as he played at being a porpoise, and a drowning man, and a fat lady afraid of wetting her hair. The bathe was uproarious, and it was necessary for Sally to be very severe to induce them all to come out.

"You're as bad as any of them," she said to Philip, in her grave, maternal way, which was at once comic and touching. "They're not anything like so naughty when you're not here."

They walked back, Sally with her bright hair streaming over one shoulder and her sunbonnet in her hand, but when they got to the huts Mrs. Athelny had already started for the hop-garden. Athelny, in a pair of the oldest trousers anyone had ever worn, his jacket buttoned up to show he had no shirt on, and in a wide-brimmed soft hat, was frying kippers over a fire of sticks. He was delighted with himself: he looked every inch a brigand. As soon as he saw the party he began to shout the witches' chorus from *Macbeth* over the odorous kippers.

"You mustn't dawdle over your breakfast or mother will be angry," he said, when they came up.

And in a few minutes, Harold and Jane with pieces of bread and butter in their hands, they sauntered through the meadow into the hop-field. They were the last to leave. A hop-garden was one of the sights connected with Philip's boyhood and the oast-houses to him the most typical feature of the Kentish scene. It was with no sense of strangeness, but as though he were at home, that Philip followed Sally through the long lines of the hops. The sun was bright now and cast a sharp shadow. Philip feasted his eyes on the richness of the green leaves. The hops were yellowing, and to him they had the beauty and the passion which poets in Sicily have found in the purple grape. As they walked along Philip felt himself overwhelmed by the rich luxuriance. A sweet scent arose from the fat Kentish soil, and the fitful September breeze was heavy with the goodly perfume of the hops. Athelstan felt the exhilaration instinctively, for he lifted up his voice and sang; it was the cracked voice of the boy of fifteen, and Sally turned round.

"You be quiet, Athelstan, or we shall have a thunderstorm."

In a moment they heard the hum of voices, and in a moment more came upon the pickers. They were all hard at work, talking and laughing as they picked. They sat on chairs, on stools, on boxes, with their baskets by their sides, and some stood by the bin throwing the hops they picked straight into it. There were a lot of children about and a good many babies, some in makeshift cradles, some tucked up in a rug on the soft brown dry earth. The children picked a little and played a great deal. The women worked busily, they had been pickers from childhood, and they could pick twice as fast as foreigners from London. They boasted about the number of bushels they had picked in a day, but they complained you could not make money now as in former times: then they paid you a shilling for five bushels, but now the rate was eight and even nine bushels to the shilling. In the old days a good picker could earn enough in the season to keep her for the rest of the year, but now there was nothing in it; you got a holiday for nothing, and that was about all. Mrs. Hill had bought herself a pianner out of what she made picking, so she said, but she was very near, one wouldn't like to be near like that, and most people thought it was only what she said; if the truth was known perhaps it would be found that she had put a bit of money from the savings bank towards it.

The hoppers were divided into bin companies of ten pickers, not counting children, and Athelny loudly boasted of the day when he would have a company consisting entirely of his own family. Each company had a bin-man, whose duty it was to supply it with strings of hops at their bins (the bin was a large sack on a wooden frame, about seven feet high, and long rows of them were placed between the rows of hops); and it was to this position that Athelny aspired when his family was old enough to form a company. Meanwhile he worked rather by encouraging others than by exertions of his own. He sauntered up to Mrs. Athelny, who had been busy for half an hour and had already emptied a basket into the bin, and with his cigarette between his lips began to pick. He asserted that he was going to pick more than anyone that day but mother; of course no one could pick so much as mother; that reminded him of the trials which Aphrodite put upon the curious Psyche, and he began to tell his children the story of her love for the unseen bridegroom. He told it very well. It seemed to Philip, listening with a smile on his lips, that the old tale fitted in with the scene. The sky was very blue now, and he thought it could not be more lovely even in Greece. The children with their fair hair and rosy cheeks, strong, healthy, and vivacious; the delicate form of the hops; the challenging emerald of the leaves, like a blare of trumpets; the magic of the green alley, narrowing to a point as you looked down the row, with the pickers in their sunbonnets: perhaps there was more of the Greek spirit there than you could find in the books of professors or in museums. He was thankful for the beauty of England. He thought of the winding white roads and the hedgerows, the green meadows with their elm-trees, the delicate line of the hills and the copses that crowned them, the flatness of the marshes, and the melancholy of the North Sea. He was very glad that he felt its loveliness. But presently Athelny grew restless and announced that he would go and ask how Robert Kemp's mother was. He knew everyone in the garden and called them all by their Christian names; he knew their family histories and all that had happened to them from birth. With harmless vanity he played the fine gentleman among them, and there was a touch of condescension in his familiarity. Philip would not go with him.

"I'm going to earn my dinner," he said.

"Quite right, my boy," answered Athelny, with a wave of the hand, as he strolled away. "No work, no dinner."

Chapter 119

Philip had not a basket of his own, but sat with Sally. Jane thought it monstrous that he should help her elder sister rather than herself, and he had to promise to pick for her when Sally's basket was full. Sally was almost as quick as her mother.

"Won't it hurt your hands for sewing?" asked Philip.

"Oh, no, it wants soft hands. That's why women pick better than men. If your hands are hard and your fingers are stiff with a lot of rough work you can't pick near so well."

He liked to see her deft movements, and she watched him too now and then with that maternal spirit of hers which was so amusing and yet so charming. He was clumsy at first, and she laughed at him. When she bent over and showed him how best to deal with a whole line their hands met. He was surprised to see her blush. He could not persuade himself that she was a woman; because he had known her as a flapper, he could not help looking upon her as a child still; yet the number of her admirers showed that she was a child no longer; and though they had only been down a few days one of Sally's cousins was already so attentive that she had to endure a lot of chaffing. His name was Peter Gann, and he was the son of Mrs. Athelny's sister, who had married a farmer near Ferne. Everyone knew why he found it necessary to walk through the hop-field every day.

A call-off by the sounding of a horn was made for breakfast at eight, and though Mrs. Athelny told them they had not deserved it, they ate it very heartily. They set to work again and worked till twelve, when the horn sounded once more for dinner. At intervals the measurer went his round from bin to bin, accompanied by the booker, who entered first in his own book and then in the hopper's the number of bushels picked. As each bin was filled it was measured out in bushel baskets into a huge bag called a poke; and this the measurer and the pole-puller carried off between them and put on the waggon. Athelny came back now and then with stories of how much Mrs. Heath or Mrs. Jones had picked, and he conjured his family to beat her: he was always wanting to make records, and sometimes in his enthusiasm picked steadily for an hour. His chief amusement in it, however, was that it showed the beauty of his graceful hands, of which he was excessively proud. He spent much time manicuring them. He told Philip, as he stretched out his tapering fingers, that the Spanish grandees had always slept in oiled gloves to preserve their whiteness. The hand that wrung the throat of Europe, he remarked dramatically, was as shapely and exquisite as a woman's; and he looked at his own, as he delicately picked the hops, and sighed with self-satisfaction. When he grew tired of this he rolled himself a cigarette and discoursed to Philip of art and literature. In the afternoon it grew very hot. Work did not proceed so actively and conversation halted. The incessant chatter of the morning dwindled now to desultory remarks. Tiny beads of sweat stood on Sally's upper lip, and as she worked her lips were slightly parted. She was like a rosebud bursting into flower.

Calling-off time depended on the state of the oast-house. Sometimes it was filled early, and as many hops had been picked by three or four as could be dried during the night. Then work was stopped. But generally the last measuring of the day began at five. As each company had its bin measured it gathered up its things and, chatting again now that work was over, sauntered out of the garden. The women went back to the huts to clean up and prepare the supper, while a good many of the men strolled down the road to the public-house. A glass of beer was very pleasant after the day's work.

The Athelnys' bin was the last to be dealt with. When the measurer came Mrs. Athelny, with a sigh of relief, stood up and stretched her arms: she had been sitting in the same position for many hours and was stiff.

"Now, let's go to 'The Jolly Sailor'," said Athelny. "The rites of the day must be duly performed, and there is none more sacred than that."

"Take a jug with you, Athelny," said his wife, "and bring back a pint and a half for supper."

She gave him the money, copper by copper. The bar-parlour was already well filled. It had a sanded floor, benches round it, and yellow pictures of Victorian prize-fighters on the walls. The licencee knew all his customers by name, and he leaned over his bar smiling benignly at two young men who were throwing rings on a stick that stood up from the floor: their failure was greeted with a good deal of hearty chaff from the rest of the company. Room was made for the new arrivals. Philip found himself sitting between an old labourer in corduroys, with string tied under his knees, and a shiny-faced lad of seventeen with a love-lock neatly plastered on his red forehead. Athelny insisted on trying his hand at the throwing of rings. He backed himself for half a pint and won it. As he drank the loser's health he said:

"I would sooner have won this than won the Derby, my boy."

He was an outlandish figure, with his wide-brimmed hat and pointed beard, among those country folk, and it was easy to see that they thought him very queer, but his spirits were so high, his enthusiasm so contagious, that it was impossible not to like him. Conversation went easily. A certain number of pleasantries were exchanged in the broad, slow accent of the Isle of Thanet, and there was uproarious laughter at the sallies of the local wag. A pleasant gathering! It would have been a hard-hearted person who did not feel a glow of satisfaction in his fellows. Philip's eyes wandered out of the window, where it was bright and sunny still; there were little white curtains in it tied up with red ribbon like those of a cottage window, and on the sill were pots of geraniums. In due course one by one the idlers got up and sauntered back to the meadow where supper was cooking.

"I expect you'll be ready for your bed," said Mrs. Athelny to Philip. "You're not used to getting up at five and staying in the open air all day."

"You're coming to bathe with us, Uncle Phil, aren't you?" the boys cried.

"Rather."

He was tired and happy. After supper, balancing himself against the wall of the hut on a chair without a back, he smoked his pipe and looked at the night. Sally was busy. She passed in and out of the hut, and he lazily watched her methodical actions. Her walk attracted his notice; it was not particularly graceful, but it was easy and assured; she swung her legs from the hips, and her feet seemed to tread the earth with decision. Athelny had gone off to gossip with one of the neighbours, and presently Philip heard his wife address the world in general.

"There now, I'm out of tea and I wanted Athelny to go down to Mrs. Black's and get some." A pause, and then her voice was raised: "Sally, just run down to Mrs. Black's and get me half a pound of tea, will you? I've run quite out of it."

"All right, mother."

Mrs. Black had a cottage about half a mile along the road, and she combined the office of postmistress with that of universal provider. Sally came out of the hut, turning down her sleeves.

"Shall I come with you, Sally?" asked Philip.

"Don't you trouble. I'm not afraid to go alone."

"I didn't think you were; but it's getting near my bedtime, and I was just thinking I'd like to stretch my legs."

Sally did not answer, and they set out together. The road was white and silent. There was not a sound in the summer night. They did not speak much.

"It's quite hot even now, isn't it?" said Philip.

"I think it's wonderful for the time of year."

But their silence did not seem awkward. They found it was pleasant to walk side by side and felt no need of words. Suddenly at a stile in the hedgerow they heard a low murmur of voices, and in the darkness they saw the outline of two people. They were sitting very close to one another and did not move as Philip and Sally passed.

"I wonder who that was," said Sally.

"They looked happy enough, didn't they?"

"I expect they took us for lovers too."

They saw the light of the cottage in front of them, and in a minute went into the little shop. The glare dazzled them for a moment.

"You are late," said Mrs. Black. "I was just going to shut up." She looked at the clock. "Getting on for nine."

Sally asked for her half pound of tea (Mrs. Athelny could never bring herself to buy more than half a pound at a time), and they set off up the road again. Now and then some beast of the night made a short, sharp sound, but it seemed only to make the silence more marked.

"I believe if you stood still you could hear the sea," said Sally.

They strained their ears, and their fancy presented them with a faint sound of little waves lapping up against the shingle. When they passed the stile again the lovers were still there, but now they were not speaking; they were in one another's arms, and the man's lips were pressed against the girl's.

"They seem busy," said Sally.

They turned a corner, and a breath of warm wind beat for a moment against their faces. The earth gave forth its freshness.

There was something strange in the tremulous night, and something, you knew not what, seemed to be waiting; the silence was on a sudden pregnant with meaning. Philip had a queer feeling in his heart, it seemed very full, it seemed to melt (the hackneyed phrases expressed precisely the curious sensation), he felt happy and anxious and expectant. To his memory came back those lines in which Jessica and Lorenzo murmur melodious words to one another, capping each other's utterance; but passion shines bright and clear through the conceits that amuse them. He did not know what there was in the air that made his senses so strangely alert; it seemed to him that he was pure soul to enjoy the scents and the sounds and the savours of the earth. He had never felt such an exquisite capacity for beauty. He was afraid that Sally by speaking would break the spell, but she said never a word, and he wanted to hear the sound of her voice. Its low richness was the voice of the country night itself.

They arrived at the field through which she had to walk to get back to the huts. Philip went in to hold the gate open for her.

"Well, here I think I'll say good night."

"Thank you for coming all that way with me."

She gave him her hand, and as he took it, he said: "If you were very nice you'd kiss me good night like the rest of the family."

"I don't mind," she said.

Philip had spoken in jest. He merely wanted to kiss her because he was happy and he liked her and the night was so lovely.

"Good night then," he said, with a little laugh, drawing her towards him.

She gave him her lips; they were warm and full and soft; he lingered a little, they were like a flower; then, he knew not how, without meaning it, he flung his arms round her. She yielded quite silently. Her body was firm and strong. He felt her heart beat against his. Then he lost his head. His senses overwhelmed him like a flood of rushing waters. He drew her into the darker shadow of the hedge.

Chapter 120

Philip slept like a log and awoke with a start to find Harold tickling his face with a feather. There was a shout of delight when he opened his eyes. He was drunken with sleep.

"Come on, lazy bones," said Jane. "Sally says she won't wait for you unless you hurry up."

Then he remembered what had happened. His heart sank, and, half out of bed already, he stopped; he did not know how he was going to face her; he was overwhelmed with a sudden rush of self-reproach, and bitterly, bitterly, he regretted what he had done. What would she say to him that morning? He dreaded meeting her, and he asked himself how he could have been such a fool. But the children gave him no time; Edward took his bathing-drawers and his towel, Athelstan tore the bed-clothes away; and in three minutes they all clattered down into the road. Sally gave him a smile. It was as sweet and innocent as it had ever been.

"You do take a time to dress yourself," she said. "I thought you was never coming."

There was not a particle of difference in her manner. He

had expected some change, subtle or abrupt; he fancied that there would be shame in the way she treated him, or anger, or perhaps some increase of familiarity; but there was nothing. She was exactly the same as before. They walked towards the sea all together, talking and laughing; and Sally was quiet, but she was always that, reserved, but he had never seen her otherwise, and gentle. She neither sought conversation with him nor avoided it. Philip was astounded. He had expected the incident of the night before to have caused some revolution in her, but it was just as though nothing had happened; it might have been a dream; and as he walked along, a little girl holding on to one hand and a little boy to the other, while he chatted as unconcernedly as he could, he sought for an explanation. He wondered whether Sally meant the affair to be forgotten. Perhaps her senses had run away with her just as his had, and, treating what had occurred as an accident due to unusual circumstances, it might be that she had decided to put the matter out of her mind. It was ascribing to her a power of thought and a mature wisdom which fitted neither with her age nor with her character. But he realized that he knew nothing of her. There had been in her always something enigmatic.

They played leap-frog in the water, and the bathe was as uproarious as on the previous day. Sally mothered them all, keeping a watchful eye on them, and calling to them when they went out too far. She swam staidly backwards and forwards while the others got up to their larks, and now and then turned on her back to float. Presently she went out and began drying herself; she called to the others more or less peremptorily, and at last only Philip was left in the water. He took the opportunity to have a good hard swim. He was more used to the cold water this second morning, and he revelled in its salt freshness; it rejoiced him to use his limbs freely, and he covered the water with long, firm strokes. But Sally, with a towel round her, went down to the water's edge.

"You're to come out this minute, Philip," she called, as though he were a small boy under her charge.

And when, smiling with amusement at her authoritative way, he came towards her, she upbraided him.

"It is naughty of you to stay in so long. Your lips are quite blue, and just look at your teeth, they're chattering."

"All right. I'll come out."

She had never talked to him in that manner before. It was as though what had happened gave her a sort of right over him, and she looked upon him as a child to be cared for. In a few minutes they were dressed, and they started to walk back. Sally noticed his hands.

"Just look, they're quite blue."

"Oh, that's all right. It's only the circulation. I shall get the blood back in a minute."

"Give them to me."

She took his hands in hers and rubbed them, first one and then the other, till the colour returned. Philip, touched and puzzled, watched her. He could not say anything to her on account of the children, and he did not meet her eyes; but he was sure they did not avoid his purposely, it just happened that they did not meet. And during the day there was nothing in her behaviour to suggest a consciousness in her that anything had passed between them. Perhaps she was a little more talkative than usual. When they were all sitting again in the hop-field she told her mother how naughty Philip had been in not coming out of the water till he was blue with cold. It was incredible, and yet it seemed that the only effect of the incident of the night before was to arouse in her a feeling of protection towards him: she had the same instinctive desire to mother him as she had with regard to her brothers and sisters.

It was not till the evening that he found himself alone with her. She was cooking the supper, and Philip was sitting on the grass by the side of the fire. Mrs. Athelny had gone down to the village to do some shopping, and the children were scattered in various pursuits of their own. Philip hesitated to speak. He was very nervous. Sally attended to her business with serene competence, and she accepted placidly the silence which to him was so embarrassing. He did not know how to begin. Sally seldom spoke unless she was spoken to or had something particular to say. At last he could not bear it any longer.

"You're not angry with me, Sally?" he blurted out suddenly.

She raised her eyes quietly and looked at him without emotion.

"Me? No. Why should I be?"

He was taken aback and did not reply. She took the lid off the pot, stirred the contents, and put it on again. A savoury smell spread over the air. She looked at him once more, with a quiet smile which barely separated her lips; it was more a smile of the eyes.

"I always liked you," she said.

His heart gave a great thump against his ribs, and he felt the blood rushing to his cheeks. He forced a faint laugh.

"I didn't know that."

"That's because you're a silly."

"I don't know why you liked me."

"I don't either." She put a little more wood on the fire. "I knew I liked you that day you came when you'd been sleeping out and hadn't had anything to eat, d'you remember? And me and mother, we got Thorpy's bed ready for you."

He flushed again, for he did not know that she was aware of that incident. He remembered it himself with horror and shame.

"That's why I wouldn't have anything to do with the others. You remember that young fellow mother wanted me to have? I let him come to tea because he bothered me so, but I knew I'd say no."

Philip was so surprised that he found nothing to say. There was a queer feeling in his heart; he did not know what it was, unless it was happiness. Sally stirred the pot once more.

"I wish those children would make haste and come. I don't know where they've got to. Supper's ready now."

"Shall I go and see if I can find them?" said Philip.

It was a relief to talk about practical things.

"Well, it wouldn't be a bad idea, I must say.... There's mother coming."

Then, as he got up, she looked at him without embarrassment.

"Shall I come for a walk with you tonight when I've put the children to bed?"

"Yes."

"Well, you wait for me down by the stile, and I'll come when I'm ready."

He waited under the stars, sitting on the stile, and the hedges with their ripening blackberries were high on each side of him. From the earth rose rich scents of the night, and the air was soft and still. His heart was beating madly. He could not understand anything of what happened to him. He associated passion with cries and tears and vehemence, and there was nothing of this in Sally; but he did not know what else but passion could have caused her to give herself. But passion for him? He would not have been surprised if she had fallen to her cousin, Peter Gann, tall, spare, and straight, with his sunburned face and long, easy stride. Philip wondered what she saw in him. He did not know if she loved him as he reckoned love. And yet? He was convinced of her purity. He had a vague inkling that many things had combined, things that she felt though was unconscious of, the intoxication of the air and the hops and the night, the healthy instincts of the natural woman, a tenderness that overflowed, and an affection that had in it something maternal and something sisterly, and she gave all she had to give because her heart was full of charity.

He heard a step on the road, and a figure came out of the darkness.

"Sally," he murmured.

She stopped and came to the stile, and with her came sweet, clean odours of the countryside. She seemed to carry with her scents of the new-mown hay, and the savour of ripe hops, and the freshness of young grass. Her lips were soft and full against his, and her lovely, strong body was firm within his arms.

"Milk and honey," he said. "You're like milk and honey."

He made her close her eyes and kissed her eyelids, first one and then the other. Her arm, strong and muscular, was bare to the elbow; he passed his hand over it and wondered at its beauty; it gleamed in the darkness; she had the skin that Rubens painted, astonishingly fair and transparent, and on one side were little golden hairs. It was the arm of a Saxon goddess; but no immortal had that exquisite, homely naturalness; and Philip thought of a cottage garden with the dear flowers which bloom in all men's hearts, of the hollyhock and the red and white rose which is called York and Lancaster, and of love-in-a-mist and Sweet William, and honeysuckle, larkspur, and London Pride.

"How can you care for me?" he said. "I'm insignificant and crippled and ordinary and ugly."

She took his face in both her hands and kissed his lips.

"You're an old silly, that's what you are," she said.

Chapter 121

When the hops were picked, Philip, with the news in his pocket that he had got the appointment as assistant house-physician at St. Luke's, accompanied the Athelnys back to London. He took modest rooms in Westminster and at the beginning of October entered upon his duties. The work was interesting and varied; every day he learned something new; he felt himself of some consequence; and he saw a good deal of Sally. He found life uncommonly pleasant. He was free about six, except on the days on which he had out-patients, and then he went to the shop at which Sally worked to meet her when she came out. There were several young men, who hung about opposite the "trade entrance" or a little further along, at the first corner; and the girls, coming out two and two or in little groups, nudged one another and giggled as they recognized them. Sally in her plain black dress looked very different from the country lass who had picked hops side by side with him. She walked away from the shop quickly, but she slackened her pace when they met, and greeted him with a quiet smile. They walked together through the busy street. He talked to her of his work at the hospital, and she told him what she had been doing in the shop that day. He came to know the names of the girls she worked with. He found that Sally had a restrained, but keen, sense of the ridiculous, and she made remarks about the girls or the men who were set over them which amused him by their unexpected drollery. She had a way of saying a thing which was very characteristic, quite gravely, as though there were nothing funny in it at all, and yet it was so sharp-sighted that Philip broke into delighted laughter. Then she would give him a little glance in which the smiling eyes showed she was not unaware of her own humour. They met with a handshake and parted as formally. Once Philip asked her to come and have tea with him in his rooms, but she refused.

"No, I won't do that. It would look funny."

Never a word of love passed between them. She seemed not to desire anything more than the companionship of those walks. Yet Philip was positive that she was glad to be with him. She puzzled him as much as she had done at the beginning. He did not begin to understand her conduct; but the more he knew her the fonder he grew of her; she was competent and self controlled, and there was a charming honesty in her: you felt that you could rely upon her in every circumstance.

"You are an awfully good sort," he said to her once apropos of nothing at all.

"I expect I'm just the same as everyone else," she answered.

He knew that he did not love her. It was a great affection that he felt for her, and he liked her company; it was curiously soothing; and he had a feeling for her which seemed to him ridiculous to entertain towards a shop-girl of nineteen: he respected her. And he admired her magnificent healthiness. She was a splendid animal, without defect; and physical perfection filled him always with admiring awe. She made him feel unworthy.

Then one day, about three weeks after they had come back to London as they walked together, he noticed that she was unusually silent. The serenity of her expression was altered by a slight line between the eyebrows: it was the beginning of a frown.

"What's the matter, Sally?" he asked.

She did not look at him, but straight in front of her, and her colour darkened.

"I don't know."

He understood at once what she meant. His heart gave a sudden, quick beat, and he felt the colour leave his cheeks.

"What d'you mean? Are you afraid that…?"

He stopped. He could not go on. The possibility that anything of the sort could happen had never crossed his mind. Then he saw that her lips were trembling, and she was trying not to cry.

"I'm not certain yet. Perhaps it'll be all right."

They walked on in silence till they came to the corner of Chancery Lane, where he always left her. She held out her hand and smiled.

"Don't worry about it yet. Let's hope for the best."

He walked away with a tumult of thoughts in his head. What a fool he had been! That was the first thing that struck him, an abject, miserable fool, and he repeated it to himself a dozen times in a rush of angry feeling. He despised himself. How could he have got into such a mess? But at the same time, for his thoughts chased one another through his brain and yet seemed to stand together, in a hopeless confusion, like the pieces of a jig-saw puzzle seen in a nightmare, he asked himself what he was going to do. Everything was so clear before him, all he had aimed at so long within reach at last, and now his inconceivable stupidity had erected this new obstacle. Philip had never been able to surmount what he acknowledged was a defect in his resolute desire for a well-ordered life, and that was his passion for living in the future; and no sooner was he settled in his work at the hospital than he had busied himself with arrangements for his travels. In the past he had often tried not to think too circumstantially of his plans for the future, it was only discouraging; but now that his goal was so near he saw no harm in giving away to a longing that was so difficult to resist. First of all he meant to go to Spain. That was the land of his heart; and by now he was imbued with its spirit, its romance and colour and history and grandeur; he felt that it had a message for him in particular which no other country could give. He knew the fine old cities already as though he had trodden their tortuous streets from childhood. Cordova, Seville, Toledo, León, Tarragona, Burgos. The great painters of Spain were the painters of his soul, and his pulse beat quickly as he pictured his ecstasy on standing face to face with those works which were more significant than any others to his own tortured, restless heart. He had read the great poets, more characteristic of their race than the poets of other lands; for they seemed to have drawn their inspiration not at all from the general currents of the world's literature but directly from the torrid, scented plains and the bleak mountains of their country. A few short months now, and he would hear with his own ears all around him the language which seemed most apt for grandeur of soul and passion. His fine taste had given him an inkling that Andalusia was too soft and sensuous, a little vulgar even, to satisfy his ardour; and his imagination dwelt more willingly among the wind-swept distances of Castile and the rugged magnificence of Aragon and León. He did not know quite what those unknown contacts would give him, but he felt that he would gather from them a strength and a purpose which would make him more capable of affronting and comprehending the manifold wonders of places more distant and more strange.

For this was only a beginning. He had got into communication with the various companies which took surgeons out on their ships, and knew exactly what were their routes, and from men who had been on them what were the advantages and disadvantages of each line. He put aside the Orient and the P. & O. It was difficult to get a berth with them; and besides their passenger traffic allowed the medical officer little freedom; but there were other services which sent large tramps on leisurely expeditions to the East, stopping at all sorts of ports for various periods, from a day or two to a fortnight, so that you had plenty of time, and it was often possible to make a trip inland. The pay was poor and the food no more than adequate, so that there was not much demand for the posts, and a man with a London degree was pretty sure to get one if he applied. Since there were no passengers other than a casual man or so, shipping on business from some out-of-the-way port to another, the life on board was friendly and pleasant.

Philip knew by heart the list of places at which they touched; and each one called up in him visions of tropical sunshine, and magic colour, and of a teeming, mysterious, intense life. Life! That was what he wanted. At last he would come to close quarters with Life. And perhaps, from Tokyo or Shanghai, it would be possible to tranship into some other line and drip down to the islands of the South Pacific. A doctor was useful anywhere. There might be an opportunity to go up country in Burma, and what rich jungles in Sumatra or Borneo might he not visit? He was young still and time was no object to him. He had no ties in England, no friends; he could go up and down the world for years, learning the beauty and the wonder and the variedness of life.

Now this thing had come. He put aside the possibility that Sally was mistaken; he felt strangely certain that she was right; after all, it was so likely; anyone could see that Nature had built her to be the mother of children. He knew what he ought to do. He ought not to let the incident divert him a hair's breadth from his path. He thought of Griffiths; he could easily imagine with what indifference that young man would have received such a piece of news; he would have thought it an awful nuisance and would at once have taken to his heels, like a wise fellow; he would have left the girl to deal with her troubles as best she could. Philip told himself that if this had happened it was because it was inevitable. He was no more to blame than Sally; she was a girl who knew the world and the facts of life, and she had taken the risk with her eyes open. It would be madness to allow such an accident to disturb the whole pattern of his life. He was one of the few people who was acutely conscious of the transitoriness of life, and how necessary it was to make the most of it. He would do what he could for Sally; he could afford to give her a sufficient sum of money. A strong man would never allow himself to be turned from his purpose.

Philip said all this to himself, but he knew he could not do it. He simply could not. He knew himself.

"I'm so damned weak," he muttered despairingly.

She had trusted him and been kind to him. He simply could not do a thing which, notwithstanding all his reason, he felt was horrible. He knew he would have no peace on his travels if he had the thought constantly with him that she was wretched. Besides, there were her father and mother: they had always treated him well; it was not possible to repay them with ingratitude. The only thing was to marry Sally as quickly as possible. He would write to Doctor South, tell him he was going to be married at once, and say that if his offer still held he was willing to accept it. That sort of practice, among poor people, was the only one possible for him; there his deformity did not matter, and they would not sneer at the simple manners of his wife. It was curious to think of her as his wife, it gave him a queer, soft feeling; and a wave of emotion spread over him as he thought of the child which was his. He had little doubt that Doctor South would be glad to have him, and he pictured to himself the life he would lead with Sally in the fishing village. They would have a little house within sight of the sea, and he would watch the mighty ships passing to the lands he would never know. Perhaps that was the wisest thing. Cronshaw had told him that the facts of life mattered nothing to him who by the power of fancy held in fee the twin realms of space and time. It was true. *Forever wilt thou love and she be fair!*

His wedding present to his wife would be all his high hopes. Self-sacrifice! Philip was uplifted by its beauty, and all through the evening he thought of it. He was so excited that he could not read. He seemed to be driven out of his rooms into the streets, and he walked up and down Birdcage Walk, his heart throbbing with joy. He could hardly bear his impatience. He wanted to see Sally's happiness when he made her his offer, and if it had not been so late he would have gone to her there and then. He pictured to himself the long evenings he would spend with Sally in the cosy sitting-room, the blinds undrawn so that they could watch the sea; he with his books, while she bent over her work, and the shaded lamp made her sweet face more fair. They would talk over the growing child, and when she turned her eyes to his there was in them the light of love. And the fishermen and their wives who were his patients would come to feel a great affection for them, and they in their turn would enter into the pleasures and pains of those simple lives. But his thoughts returned to the son who would be his and hers. Already he felt in himself a passionate devotion to it. He thought of passing his hands over his little perfect limbs, he knew he would be beautiful; and he would make over to him all his dreams of a rich and varied life. And thinking over the long pilgrimage of his past he accepted it joyfully. He accepted the deformity which had made life so hard for him; he knew that it had warped his character, but now he saw also that by reason of it he had acquired that power of introspection which had given him so much delight. Without it he would never have had his keen appreciation of beauty, his passion for art and literature, and his interest in the varied spectacle of life. The ridicule and the contempt which had so often been heaped upon him had turned his mind inward and called forth those flowers which he felt would never lose their fragrance. Then he saw that the normal was the rarest thing in the world. Everyone had some defect, of body or of mind: he thought of all the people he had known (the whole world was like a sick-house, and there was no rhyme or reason in it), he saw a long procession, deformed in body and warped in mind, some with illness of the flesh, weak hearts or weak lungs, and some with illness of the spirit, languor of will, or a craving for liquor. At this moment he could feel a holy compassion for them all. They were the helpless instruments of blind chance. He could pardon Griffiths for his treachery and Mildred for the pain she had caused him. They could not help themselves. The only reasonable thing was to accept the good of men and be patient with their faults. The words of the dying God crossed his memory:

Forgive them, for they know not what they do.

Chapter 122

He had arranged to meet Sally on Saturday in the National Gallery. She was to come there as soon as she was released from the shop and had agreed to lunch with him. Two days had passed since he had seen her, and his exultation had not left him for a moment. It was because he rejoiced in the feeling that he had not attempted to see her. He had repeated to himself exactly what he would say to her and how he should say it. Now his impatience was unbearable. He had written to Doctor South and had in his pocket a telegram from him received that morning: *"Sacking the mumpish fool. When will you come?"* Philip walked along Parliament Street. It was a fine day, and there was a bright, frosty sun which made the light dance in the street. It was crowded. There was a tenuous mist in the distance, and it softened exquisitely the noble lines of the buildings. He crossed Trafalgar Square. Suddenly his heart gave a sort of twist in his body; he saw a woman in front of him who he thought was Mildred. She had the same figure, and she walked with that slight dragging of the feet which was so characteristic of her. Without thinking, but with a beating heart, he hurried till he came alongside, and then, when the woman turned, he saw it was someone unknown to him. It was the face of a much older person, with a lined, yellow skin. He slackened his pace. He was infinitely relieved, but it was not only relief that he felt; it was disappointment too; he was seized with horror of himself. Would he never be free from that passion? At the bottom of his heart, notwithstanding everything, he felt that a strange, desperate thirst for that vile woman would always linger. That love had caused him so much suffering that he knew he would never, never quite be free of it. Only death could finally assuage his desire.

But he wrenched the pang from his heart. He thought of Sally, with her kind blue eyes; and his lips unconsciously formed themselves into a smile. He walked up the steps of the National Gallery and sat down in the first room, so that he should see her the moment she came in. It always comforted him to get among pictures. He looked at none in particular, but allowed the magnificence of their colour, the beauty of their lines, to work upon his soul. His imagination was busy with Sally. It would be pleasant to take her away from that London in which she seemed an unusual figure, like a cornflower in a shop among orchids and azaleas; he had learned in the Kentish hop-field that she did not belong to the town; and he was sure that she would blossom under the soft skies of Dorset to a rarer beauty. She came in, and he got up to meet her. She was in black, with white cuffs at her wrists and a lawn collar round her neck. They shook hands.

"Have you been waiting long?"

"No. Ten minutes. Are you hungry?"

"Not very."

"Let's sit here for a bit, shall we?"

"If you like."

They sat quietly, side by side, without speaking. Philip enjoyed having her near him. He was warmed by her radiant health. A glow of life seemed like an aureole to shine about her.

"Well, how have you been?" he said at last, with a little smile.

"Oh, it's all right. It was a false alarm."

"Was it?"

"Aren't you glad?"

An extraordinary sensation filled him. He had felt certain that Sally's suspicion was well founded; it had never occurred to him for an instant that there was a possibility of error. All his plans were suddenly overthrown, and the existence, so elaborately pictured, was no more than a dream which would never be realized. He was free once more. Free! He need give up none of his projects, and life still was in his hands for him to do what he liked with. He felt no exhilaration, but only dismay. His heart sank. The future stretched out before him in desolate emptiness. It was as though he had sailed for many years over a great waste of waters, with peril and privation, and at last had come upon a fair haven, but as he was about to enter, some contrary wind had arisen and drove him out again into the open sea; and because he had let his mind dwell on these soft meads and pleasant woods of the land, the vast deserts of the ocean filled him with anguish. He could not confront again the loneliness and the tempest. Sally looked at him with her clear eyes.

"Aren't you glad?" she asked again. "I thought you'd be as

pleased as Punch."

He met her gaze haggardly.

"I'm not sure," he muttered.

"You are funny. Most men would."

He realized that he had deceived himself; it was no self-sacrifice that had driven him to think of marrying, but the desire for a wife and a home and love; and now that it all seemed to slip through his fingers he was seized with despair. He wanted all that more than anything in the world. What did he care for Spain and its cities, Cordova, Toledo, León; what to him were the pagodas of Burma and the lagoons of South Sea Islands? America was here and now. It seemed to him that all his life he had followed the ideals that other people, by their words or their writings, had instilled into him, and never the desires of his own heart. Always his course had been swayed by what he thought he should do and never by what he wanted with his whole soul to do. He put all that aside now with a gesture of impatience. He had lived always in the future, and the present always, always had slipped through his fingers. His ideals? He thought of his desire to make a design, intricate and beautiful, out of the myriad, meaningless facts of life: had he not seen also that the simplest pattern, that in which a man was born, worked, married, had children, and died, was likewise the most perfect? It might be that to surrender to happiness was to accept defeat, but it was a defeat better than many victories.

He glanced quickly at Sally, he wondered what she was thinking, and then looked away again.

"I was going to ask you to marry me," he said.

"I thought p'raps you might, but I shouldn't have liked to

stand in your way."

"You wouldn't have done that."

"How about your travels, Spain and all that?"

"How d'you know I want to travel?"

"I ought to know something about it. I've heard you and Dad talk about it till you were blue in the face."

"I don't care a damn about all that." He paused for an instant and then spoke in a low, hoarse whisper. "I don't want to leave you! I can't leave you."

She did not answer. He could not tell what she thought.

"I wonder if you'll marry me, Sally."

She did not move and there was no flicker of emotion on her face, but she did not look at him when she answered:

"If you like."

"Don't you want to?"

"Oh, of course I'd like to have a house of my own, and it's about time I was settling down."

He smiled a little. He knew her pretty well by now, and her manner did not surprise him.

"But don't you want to marry *me*?"

"There's no one else I would marry."

"Then that settles it."

"Mother and Dad will be surprised, won't they?"

"I'm so happy."

"I want my lunch," she said.

"Dear!"

He smiled and took her hand and pressed it. They got up and walked out of the gallery. They stood for a moment at the balustrade and looked at Trafalgar Square. Cabs and omnibuses hurried to and fro, and crowds passed, hastening in every direction, and the sun was shining.